CONSUMER BEHAVI
and *MATERIAL* *CUL*
in *BRITAIN* *1660-*

LORNA WEATHERILL

CONSUMER BEHAVIOUR and MATERIAL CULTURE in BRITAIN 1660–1760

ROUTLEDGE
LONDON AND NEW YORK

First published in 1988 by
Routledge
a division of Routledge, Chapman and Hall
11 New Fetter Lane, London EC4P 4EE

Published in the USA by
Routledge
a division of Routledge, Chapman and Hall, Inc.
29 West 35th Street, New York NY 10001

Printed in Great Britain at the University Press,
Cambridge

British Library Cataloguing in Publication Data
Weatherill, Lorna
   Consumer behaviour and material culture
   in Britain 1660–1760.
   1. Consumers——Great Britain——History
   2. Middle classes——Great Britain——
   History
   I. Title
   339.4′7′0941   HC260.C6

   ISBN 0–415–00723–2

Library of Congress Cataloging in Publication Data
Weatherill, Lorna.
   Consumer behaviour and material culture in Britain,
   1660–1760/Lorna Weatherill.
       p.   cm.
   Bibliography: p
   Includes index.
   1. Consumers — Great Britain — History — 17th
   century. 2. Consumers — Great Britain — History
   — 18th century. 3. Great Britain — Economic
   conditions — 17th century. 4. Great Britain —
   Economic conditions — 18th century. 5. Great
   Britain — Social conditions — 17th century. 6.
   Great Britain — Social conditions — 18th century.
   I. Title. II Title: Consumer behaviour and material
   culture in Britain, 1660–1760.
   HC260.C6W4   1988
   306′.3 — dc 19   88–4033

   ISBN 0 415 00723 2

For
my children
and
my friends

with love

CONTENTS

List of plates   viii
List of tables   ix
Preface   xi
1 Introduction   1

Part 1   *THE NATION*   23
2 Growth   25
3 Contrasting localities   43
4 The influence of towns   70

Part 2   *THE HOUSEHOLD*   91
5 Financing the household: income, wealth, and prices   93
6 Financing the household: expenditure and priorities   112
7 The domestic environment   137
8 Ownership of goods, social status, and occupation   166

9 Conclusions and implications   191
  Appendix 1: Ways of using probate inventories   201
  Appendix 2: Occupations and status in inventories   208
  Notes   215
  Bibliography of contemporary sources   240
  Index   244

PLATES

1 *Grace before a Meal*, J. Van Aken, *c.*1720 (Ashmolean
Museum, Oxford)   7

2 *Claud and Peggy*, David Allan, *c.*1780s (National
Galleries of Scotland, Edinburgh)   12

3 *Family at Tea*, R. Colius, 1732 (Victoria and Albert
Museum, London)   35

4 Mid-eighteenth-century cutlery (photographs from the
collection in Sheffield City Museum)   36

5 *Penny Wedding*, David Allan, 1785 (National Galleries
of Scotland, Edinburgh)   68

6 *Covent Garden, London*, J. Van Aken, *c.*1720 (Museum
of London)   82

7 *Dixton Manor House*, eighteenth-century British school
(Art Gallery and Museum, Cheltenham)   82

8 *High Life Below Stairs*, John Collett, *c.*1750s (British
Museum)   140

9 Kitchen scene: women washing, Paul Sandby, 1765
(Royal Library, Windsor Castle)   141

10 A kitchen at Steeple, Isle of Wight, anon., no date
(Carisbrooke Castle, Isle of Wight)   141

11 *Making Pies*, Paul Sandby, *c.*1765 (Royal Library,
Windsor Castle)   148

12 A domestic scene by David Allan, *c.*1780 (Glasgow Art
Gallery and Museum)   154

13 *An English Family at Tea*, J. Van Aken, *c.*1720 (Tate
Gallery, London)   158

TABLES

2.1 Frequencies of ownership of selected household goods
    in a sample of inventories from England, 1675–1725   26
2.2 Frequencies with which selected goods were recorded
    in a sample of inventories from the London Orphans'
    Court, 1675–1725   27
3.1 Ownership of selected goods in a sample of inventories
    from eight English regions, 1675–1725   44
3.2 Some characteristics of inventories from eight regions of
    England, 1675–1725   46
3.3 Changing ownership of selected goods in each of eight
    English regions, 1675–1725   49
3.4 Numbers of dealers in coffee and tea in the 1730s in the
    counties covered by the sample of inventories,
    population, and the frequency of ownership of utensils
    for hot drinks in 1725   62
4.1 Frequencies of ownership of selected goods in towns and
    country areas in a sample of English inventories,
    1675–1725   76
4.2 Frequencies of ownership of selected goods in farmers'
    and tradesmen's inventories, in town and country,
    1675–1725   78
4.3 Frequencies of ownership of selected goods in a
    sample of inventories in towns and country areas in
    eight regions of England, 1675–1725   80
4.4 Changing frequencies of ownership of selected goods in
    towns and country areas, 1675–1725   88

5.1 Percentages of a sample of inventories with selected household goods in wealth groups defined by the value of the inventory 107

5.2 Percentages of a sample of inventories with selected household goods divided according to the value of household goods 108

5.3 Ranges of values given to selected goods in inventories 110

6.1 Household and other expenditure of Richard Latham of Scarisbrick, Lancashire, 1724–1740 116

6.2 Household and other expenditure of Rachael Pengelly of Finchley, 1694–1708 124

6.3 Household and other expenditure of Sarah Fell of Swarthmoor Hall in 1675 and 1676 129

6.4 Household and personal expenditure in several households as a proportion of recorded annual expenses 133

7.1 Household activities: estimates of time spent doing them 143

8.1 A social-status hierarchy: frequencies of ownership of goods in a sample of inventories in England, 1675–1725 168

8.2 A consumption hierarchy: frequencies of ownership of goods in a sample of inventories in England, 1675–1725 184

8.3 Frequencies of ownership of selected goods in a sample of inventories in England, 1675–1725, subdivided by economic sector of occupations 186

8.4 Frequencies of ownership of selected goods in a sample of inventories in England, 1675–1725: selected occupations 188

A2.1 Occupations and status in the sample of inventories 209

A2.2 Some characteristics of inventories in ten social-status groups 212

A2.3 Some characteristics of inventories in eight general occupational groups 213

A2.4 Some characteristics of inventories in different economic sectors 214

PREFACE

The research upon which this book was based was undertaken as a project funded by the Economic and Social Research Council from 1981 to 1985, with the title 'Consumer behaviour and material culture in Britain 1660–1760'. I am ever grateful to the Economic Affairs Committee for making it possible for me to undertake the work and travel. The research was done in many libraries and record offices, and I thank all the librarians and archivists who helped me to find what I needed; without them research would be impossible. The University of St Andrews generously gave me the facilities to work and to meet other scholars, and I am particularly grateful to have used St John's House Centre for Advanced Historical Studies.

I have also been helped by many people in practical, intellectual, and personal ways. Without Angie Lamb the computing would have been done in a very clumsy way. Pene Corfield and Peter Earle contributed insights into social structures and wealth. Without Mark Overton my appreciation of inventories and of geographical regions would have been much less, and I have enjoyed my conversations with him. Many other people have talked to me about this or that aspect of the subject, or encouraged me in one way or another. Among them are John Hatcher, John Chartres, Helen Irwin, Roger Mason, John Styles, Pat Hudson, Kay Young, Sarah Bankes, Maxine Berg, Tony Upton, David Gascoigne, Judith George, and Geoffrey Parker. Catherine King showed me the pitfalls of interpreting apparently realistic pictures, and without her I would never have unearthed so many. Without Keith Wrightson this would have been a much less interesting book, and I thank him for his time, patience, and perception in the knowledge that such debts can never properly be repaid. Nor can I properly thank Christopher Smout for encouraging me to see the importance of what I found and for a wider inspiration. Rhoda and Aidan Weatherill breathed life into the household.

St Johns House, St Andrews

1

INTRODUCTION

the middle state ... was the best state in the world, the most
suited to human happiness; not exposed to the miseries and
hardships, the labour and sufferings of the mechanic part of
mankind and not embarrassed with the pride, luxury, ambition
and envy of the upper part of mankind.

(Daniel Defoe, *Robinson Crusoe*, 1719)

the *Middling Class* of People, which Class we know are vastly, I
had almost said, infinitely superior, in number to the Great.

(Josiah Wedgwood, 1772)[1]

This book is about consumption and consumer behaviour in the
early modern period.[2] It is hardly a new subject, for perceptive
contemporaries puzzled over other people's expenditure, accepting or rejecting new habits and new goods according to their
preconceptions. Defoe, writing here from the viewpoint of consumers, makes the fundamental distinction between people who
cannot afford to consume, those who consume too much, and
those in the middle, of whom he approved. Wedgwood, from a
manufacturer's viewpoint, makes a similar distinction, but adding
that those in the middle were a potentially large and attractive
market. The interesting thing about these comments is that they
both take it that upper, middle, and lower ranks could be distinguished on the basis of their consumption habits. Consumer
behaviour does indeed imply a great deal more than whether or
not some goods or services were available and used, which means
that consumption cannot be discussed in isolation from other
aspects of social and economic life.

Historians have also puzzled over consumption, for it has long been recognized that increasing demand for a wide range of goods and clothing was as important in industrialization as the invention of new methods of production. Yet, although the importance of the subject can be simply stated in general terms and although it is evident that consumption habits were a fundamental part of life, answers to questions about who consumed what, where they did so, and why have not been firmly established. So it is the purpose of this book to present new evidence about consumers in the early modern period and to look at this evidence in new ways. The main question, underlying the whole of it, is whether people's material lives reflected their social position. To discuss this, and to present different viewpoints on the processes involved, the argument is divided into two main sections. Part 1 deals with consumption at national, regional, and local levels. Part 2 looks more closely at household expenditure and behaviour before discussing the role of social position directly. This introduction explains the research methods and some of the concepts used, as well as outlining some approaches taken by previous writers.

New evidence: inventories

The main framework of the book is based on new factual evidence from a comprehensive collection of probate inventories from eight parts of England.[3] These listings of movable goods were made by neighbours shortly after a person's death, and the executors or administrators of an estate were required to exhibit the inventory at the time of probate. They were commonly made throughout the seventeenth century and became rare only after the 1720s, although the precise date varies in different dioceses. In them are listed, sometimes in considerable detail, the farming, trade, and household goods of the deceased person, together with cash and debts due. They do not record debts owed or any real estate, so they do not give a complete account of the person's wealth, although they normally give a full account of household contents. They also record other information, notably the date, the parish of residence, and the occupation or status. Each inventory contains some information about factors that may have influenced ownership, with the exception of age at death and details about the size and structure of the household. Thus it is possible to gain a considerable body of information from inventories about who exactly owned domestic goods, especially before 1725.

Many goods are listed in the documents, and it simplifies the problem of data collection and analysis to select some of them for particular study. Two criteria were used to select about twenty items for special attention: they had to be reliably and consistently listed in the documents, and they had to be representative of other goods or of people's domestic behaviour. They range from basic furniture and utensils (tables, pewter, and cooking pots) to newly available things like china. Many of them, like knives and forks or utensils for hot drinks, point towards gradual changes in eating and drinking habits. Some, such as books and clocks, show something of a household's cultural interests and indicate contacts with a wider world. The main omission is that textiles are poorly listed, and clothing was not valued in a reliable way. The full list of goods is discussed in appendix 1, together with other observations about the way in which the data were collected.

Ownership patterns of the selected goods can be analysed by cross-tabulating whether or not they were recorded in an inventory. There are a number of variables derived from the inventories themselves, and these form a framework for discussing the role of social status, occupation, wealth, place of residence, and change over time. That variations can be shown in all of these confirms that there were a large number of influences over ownership, and these are an important starting-point in discussing consumer behaviour.

The validity of these observations rests on the way in which the inventories examined were selected and the extent to which they are a meaningful sample. There are many problems in selecting inventories in a comprehensive way; one of these is that they were not made on behalf of everyone who died, and they give their best results for the middle ranks, from the lesser gentry down to the lesser yeomen. They are extremely rare for labourers. The sample for this book amounted to almost 3,000 inventories, taken from eight parts of England (Kent, Hampshire, Cambridgeshire, the north-east, the north-west, Staffordshire, Cumbria, and London) in the middle year of each decade from 1675 to 1725. The documents were taken unseen from the boxes, and no bias due to this simple technique has been noted in analysing the data. Scottish testaments usually contain only partial lists of goods and credits so cannot be sampled in this way.

At the same time, a sample of 300 for the same years was taken from the inventories of the Court of Orphans in the City of London, in order to include a wealthy group of consumers not covered in the main sample.[4] The information from these is of particular value in enabling comparisons to be made between some very well-off merchants and tradesmen and those of modest means. For instance, the median value of the inventories of the sample from the Orphans' Court was £2,034 (maximum £47,000), but for the probate sample it was £63 (maximum £4,132). These people more often owned all the goods listed than those in the main sample, as is demonstrated in chapter 2.

Inventories are a familiar documentary source of information for scholars working on early modern England; they have been widely used in studies of agriculture, trades, towns, and other communities. There are also a few studies that focus on living standards, as well as several printed collections with introductory sections discussing housing, furnishings, and changing expectations.[5] The sample used in this book, and the selection of goods for detailed examination, approaches the problem in a different way, for the documents have been taken from eight contrasting parts of the country, rather than from one area or community or occupational group. This means that the results are meaningful for much of the country, and comparisons can be made between different regions and between town and country.[6]

New evidence: diaries, household papers, and illustrations

Diaries, accounts, and domestic manuals are gradually becoming more familiar to historians than formerly, especially to those interested in family life.[7] They were made for many purposes and give a depth of detail not obtainable from inventories, and their range can be seen from the Bibliography. In this book I have used spiritual and personal diaries for their insight into daily routines and infrequent comments on material goods. Household accounts are much undervalued as a source for social history, although they are very rare and, for this reason, unrepresentative. They are often obscure in their meaning and time-consuming to analyse. Three full and interesting accounts have been used, especially in tracing household expenditure patterns in chapter 6. Like inventories, these sources of evidence about middle-ranking households are not unfamiliar to historians. The main problem in using them is that they originated from people's inner needs to record experiences, feelings, or financial affairs, and the contents reflect individual idiosyncrasies as well as individual experiences. Their reasons for writing were not to tell us about domestic routines and consumption patterns, so there are many gaps and unanswerable questions. Yet they are as close as we can get to the inner lives of households, and I have drawn on them extensively for general insights as well as specific examples.

Pictures, prints, and drawings of domestic interiors, especially British ones and especially those depicting interiors of middle rank, are potentially valuable in giving coherence to descriptions from written sources. They show 'images' of household activities, mealtimes, and leisure, and they confirm information from inventories and elsewhere. For instance, knives and forks were not used, interiors were bare, curtains were unusual, and so on. The best pictures are by Flemish and Dutch painters who visited England. However, great care is needed in using them because artists were concerned with images and ideas as well as with description. There was, it is true, a longstanding tradition of painting graphically, but how 'real' the reality is impossible to tell. Their importance is that they convey atmosphere and physical presence in a way that no written record can do. The same is true of the work of David Allan in Scotland in the late eighteenth century, although he was influenced by Italian styles.[8]

Interpretations: household consumption

A new body of evidence about ownership patterns of household goods and the contexts in which they were bought and used is not, however, enough. It is also necessary to seek new ways of interpreting consumer behaviour in the early modern period. This can be difficult and uncertain because there are no obvious, accepted concepts that the historian (or anyone else) can readily use to analyse all aspects of the material side of people's lives.

One starting-point implicit throughout this study is that material goods were, as they still are, indicative of behaviour and attitudes. They had symbolic importance as well as physical attributes and practical uses.[9] If this is taken into account, it is possible to move beyond whether or not something was recorded in a list to the meaning of ownership in social and other terms. At a simple level this is done by analysing the results from the sample of inventories, using cross-tabulations of social position or occupation. Even this shows complex patterns, but it is necessary to go further and examine the dynamics of ownership at the level of the 'unit of consumption', the household. Through exploring the organization of day-to-day life in households we can understand the specific practical and social situations with which consumption was associated. In turn, this leads to an appreciation of some of the mechanisms behind the spread of new goods throughout society from the perspective of the lives of the consumers themselves. From this point of view it is important to emphasize that the housholds of the middle ranks were organized on a scale that we would recognize. Most early modern households in England and Scotland had between four and seven people in them.[10] There were no massive feasts, no accommodation problems for large numbers of servants, and no need for formal rules for good behaviour. This must be emphasized because many accounts of early modern households are based on evidence from large establishments.

Interpretations: the house as a physical environment

In early modern houses, as now, space was used in coherent and socially meaningful ways. There is a great deal of evidence about buildings; indeed, there is almost too much, because studies of particular buildings tend to emphasize individual variation rather than general features.[11] Inventories show that most households of middle rank had houses with between three and six rooms, although some of the farmhouses were very much larger.[12] Houses surveyed in Gloucestershire were larger, probably because only the larger houses have survived; here most had eight to ten rooms.[13] The most common arrangement was two or three rooms on a ground floor, with rooms over them. The ground-floor rooms were variously called parlour, hall, houseplace, and kitchen; the rooms above were normally called chambers.[14] There were also outhouses for working tools and farming equipment. This meant that there were enough rooms for activities to be carried out in separate parts of the house, and this has significance for the ways in which space was used within the house.

Houses also had movable goods which were, by our standards, sparse, although less so than they had been in the earlier part of the seventeenth century. There were increases in domestic utensils and furnishings by the early eighteenth century, and some houses had a wide variety of such things, but many did not. It is here that illustrations can help us to visualize how bare some

Plate 1   Grace before a Meal, J. Van Aken, *c.*1720 (Ashmolean Museum, Oxford). The best and most realistic illustration of a middle-rank lifestyle.

interiors could be. Paintings and engravings of domestic interiors show that tables were laid for meals in very simple ways, ornamentation was rare, curtains at windows were unusual, armchairs and carpets were confined to a very few houses, and there were generally few pieces of furniture. Van Aken's *Grace before a Meal* is a good instance of an evocation of one corner of an English room. The bare floor and walls are immediately striking, as is the absence of curtains, ornaments, or wall hangings. In the sample of 3,000 inventories only a small proportion recorded window curtains (13 per cent), pictures (13 per cent), or decorative china (4 per cent). The wealthier London tradesmen more often had these things (81 per cent recorded window curtains and 41 per cent china), but these people were exceptional in that they were more likely than any others in England, apart from the wealthiest gentry, to own such new or decorative goods. So Van Aken does seem to be portraying a likeness that was not untypical of middle-ranking homes at the time. The picture shows very simple table-ware, with no cutlery as we would use it and no table ornaments; this too was typical, in that knives and forks were recorded in only 4 per cent of the whole sample of inventories (14 per cent in London and 33 per cent in the London Orphans' Court sample). The plates are of pewter, and this too would be expected, for china and earthenware plates were very unusual until the middle of the eighteenth century. The painting also illustrates that a living room of this kind was used for different purposes; in this case there is furniture for storage, a table set for a meal, and a spit for roasting over the fire. These and other aspects of domestic use of space are fully discussed in chapter 7, although they are implicit in the general approaches of the whole book. Differences between consumption of furnishings and consumption of clothing are also suggested by the fact that the clothing is more elaborate than the background, just as a higher proportion of expenditure was devoted to it, as is shown in chapter 6.

Interpretations: domestic space and social meaning

There is no single analysis of relationships between material and social life, but there are several interrelated approaches that are suggestive of the social meanings of physical surroundings. Behind all of them is the assumption that buildings and interiors were constructed to convey social meanings as well as for practical purposes. Sometimes the symbolism is obvious, such as the wealth and power conveyed by the architecture of large country houses. More often, at a domestic level, the impact of a place or interior was more subtle and its meanings subconsciously achieved. This impact arose partly (as it still does) from the shared expectations and culture of the people using it. Material goods, such as furnishings, made physical and visible statements about accepted values and expected behaviour. They were used to draw lines in social relationships, at the same time as providing shelter and subsistence. The notion that the built environment and the domestic space had social meanings has been effectively explored by historians of nineteenth-century housing but has been less in evidence in the work of historians of the early modern period. Likewise, those studying the buildings have made more use of these ideas than historians of their contents.[15]

One useful way of interpreting behaviour and responses to the environment is to take specific account of how people endeavoured to present themselves to others in everyday situations, using ideas derived from studies of the present day.[16] In order to foster particular images, people present themselves to others in ways that are analogous to actors' methods of presenting themselves to an audience. Various techniques are used for fostering particular impressions, such as facial expression, tones of voice, clothing, and, of course, physical surroundings. This kind of 'presentation of self' does not apply in all situations and normally takes place at an automatic and subconscious level, but it is an everyday activity, both in the home and elsewhere. In putting forward these views, Goffman and, later, Portnoy have distinguished between use of space in different parts of the living area.[17] When people are in the presence of others or when they are actively fostering their image, their behaviour is different from when they are doing essentially private things. Thus there are 'front stages', which are the settings of activities in which people present themselves to others, and can be likened to a theatrical stage. The appearance and ambiance of the 'front stage' affect the way in which individuals or households can present themselves. Likewise, the 'back stage' is analogous to the back stage of a theatre. Thus we can attempt to interpret the social roles of some possessions by observing use of space and assessing the values that were placed on activities from the point of view both of the kinds of goods that were found in different parts of the house and of the kinds of activities that took place there.

That this is a useful approach is shown by the fact that some parts of houses were more valued than others. Rooms were used for different purposes because different values were attached to different parts of the living space. In both England and Scotland households had a general living room, which in England was variously called the houseplace, house, or hall.[18] In the smaller houses this contained furniture and equipment for many household activities, such as tables, seating, cooking equipment, storage space, pewter, and miscellaneous other goods associated with daytime living. In England it was virtually unknown to have a bed in the main living room, although in Scotland enclosed and folding beds were normally to be found in the main living area. In England the main room sometimes had decorative things such as pictures, a looking glass, a clock, or books. A room used for many activities, such as that of Elizabeth Bullock of Wrockwardine in Shropshire (she was a spinster and schoolmistress), was only unusual in that she carried on her trade (schoolteaching), had a bed, and cooked in the same room.

	£	s	d
In the loft which was the place where shee kept schoole in one Truckelbed with the furniture thereunto.	1	0	0
Itm In the same Roome one little table Three buffet stooles & a low ioyned stoole with a drawer Two Greene Chaires seven benches & four little stooles.	0	10	0
Itm In the same Roome one brasse pot three little iron pots one very little kettle one boxe to hold salt a paire of bellowes one grate a paire of pothookes a paire of tounges a fire shouvl one plate to warme drinke before the fire a paire of Pot Geales and a ffrying pan.	1	0	0

She had a two-room dwelling, and the other room was 'her lodging Chamber', which was nicely furnished, with a bed (valued at £5, quite a high sum), tables, trunks, shelves, pewter, a looking glass, 'three Jugs with blue spots', linen and sheets (£5), cloth and clothes (£4. 6s. 8d.), and books (£1).[19]

In Scotland, even among the better-off tenants (roughly the equivalent of yeomen) room use was less specialized and houses were small, even in the mid-eighteenth century. A retrospective description of the farmers' living conditions around 1765 mentions two rooms, the but (or kitchen) and the ben (or parlour). The kitchen was used for a large number of activities, much as the English houseplace was, but with some important differences:

it was the general eating chamber, and one of the principal sleeping-rooms. Besides, it was the place where all the victuals were prepared: where they baked the bread, kirned the milk, washed the clothes and ironed them; ... it was the general rendezvous of all the *comers* and *gangers* about the family.[20]

This in a room 14 by 16 feet and containing standing beds. The other room, the ben, was something like an English parlour, with the master's bed and personal possessions, the Bible, linen, and food storage. In houses such as these the distinction between 'front' and 'back' becomes blurred, for there were no places devoted to specific activities, although the ben clearly served more private needs for some of the household members, while the but was more public.[21] This kind of use of space is illustrated in *Claud and Peggy* by David Allan, which depicts various kinds of activity in a very small space.

Rooms could be more specialized when the house was larger. The evidence from England is better here, and many inventories show that there were service areas, such as a kitchen, a dairy, or a buttery, for some of the messier activities. Chambers were common in all houses in England, where they were used for both sleeping and storage. In Scotland, houses larger than the 'but and ben' also contained separate rooms devoted to sleeping and storage. Chambers were normally sparsely furnished and, although some had decorative objects in them, they had the characteristics of 'backstage' areas.

That the use of space in houses served social functions, and was subject to modification, can be seen from changes in room use. The most interesting change in England in the late seventeenth century was that the parlour, formerly a best bedroom with some seating and storage, became a best living room, containing decorative things and new types of furniture. These contrasting parlours of urban tradesmen illustrate the change. The first dates from 1674/5.[22]

	£	s	d
In the Parlour			
A fether bedd bedsted and Furniture a Truckle bedd			
with Furniture a Chest Three Trunckes one Shelfe			
an old viol & a little range	4	0	0

The second, from 1717, illustrates how the parlour could be used in new ways, in this case as a room for meals, although sometimes they were furnished for other activities too.[23]

Plate 2   Claud and Peggy, David Allan, *c*.1780s (National Galleries of Scotland, Edinburgh). Many activities at the same time in one Scottish living room. There is an enclosed bed in the background.

	£	s	d
In the Parlour			
6 cane chaires 2 Elbow chaires One ovell Table			
25 picktures great and small One tea Tabble 6 sawcers			
6 cupps, two slopp basons one Tea pott One dish one			
cannister and stand one glass lanthorne 2 bird cages			
Window curtains and vallence one house Cloath	3	3	6

Yet there was also continuity, for parlours like the first could be found well into the eighteenth century, as this example of 1748 shows.[24]

	£	s	d
In the Parlour			
a Feather Bed, Bedsteads, Bolsters, sheets, Blanketts hangings & furniture	1	10	0
a Chest of drawes, one Ovall Table and Eight join'd Chairs	1	2	0
a Clock and Hanging Press	1	19	0

Whether they changed or not, the furniture, fittings, and utensils of a house made up the material culture of domestic life. This, in turn, was closely associated with the practical functions and social purposes of households. Relationships between ordinary activities, social mores and material life need to be explored in order that consumption, and specifically ownership, of household goods, can be properly placed within the contexts in which they were used. This means that it is essential to describe the numerous, time-consuming, and arduous activities necessarily undertaken in all households. These were central to the organization of space within the house, and only the larger houses had space devoted exclusively to things other than cookery, eating, cleaning, sleeping, and resting. This is the particular subject of chapter 7, but the observation that all domestic activities contributed towards the generation of the material environment is of central importance to the arguments in the book. If ownership patterns and consumer behaviour are to be understood in a social context, then patterns of household activities and their meanings need careful consideration.

Social status and occupation: the middle ranks

There are several possible ways of defining the 'middling' parts of society in the seventeenth and early eighteenth centuries. For the purposes of this book, the middle ranks are taken to encompass people who were neither at the bottom (servants, labourers, and wage-earners) nor at the top (county gentry and aristocracy) of the social hierarchy as outlined by King and Massie.[25] They therefore include the lesser gentry, professions, merchants, shopkeepers, farmers, yeomen, husbandmen, and craftsmen. About half the households in the country fell into these groups in the late seventeenth century (about 700,000 out of 1,400,000). In the mid-eighteenth century there may have been rather more than half in the middle ranks, Massie's estimate suggesting about a million out of one and a half million. It is important to realize that the boundaries between the middle and lower ranks are not clear. Husbandmen, for instance, were sometimes barely able to maintain themselves and were quite unlike the better-off farmers or even craftsmen. In tracing their incomes and consumption, one must take into account the nuances of difference within occupations, a point developed more fully in chapters 5 and 8. In order to draw on as large a part of society as possible, and to remain sensitive to differences and complexities in occupation and status, I have taken as broad and pragmatic a definition as possible.

The middle ranks were economically, socially, and politically important. Even in the seventeenth century the largest market for new and imported goods was among these consumers, and the wealthiest had an impressive range of household goods. They also made up the local social and political élites in villages and towns; many were enfranchised. The professions were of increasing importance, as were merchants and shopkeepers. Many were the forerunners of the nineteenth-century 'middle classes', a term already in use in the later eighteenth century. Some in the middle ranks had distinctly consumerist tastes and a need to assert their position in society in subtle ways. What is less obvious is that there were very many of modest means who sought to live 'not exposed to the miseries and hardships ... and not embarrassed with the pride, luxury, ambition and envy'.[26]

Consumption, luxury, and necessity

Other concepts have been used to link consumption and social life. Much writing on living standards is based on an attempt to distinguish between expenditure that was, in some sense, essential to maintaining physical life, and other goods and services. Here the vocabulary of 'necessity' and 'luxury' is frequently deployed. The contrast has some point in enabling us to gauge what kinds of things were held to be important, but in practice it is not a sophisticated enough approach to enable us to understand the meanings of consumption, especially among the middle ranks.

What were basic necessities? Did people die without them or were they just uncomfortable? It is hard to know how to define a necessity in our own culture; different people have different purposes for wanting to do so. It is harder still to do so in retrospect, but our views on the necessity for running water, sewage disposal, and central heating cannot usefully be translated into a critique of early modern consumption. But the distinction between 'necessity' and 'luxury' is one that has attracted historians, and we need to consider the meaning and impact of this well-known, if misleading, vocabulary.[27]

The meanings of these terms vary with circumstances: the word 'luxury' is normally used to convey the idea of consumption of costly and high-quality goods, food, or services; it can also carry some implicit judgement that luxuries are immoral. There is also an implied contrast with 'necessity', so that 'luxury' can also contain the meaning that 'If it had been done without by an earlier age, it was unnecessary and therefore a luxury'.[28] The word has also commonly meant something that is desirable but not in-dispensable, but possibly of higher quality and price than other goods of a similar nature: 'all that assemblage which is rather intended to please the fancy, than obviate the real wants, and which is rather ornamental than useful'.[29] The cultural aspect of luxuries is also recognized by their ability to mark the rank of the owner and thus communicate social position in a non-verbal way.[30] This frequently used word is a shorthand for a number of social and economic ideas, and its use has a certain interest in showing how ownership of some goods could be seen in polemic terms, but it does not provide a firm basis for understanding consumer behaviour. Nor does it provide any means of identifying whether particular goods should be identified as 'luxuries' or not.

It is equally difficult to pinpoint a 'necessity'. In the late seven-teenth century most household goods did not 'obviate the real wants' in the sense that some form of physical life could have been uncomfortably maintained without them. While it is amusing to speculate on the minimal food, clothing, and utensils needed for people to survive, it does not make sense to interpret behaviour in these terms, for this was already a society in which people expected to have a selection of domestic goods, although their homes seem sparsely furnished to modern eyes. So, while a 'necessity' could be defined as something necessary to main-tain life, this is an abstract definition and not a meaningful starting-point for discussing consumption. One reason for this is fundamental to the way in which social historians approach these matters, for people did not just have physical requirements; they valued the non-material aspects of their lives, such as reading, religion, family life, friends, gossip, and games; they were aware of many satisfactions in life. What people as individuals, or together as a society, felt was 'necessary' has also to be taken into account and can be understood only by observing their behaviour and priorities, as well as what they chose to own. The idea that there were classes of goods between 'luxuries' and 'necessities', usually referred to as 'decencies', modifies the stark contrasts in the vocabulary but does not remove the need to take account of the priorities shown within a society. These terms should be as carefully used as words about class.

Consumption and society have also been linked in characterizations of the 'consumer society' or 'consumerism' in the eighteenth century. Accounts of the exuberant enjoyments, increasingly available as the century progressed, make compulsive reading, with amusing anecdotes about the consumerist pleasures of the wealthy, the excesses of those who strived to be fashionably dressed, and the attempts of tradesmen to satisfy this kind of demand.[31] This social history of consumerism is confined to the wealthier tradesmen and the gentry, who had the time and resources for an increasing range of goods and services by the later eighteenth century. It is hard to see through this to other consumers, whose behaviour is difficult to dramatize, but whose experience was that of a larger proportion of the middle-ranking population. Excitement about new goods and services became much greater towards the end of the eighteenth century and, although fashion and enjoyment were clearly experienced in the late seventeenth century, the 'consumerist' approach is not so appropriately applied either to the earlier period or to the bulk of the middle ranks.

Consumption and economic change

The main themes in this study are essentially social and cultural. These have not, however, been the approaches favoured by most writers about consumption. A very large amount written on this subject arises from attempts to explain industrialization in the second half of the eighteenth century,[32] although there are also studies of the pre-industrial era that refer to consumption.[33]

These works discuss the role of the home market and of demand, as opposed to production and overseas trade. Early writers, especially Gilboy in the 1930s, and later Eversley, outlined ideas and possibilities that still have not been properly tested and developed. To use Gilboy's words:

'Obviously the factory system with its complicated industrial mechanism cannot function profitably without a large and growing demand ready and willing to absorb its products as fast as they are produced. ... Why ... should the home population suddenly afford a market for a greater number of products?'[34]

Gilboy's explanations were that there were increases in real incomes (by which she meant wages) and that new 'wants' were spread throughout the population partly as a result of inter-class competition and mobility. But, although she recognized the limitations of the evidence then available, she called for 'continued investigation of demand in relation to the Industrial Revolution'. This has certainly been done in the half-century or so since she wrote, and no account of the economy in the eighteenth century is without a discussion of 'demand' in some form or other; but, as a recent survey puts it, 'the study of the subject is still severely handicapped by the lack of adequate quantitative data'.[35] There continues to be an uncertainty in the literature as to the importance of demand in economic change, and whether it came primarily from the home market or from exports.[36] Eversley's work is important here because it emphasizes the role of the middle ranks within the home market and thus the significance of the households that are the main subject of this book.

Economic historians have also looked at consumption from the perspective of single industries, or even single businesses. Most business or industrial histories make some attempt to outline the markets for the products made, in order to provide a context for discussions of growth, business decisions, or the fortunes of individuals.[37] These studies often point towards the industrial revolution, but they are normally based on well-documented accounts of particular parts of the economy that cover a longer time span than the late eighteenth century. Coleman's study of the silk industry, at the beginning of his larger study of one company within it, exemplifies this, for here the focus is clearly on production, manufacturing techniques, and supplies of raw material, but the importance of a broader market for simple silks is recognized and production explained in terms of available markets.

The meanings that the consumers themselves attached to silk, and any other implications of its use, go unremarked.[38] In this, as in all studies of industrial change, the focus is on production, while the consumers themselves are taken for granted. Business decisions are seen as influencing the market and thus consumption, but the responses and choices made by consumers are not the central issue. This approach is found in a very large and distinguished body of writing on industrial change, although some recent writers have shown a greater sensitivity to the importance of understanding the people who bought things.[39] On the other hand, there is a valuable sensitivity to the economic and other constraints on producers and a regard for the qualities of different kinds of products in these writings, which are also less limited chronologically to explaining the industrial revolution; they tend to trace developments as far back in time as documentary and other evidence allows, and especially into the late seventeenth century.

Approaches to consumption by way of enquiries into increasing demand in the eighteenth century are, as already implied, beset with problems. The factual basis is extremely insecure at a national level. For instance, the production series for 'home industries' presented by Deane and Cole are narrowly based on a few products, namely soap, leather, candles, and beer. These were unfortunate enough to catch the eye of the eighteenth-century excise, and as such were by no means representative of all, or even many, products for the home market.[40] No domestic durables were included, although other studies have shown that these were liable to rapid change.[41] The output of this narrow range of 'home' industries is shown as virtually static from 1700 to 1750 at a time when 'export' industries were estimated almost to have doubled. But there were some rapidly expanding trades at this time, making a hitherto unknown range of goods available to some of the population.

There are also problems with chronology. Studying demand in the economy arose out of a longstanding desire to explain and understand the industrial revolution. This has meant that the late seventeenth and the early eighteenth centuries have been presented as a time when nothing much happened. Later developments in the structure of production, in imports of materials, and the output of many industries are seen as completely overshadowing the less dramatic changes of the earlier period. Likewise interest is strongest in those issues that seem to offer explanations for later growth. These essentially macro-economic approaches do not go very far in describing and explaining the processes of consumption because they are asking questions about economic transformation, statistical aggregation, and the causes of the industrial revolution. As an instance of this, it is notable that an economic study of brewing was published in 1959, but historians have only recently tried to put the consumption of ale in a social perspective through studies of inns and alehouses.[42] So this kind of approach does not aim to illuminate the experiences of consumers themselves, and especially not consumers in the earlier part of the eighteenth century. Nevertheless, the chronology of change is important, and chapter 2 examines patterns of growth derived from the sample of probate inventories.

Consumption, wages, and living standards

A further economic approach to consumption in the historical literature focuses on wages and living standards. This too arises from interest in economic growth and production, rather than from a concern for the behaviour of consumers themselves, but questions are sometimes posed about the expenditure patterns of individuals and their behaviour as consumers. For instance, A. H. John and others following him have argued that lower food prices between about 1730 and 1750 enabled wage-earners to have a small surplus to spend on domestic goods and clothing, thus stimulating innovation in industrial production in the early stages of economic growth. Eversley has argued that a similar momentum continued until 1780.[43] These ideas have not gone unchallenged and are based on fragile evidence, but they exemplify the way in which writers have made broad generalizations about consumption habits and economic growth. Evidence from inventories about these issues is presented in chapter 8, and the conclusion that wage-earners were unlikely to have been important in consumption is stressed again in chapter 9.

In a different context, assumptions have necessarily been made about consumption patterns of wage-earners when calculations are made for price series. Here consumption is seen in terms of a 'basket of goods' needed to define the weightings of price series. Any attempt to estimate 'cost of living' is based on assumptions about, or observations of, consumer behaviour, but the main problem with these studies in the early modern period is that the factual basis for many statements about living standards is founded on very little evidence about expenditure, and on too narrow an approach to income – problems that those who have done the calculations acknowledge more readily than those who have used the results.[44] Recent research has adopted different viewpoints because it is apparent that living standards, incomes, and expenditure were too complex to be characterized by contrasts like wages/prices. The idea that people adopted complex strategies for survival, obtaining wages and incomes from many sources, enables us to understand individual behaviour in a less abstracted way, although it makes it harder to trace long-term changes in incomes.[45] This book does not confront these issues directly because it concentrates on the middle ranks, rather than on wage-earners. It does, however, interpret incomes in terms of the various strategies for survival and shows that incomes were derived from many sources. The two chapters about the incomes and expenditure of middle-ranking households (chapters 5 and 6) are based on an analysis of household accounts and diaries.

One suggestion about living standards has been that people copied one another for social reasons. Thus markets for industrial goods were able to develop in Britain because there was no legislation to prevent people owning what they wanted and copying the behaviour of the upper ranks. In theory people could dress how they liked and own what goods they liked and there were no institutional barriers to new goods being available to a large part of the population.[46] This important observation about the relationship between social structure and production has been developed in a number of ways. One of these has been the idea that people readily copied one another in order to keep up appearances and to follow the lead of those of higher social status than themselves in the kinds of clothing and possessions that they owned. Perkin has especially noted the tendency for people to emulate those of higher rank; Hecht suggests that the employment of servants by the wealthier people in the population helped to spread new ideas and habits to the lower classes; McKendrick and Minchinton have argued that the pursuit of fashion, and the commercialization that went with it, broke down resistance to consumption and enabled a fully fledged consumer society to emerge at the end of the eighteenth century.[47] These approaches to social relations and consumer behaviour are, however, limited to specific situations and groups of people; they do not provide a satisfactory framework for discussion of the experiences involved in consumption for the majority of people of middle rank. The cross-tabulations of ownership of goods from inventories in chapter 8 do show that there was a consumption hierarchy, with goods recorded in some groups more frequently than in others. This was not, however, the same as the social hierarchy.

The artefacts

There is also a large amount written about the artefacts themselves, that is to say clothing, costume, domestic utensils, and furniture. Surviving artefacts are cared for in museums or collected privately, and this influences the works about them, for their main intention is to provide detailed guides, descriptions, and attributions. This fact, together with the nature of the surviving objects themselves, gives a quite different view of consumption.[48] Pottery and porcelain, for instance, have generated an enormous collectors' literature with fully researched discussions on all the collectable pottery available in the eighteenth century, but the focus tends to be on the most valuable pieces; there are even specialist journals.[49] Likewise, the study and collection of furniture and costume has generated specialist collections in museums and a specialist literature.[50] The intentions of those who study the objects themselves are so different from the intentions of economic and social historians that it takes considerable imagination to bridge the gap and see any relevance in this work for the study of consumption.[51] Collectors are interested in the objects themselves, in their aesthetic qualities, origins, date, and sometimes monetary value, although there is some interest in the economic and social background to production and consumption. Thus there are some very good studies of makers, but the focus is usually on attribution of an object to a maker. On the other hand, economic and social historians tend to regard the objects as illustrative material for their studies and show a surprising disregard for the physical remains of the past.

The main problem with the very large literature on the artefacts themselves is that the surviving pieces are those of the highest quality and greatest aesthetic appeal. It is impossible to analyse the style of pottery or furnishings found in a yeoman's or tradesman's house in the early eighteenth century from displays in even the most comprehensive collections, such as the primary galleries in the Victoria and Albert Museum in London. Likewise, galleries with reconstructed interiors, such as those at the Geffrye Museum in London, or at the Victoria and Albert Museum, show objects and interiors owned by the wealthier members of society. In the same way, the otherwise enlightening and interesting books on styles of furnishings in the seventeenth and eighteenth centuries refer largely to the country houses of the gentry or to the large town houses of the well-to-do, not to the houses of the bulk of middle-ranking people.[52] Studies of design and artefacts thus provide only a partial view of the goods themselves. Even so, there is much more here than most writers of general histories and students of consumption itself admit. That physical remains can be used to illuminate consumption is shown in Spufford's study of the linen trade where she illustrates a few, rare examples of clothing worn by people in the lower parts of society.[53]

This book partly originated in these approaches, through an earlier attempt to explore consumption and production in the pottery industry.[54] Looking at consumption from the perspective of particular goods, as well as looking at surviving examples, has a great deal of merit in it. But, from the point of view of consumers themselves, we need to know about their behaviour, the goods they owned, and their priorities. Ideally we require lists of the goods, clothing, and textiles owned by all households every few years, so that we could trace who owned what, and changes could be clearly documented. But historical evidence is rarely ideal, and this book makes the most of what is available in order to explore the motivation behind consumer behaviour. This begins, in the next chapter, with an outline of changing consumption after 1670.

Part 1

THE NATION

2

GROWTH

In travelling thro' England ... which way soever we look, we see
something new.

(Daniel Defoe, 1727)[1]

The purpose of this chapter is to set the scene by demonstrating
that the ownership of domestic goods increased between 1675
and 1725. This establishes that the late seventeenth and early
eighteenth centuries were marked by brisk changes, some based
on industrial expansion, others on increasing imports of consumer
items. These years used to be thought of as ones of restricted
development, but it is now realized that there were growth areas
as well as structural changes. The impression of stagnation is
derived from figures from the excise records, but these are not
representative of the economy as a whole.[2] In the last fifteen years
many more statistical series have become available, as well as an
important study of the East India trade.[3]

One of the most important conclusions from the sample of
inventories is that ownership of all household goods increased
before 1725. This confirms the importance of the latter part of the
seventeenth century and the early years of the eighteenth century.

Table 2.1 shows the proportions of inventories in each decade
in which the selected goods were recorded in the main sample.
Table 2.2 shows the same information for the sample taken from
the inventories of the London Orphans' Court. Changes in consumer behaviour are clearly apparent; virtually all goods were
recorded more frequently in 1725 than previously. In some cases,
expansion in ownership was very dramatic. Clocks, for instance,
were over three times more frequent by 1715 than they had been
in 1685; in the wealthy households of the London freemen they

Table 2.1 Frequencies of ownership of selected household goods in a sample of inventories from England, 1675–1725

	No. of inventories	Tables %	Cooking pots %	Sauce-pans %	Pewter dishes %	Pewter plates %	Earthen-ware %	Books %	Clocks %	Pictures %	Looking glasses %	Table linen %	Window curtains %	Knives and forks %	China %	Utensils for hot drinks %	Silver or gold %
1675	520	87	66	2	39	9	27	18	9	7	22	43	7	1	0	0	23
1685	520	88	68	6	46	18	27	18	9	8	28	45	10	1	1	0	21
1695	497	89	69	8	44	21	34	18	14	9	31	41	11	3	2	1	24
1705	520	90	71	11	47	34	36	19	20	14	36	41	12	4	4	2	23
1715	455	91	74	17	56	42	47	21	33	24	44	44	19	6	8	7	29
1725	390	91	76	23	55	45	57	22	34	21	40	37	21	10	9	15	21
All	2,902	89	70	11	48	27	37	19	19	13	33	42	13	4	4	4	23

Sources and notes
Main sample: see appendices 1 and 2 for the origin of the sample and its limitations

Table 2.2 Frequencies with which selected goods were recorded in a sample of inventories from the London Orphans' Court, 1675–1725

	No. of inventories	Tables %	Cooking pots %	Sauce-pans %	Pewter %	Pewter dishes %	Pewter plates %	Earthen-ware %	Books %	Clocks %	Pictures %	Looking glasses %	Table linen %	Window curtains %	Knives and forks %	China %	Utensils for hot drinks %	Silver or gold %
1675	50	94	82	32	96	10	4	64	60	56	44	88	76	68	8	4	2	88
1685	50	96	84	32	82	4	8	56	80	54	58	86	60	68	20	10	0	94
1695	50	98	86	58	90	12	16	58	84	58	70	98	80	76	22	30	8	94
1705	50	100	96	76	78	18	18	72	90	70	80	98	86	82	36	48	48	96
1715	50	100	78	76	96	48	48	90	86	90	86	96	88	96	48	74	78	96
1725	50	100	94	84	88	70	76	88	94	88	76	98	82	94	64	80	96	94
All	300	98	87	60	88	27	28	71	82	69	69	94	79	81	33	41	39	94

Sources and notes
London Orphan's Court sample, City of London Record Office. See appendix 1 for comments on the sample.

were already recorded in over a half in 1675, but increased until nine out of ten had them by 1715. The greatest expansion was in ownership of china and utensils for hot drinks in the freemen's inventories; the latter were extremely rare, even in the 1690s, but were recorded in virtually all of these households by 1725. The period after 1670 was therefore one of changing consumption, and the changes in frequency with which goods were recorded in households offers the basis for a chronological framework within which other aspects of consumer behaviour can be seen.

Patterns of change

There were three patterns of change in the frequencies with which items were recorded in both series of inventories. A few goods were well established in the 1670s; these are representative of basic furniture and utensils (pewter, tables, and cooking pots), many associated with 'backstage' activities. These also represent well-established aspects of the economy. Secondly, some goods were already in use in 1675 but were not common; these include books, silver, table linen, pewter dishes, pewter plates, looking glasses, and earthenware. They were mostly associated with 'frontstage' activities. Change here was often rapid. Lastly, there were some important new goods, some of which were virtually unknown in 1675, such as china and various equipment for the new hot drinks, tea, coffee, and chocolate. Others were extremely rare in 1675, including clocks, pictures, window curtains, and knives and forks. They too were 'frontstage' goods and were either decorative or associated with new mealtime behaviour. Ownership of them all expanded very rapidly.

Established goods were found in most inventories in the first decade of the survey, together with many other basic items that have not been selected for particular study. They were not recorded in every inventory, but the tiny upward movement reflects growing ownership of commonplace goods. Each item had its own idiosyncrasies, and pewter is especially interesting, for it had declined slightly (4 per cent) in frequency by 1725. This is within the margins of error for the survey, but it is also in keeping with what we know about the development of pewter manufacture at this time, which reached its zenith in the late seventeenth and early eighteenth centuries and was thereafter very gradually replaced by crockery and glass. The only sign of this replacement by

GROWTH 29

1725 is in the Kent sample, where the frequency with which it was recorded was much lower (91 per cent) than it had been in 1705, when every inventory had had it. There were unusually high proportions of inventories with earthenware in this area, and earthenware plates and tablewares were often specified, also unusual at this date elsewhere. But this 'replacement' effect was mild, and pewter predominated for some time, gradually fading out in the later eighteenth century as crockery became standard.

In the wealthier households of the Orphans' Court inventories there were similar patterns of change for established goods, with high frequencies to begin with and slight growth by 1725. The main difference was that a wider range of goods was already well established in 1675, including many 'frontstage' goods. Looking glasses, for instance, were found in 86 per cent of Orphans' Court inventories as early as 1685 and in virtually all of them by 1725.

Ownership of established goods in inventories relates to those parts of the economy and society that had been functioning for some time and had relatively limited scope for expansion. Whether they can also be said to represent 'traditional' aspects of seventeenth- and eighteenth-century life is more difficult to say, for to observe that something was already there is not the same as to say that it had had long acceptance or was an underlying part of the structure of society. But it is clear that there were many well-established goods which represent less rapidly changing aspects of the economy and of consumers' lives. It is also significant that these were either furniture or goods with functions in food preparation.

There were more varied patterns of change among the things that were unusual in 1675. Some showed little or no increase; book ownership, for instance, changed very little in aggregate, although this was made up of substantial increases in London by 1725 (from 18 to 56 per cent) and other towns of all kinds (from 20 to 36 per cent) and decline in rural areas (from 18 to 13 per cent). Likewise, the frequencies with which silver was recorded declined slightly overall, resulting from a combination of mild decrease in some areas and mild increases elsewhere. Silver was more common in the London sample than elsewhere; in 1675, 48 per cent in London owned silver, but only 8 per cent in Carlisle and 9 per cent in the Cambridgeshire samples, while virtually all Orphans' Court inventories recorded it. Influences on the ownership of silver were probably different from those on any other item here, because it had an intrinsic value and fluctuations in ownership could have varied with family needs and prosperity. It could have represented the 'traditional' attitude of investing in things of known value rather than spending money on other goods of a more useful or decorative nature. If it did represent anything about attitudes, the patterns of change shown here do not suggest that these altered much in this period, and, if it is taken as a material which was acquired for its relatively high value, then hoarding of increased wealth is not apparent either.

On the other hand, ownership of some goods (earthenware, pewter dishes, pewter plates, looking glasses) increased dramatically; the proportion of households with earthenware and looking glasses more than doubled between 1675 and 1725. Again there were considerable variations from place to place, both in the frequencies recorded at the beginning and in amounts of growth. In Lancashire, earthenware was recorded in most inventories (82 per cent) in 1675, with an unusual downward trend thereafter to 65 per cent in 1725. In Kent, it was recorded in only 38 per cent in 1675 but in most (88 per cent) of them by 1725. But the composite picture is of earthenware as a known, but not ubiquitous, item in 1675, ownership of which grew rapidly by 1725. In the Orphans' Court inventories, earthenware was much more common to begin with and grew to being one of the most frequently recorded materials by 1725. Looking-glass ownership was similarly varied and complex. In some dioceses, looking glasses were virtually unrecorded in 1675 (Carlisle 3 per cent, Cambridgeshire 6 per cent, for instance), but were quite common in other areas (London 34 per cent, Kent 37 per cent), and they were already well established in the Orphans' Court inventories. Growth did occur everywhere except in Carlisle and Staffordshire, while in the Orphans' Court inventories they became, with the exception of tables, the most frequently recorded item by 1725. The evidence for pewter dishes and plates is less firmly based because of residual doubts (outlined in appendix 1) that they may have been seriously under-recorded in some places; but, if omissions were reasonably consistent in the five dioceses examined in table 2.1, then interesting patterns can be seen here too. Plates were smaller than dishes and were used by individuals rather than for eating in a communal way. The differences in shape and size can be seen from illustrations of mealtimes in chapter 7 and also from valuations, for dishes were normally valued at between one and two shillings; while plates were cheaper, at about sixpence each – which is indicative of their smaller size. Rapid growth in ownership of pewter plates is therefore more important than it might seem because they are indicators, with many other goods, of changing behaviour at meals. The frequencies with which new goods were recorded changed extremely rapidly between 1700 and 1725. The Orphans' Court inventories were slightly different, in that the only goods that were rare in 1675 were those that were entirely new, but these displayed exceptionally rapid expansion. Utensils for hot drinks were found in less than 10 per cent of the Orphans' sample in 1695 but thirty years later were in virtually all of them. China similarly changed from being unknown in 1675 to being a normal part of household equipment by 1715. In the main sample there were important regional and other variations, and it is here that some of the influences over consumer behaviour and preferences stand out most clearly. The things that were already known in 1675, even if they were unusual, increased in frequency in all dioceses, although the places with fewest at the beginning usually had fewest at the end. Clock ownership was slightly different, in that Lancashire and London joined Kent as the areas with the highest proportions (about 50 per cent) with them. Clocks were also exceptional in that only a slightly lower proportion of households had them in rural than in urban areas, while ownership of the rest increased more in urban areas, with London predominating. In the Orphans' Court inventories, ownership of these things grew more rapidly from a higher starting-point, with the result that clocks, pictures, and curtains were to be found in virtually every household by 1715, at a time when they continued to be very rare in some of the main sample.

Ownership of completely new goods was more varied, for they were quite common in some places by 1725 but still virtually unknown in others. Thus china was not recorded in Staffordshire until 1725, whereas it first appeared in the Durham sample in 1685. Utensils for hot drinks, recorded in Kent in 1685, did not appear in the Cambridgeshire sample until 1725. This meant that growth was more concentrated in some areas than others; by 1725, 60 per cent of London inventories recorded utensils for hot drinks, whereas only 6 per cent of those in rural areas had them. China appeared in 35 per cent of the London sample but in only 4 per cent of rural areas by 1725. This kind of wide variation suggests that there were uneven economic, commercial, and social mechanisms at work which led to new goods being more readily

available in some places than others. In this respect, the Orphans'
Court inventories show just how fast new commodities could, in
favourable circumstances, be adopted.

Distinctions between new and established goods are useful in
showing variety in patterns of change, although observation of
increasing frequencies for new goods is implicit in this kind of
evidence, for, although households contained many of them, I
have chosen only a few that had little room for growth. What this
does show is that changing ownership was based both on new
commodities and on those that were already known, so expansion
was not confined to new wants and behaviour, but it is notable that
the most rapid growth took place in those goods used for entirely
new purposes. Thus earthenware and china spread as utensils for
hot drinks, whereas the use of new materials for tableware was a
later development which took much longer to finalize. This confirms the need to examine carefully how goods were used and the
roles that they fulfilled in the lives of the people who owned them.

Other kinds of change

Whether particular items were present in households conveys a
surprising amount about changing consumer preferences and the
ownership of goods, but there were other changes too. Utensils
and miscellaneous household goods changed in appearance and
style, while households came to own more of them, so that
the overall effect was of rooms which were less bare and more
decorative, although the chronology of these changes is difficult to
pinpoint. There were quality changes which are also hard to
pinpoint because most of the furniture, china, teawares, pictures,
and mirrors that have survived tend to be those of higher quality.
Ordinary products have long since been discarded. Thus museum
collections of china contain high-quality pieces, and discussions
of domestic interiors tend to concentrate on the élite, as do the
histories of furniture.[4] It is not, of course, improper that museums
should concentrate on artistic merit and design, but we should not
assume that the items preserved in collections are representative
of the whole of society. Likewise, the formalized interiors painted
as backgrounds in the English conversation pieces of the 1740s
depict idealized interiors of the gentry and others who were
generally richer than the majority of the people covered by this
study, and give a false picture of their environment.

The heavy architectural and artistic styles of the baroque and the lighter styles of the rococo were reflected in high-quality household goods and furniture, but these influenced fashionable style in London and had less impact on even the best locally made furniture in the provinces. As far as most middling households were concerned, these styles were of marginal relevance, for much furniture was very simply made and has not been thought worth keeping, so that any changes in appearance cannot be reconstructed. There was considerable continuity in the styles of some utensils; cooking pots and kettles, for instance, varied in shape but were basically the same in the seventeenth and eighteenth centuries as they had been before and continued to be after.

Some differences in furniture resulted in part from changes in the organization of the furniture-making trades, as well as in fashionable taste. In the seventeenth century, even in London, the joiner was the main woodworking craftsman, but the trade of cabinet-maker developed in the late seventeenth century in the London quality trade. Cabinet-makers made high-quality furniture, especially chests of drawers and tables. They also used new woods, such as walnut and mahogany, and new techniques, such as veneering, which resulted in lighter, more varied furniture. In addition, cane chairs became popular in the late seventeenth century, although they went out of fashion in the 1720s. Some of these new techniques, and the trade of cabinet-maker, spread to the provinces in the early eighteenth century, although furniture normally continued to be made locally by joiners. Many of the short-lived fashion changes were not relevant to the possessions of the middle ranks and especially not to the husbandmen or farmers who are the subject of much of this study. The pace of change in styles probably increased by the 1730s, when the value of designing properly for the high-class trades was appreciated, with the first pattern books dating from the 1750s (although full-time designers were not known until the late eighteenth century).[5]

Some changes in modest households can be seen in contrasts between living rooms in the seventeenth and early eighteenth centuries. A farmer's living room in 1676/7 had very sparse and basic furnishings.[6]

£ s d

It in the dwelling howse
one longe table 6 joyned stooles one Cubbord

	£	s	d
3 Chaires one little table one fire grate fire showell & tonges one jack three spits prised at	3	0	0
It Brass & pewter of all sorts prised at	5	0	0
It two Iron pots one dreping pan 2 frying pans & other Ware prised at	0	15	0
It Butter & Cheese hemp & flax prised	2	0	0
It in the plor one fether Bed and bedclothes & boulster prised at	0	10	0
one chest & one table Boord & other things therein prised at	0	10	0

Later examples have a different feel about them.[7]

	£	s	d
In the hall place one·Clock & Case 1 large grate 2 Tables & 2 forms 8 Joyned Chaires. 1 warming pan, 1 dreeping pan one Northprospect of London	6	4	0
In the little parlour 13 cane Chaires 1 oval Table 1 looking glass. 1 Day Table & some smal pictures	6	5	0

An unusually late example (1742) has an almost modern feel about it, although there are still relatively few pieces of furniture.[8]

	£	s	d
In the Hall a Clock & Case	1	10	0
A looking Glass	0	10	0
A Writing Desk and Table & Stand	2	10	0
A Doz of Sedge Chairs	0	6	0
a grate	0	8	0
In the Parlour A Corner Cupboard & China & a Tea Table	0	17	6
An Oval Table a Tea Table a Card Table a dressing Table & a Hand Board	1	2	6
twelve Cane Chairs	2	8	0

Utensils and other goods changed more rapidly in style than furniture because they were more readily replaced. Some changes were remarkable; earthenware, for instance, was transformed before 1750, with many new styles and finer shapes resulting in much wider variety of pieces with much more varied uses. Increasing availability of china also had a dramatic impact, although the shapes and styles of imported blue and white wares for the

Plate 3 Family at Tea, R. Colius, 1732 (Victoria and Albert Museum, London). The teawares here were more lavish than those in most houses of middle rank, and few had such extensive collections of silver. The cups and saucers are typical of those imported from China and were among the most decorative of the new utensils.

middle market remained fairly standard during the eighteenth century. Some new items, like teawares or knives and forks, were different from anything previously available, so that their use modified the physical appearance of living spaces. Take, for instance, the differences between the appearances of meals and of tea-tables in contemporary painting, such as those by Van Aken and R. Colius. The tea-tables have decorated, blue and white utensils; the meals have less colour and less varied equipment, although the households portrayed at tea were probably of higher status than those shown in the meals. They illustrate the kinds of visual impact that the changing ownership of these utensils could have.

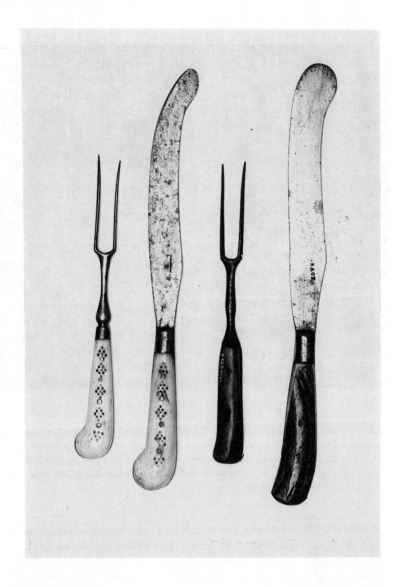

Plate 4   Mid-eighteenth-century cutlery (photographs from the collection in Sheffield City Museum). Another new commodity in the eighteenth century. Simple cutlery in museum collections dates from the middle of the eighteenth century when it was being more widely used than previously. The pair on the left have bone handles and date from the 1750s; maker Benjamin Middleton of Sheffield. The pair on the right have handles of horn and date from the 1780s; maker John Staniland of Sheffield.

Patterns after 1725

Can the same kinds of patterns and distinctions be made after 1725, when inventories become too rare to sample? Two examples illustrate that they can, at least until 1750. Imports of pictures showed little upward trend until the 1750s, but print production in England (especially in London) was increasing from the 1730s, and by 1760 there were very large numbers of engravers and print-sellers in London, as well as portrait and landscape painters.[9] The output of pictures and prints increased from the 1740s, so that ownership of such things could have continued to grow as it had done earlier in the century, and there is no reason to suppose that the expansion in the numbers of households who owned them did not continue after 1725. The capacity of the pottery industry also represents some of the complexities in the patterns shown by this group of goods, for it did not expand very much overall between 1725 and 1745, but this was the result of a mild decline in the established branches of delft and coarse earthenware, and the growth of new types of pottery. Between about 1715 and 1750 the industry underwent major structural changes in location, techniques, and organization, which only manifested themselves in rapid expansion after 1745. Ownership of earthenware would have continued to expand in the same kind of way after 1725 for perhaps two decades, but after 1750 change would have been more rapid, as the capacity of the industry, and the range of products available, expanded more rapidly. Thus patterns of change in ownership shown by inventories could have continued in the same kind of way through the 1740s, but thereafter the mechanisms may well have been different, with new patterns about which we have no evidence comparable with that from inventories.

The same kinds of conclusions are also true of new goods, for these continued to be distinguished by rapid expansion after 1725. The goods that had been new in the late seventeenth century were imported through the East India Company, and they all strongly suggest that the patterns that can be seen before 1725 continued but with more rapid change after 1750. Legally imported hot drinks, for instance, and especially tea, became much more common in the 1750s, and we would expect the utensils for these to be more common as well. Indeed, by the 1740s and 1750s tea was widely referred to as a normal part of the lifestyles of the middle ranks in society in all kinds of ways. So what we see from the sample of inventories before 1725 is the beginning of the process by which a new item entered the diet of the middle ranks, a process which continued in the following decades. However, it certainly had not spread to the whole population by 1760.

Chronology of change, 1670–1760

Change was not equally spread over the decades covered by the inventory sample, for it was more apparent from 1685 to 1715 than before or after. Inventories record a particular item at one particular time; there is no information about how long the household had owned it and whether they had formerly got rid of things. In tracing the spread of household durables, it would be best to know when they were first purchased, but this cannot be deduced from inventories; nor is it possible to measure the likely time-lags between people acquiring things and their appearance in inventories. The implicit assumption here is that the behaviour of those who were about to die (and therefore leave inventories) was much the same as that of everyone else. Goods could certainly appear quickly in inventories, as the rapid increases in newly available china in the Orphans' Court sample twenty years earlier than in the main sample shows. Ownership of most goods changed more slowly as a result of processes that took some time to work through, so that we must not necessarily expect close relationships between economic conditions (especially crises and annual trade fluctuations) and the patterns displayed in inventories. There is a reasonable similarity in some decades but in others there are surprises, such as the observation that the greatest change in ownership in both series of inventories occurred in the decade 1705–15, which does not fit with this as a decade of crisis, high prices, and disrupted trade. Likewise the last decade, 1715–25, was more prosperous in general but showed as little growth in ownership frequencies as the first decade of the sample.

In the first decade after 1675, as table 2.1 illustrates, there was little change in the proportions of households owning the goods selected from the probate inventory sample, except for a few items in the Orphans' Court sample (books, knives and forks, and pictures, together with pewter dishes and plates in the main sample). The decade was therefore one of continuity with the past as it was in the economy as a whole. It followed a period of mixed fortunes, for there had been some years of acute crisis and misfortune in the 1660s, although by 1674 confidence had returned and the economy enjoyed a period of prosperity which lasted, with setbacks, into the 1690s. Yet the impact of the availability of new goods was not as yet apparent in the 1685 sample of inventories, except for a small increase in the ownership of china in the London Orphans' Court inventories. There were signs of new developments in the economy, especially the imports of a wider range of goods, together with signs that these were influencing the behaviour of the wealthy commercial classes in London. In this way, developments in the economy as a whole 'matched' those suggested by the inventory sample, expressing basic continuity, with some slight changes.

In the decade 1685–95 there was considerable economic advance in general, and here too developments in the economy 'match' those of the inventory sample, for there were increases in ownership of both new and established goods, with much more rapid change in the Orphans' Court sample. Ownership of the established goods changed relatively little, but there were changes between 1685 and 1695 in the frequencies of things already known in households but not widely owned, both in the main sample and in the Orphans' Court inventories. In particular, this was an important decade for the expansion in ownership of items that were to become very common by 1715 (looking glasses, earthenware, clocks, pictures, and curtains) in the Orphans' Court inventories. The decade 1685–95 was characterized by considerable economic activity in general. The evidence from the inventories more or less coincides with that on the economy as a whole, with growth in ownership of known, but not widespread, items; the beginnings of growth in ownership of new goods; and very little change for established goods. From a chronological viewpoint, this must not be dated too precisely because there were many variations and there were time-lags that we cannot measure between general economic change and recorded changes in ownership of domestic durables in inventories. But the basic prosperity of the 1680s and 1690s was manifesting itself by 1695 in increasing frequency of ownership of most goods, new and known.

From 1695 to 1705 the economy as a whole was more troubled and more liable to wide fluctuations and periodic crises, with greater or lesser influence depending on the part of the economy examined. Bread prices in London, for instance, were high for the whole of the 1690s, although they reached unusually low levels in 1701 and 1702. Some of this variation is reflected in the inventories, for it was at this time that the new goods began, as yet unevenly, to establish themselves. Variation and unevenness can be seen in comparisons between the Orphans' Court sample, measuring the most advanced aspects of ownership, and the rest. By 1705 many things which were as yet uncommon in the main sample had become standard household equipment in the Orphans' Court sample (earthenware, looking glasses, pictures, clocks, books), and this alone identifies it as an important decade, although in the main sample itself expansion was at a lesser rate and, in some things, insignificant. Thus china and utensils for hot drinks increased dramatically in frequency in the Orphans' Court inventories but had only just appeared in some parts of the main sample.

The decade 1705–15 stands out as the one in which most change took place in both sets of inventories. Every item recorded some increase between 1705 and 1715, even the well-established ones and even those that expanded very little over the whole period 1675–1725. The previously known things, such as clocks, pictures, looking glasses, earthenware, and curtains, became much more common everywhere. New goods increased, and some became, by 1715, normal equipment in the London households represented by the Orphans' Court inventories. Change was uneven in other ways, for growth was more rapid in some places than in others. In particular, all goods were more frequent in the London inventories by 1715 than elsewhere, although this had not previously been the case. It is as if these changes in ownership were exaggerating previously existing inequalities; issues such as the role of towns and the growth of London clearly warrant further consideration and are the subject of later chapters. Yet this decade of change was varied and troubled in the economy as a whole; it began in crisis, and recorded the highest bread and other prices (1709–10) of the period 1660–1760. There is no reason why ownership of household durables should not expand in conditions of economic fluctuation and variation of this kind, for there were growth areas in the economy which were, to some extent, aimed at household consumption. Furthermore, changing patterns of ownership were not related to the immediate ups and downs of the economy, and this decade was the culmination of a long period of gradual but varied economic change.

In the last decade before 1725 there was much less expansion in both series of inventories. Ownership of the well-established goods barely changed, which is not surprising, in that they were already very common by 1715, but there was even a very mild decline in pewter ownership. Some of the other things that had become more common by 1715 also appeared slightly less often, among them pictures and looking glasses. The only goods to be recorded more frequently were those associated with the East India trade, namely china and utensils for hot drinks, together with earthenware. On the other hand, and apparently in contrast, this was a more prosperous decade in the economy as a whole (except for the financial collapse of 1720–1), with low bread prices and increases in many series measuring trade and production. Tea and coffee imports increased very rapidly, while many other indicators, such as imports of china, pottery, printed goods, paper, and beer output, at least remained steady, and there were fewer violent fluctuations in annual trade. The differences in frequencies of ownership of goods between 1715 and 1725 seem out of keeping with some of the patterns for this decade in general and indicate that the influences over changes in the frequency of ownership of household goods were not necessarily immediate ones, and fluctuations in the economy could work in a number of directions.

After 1725 similar mechanisms were at work until more rapid growth occurred in some sectors of the economy by the 1750s. In the economy as a whole the two decades after 1725 were not dissimilar to the ones before, in that there was both change and continuity, but without the intense crises of the earlier part of the century and with a steady decline in the prices of basic foodstuffs after 1730. This has led some historians to argue that these years were favourable for the consumer of household goods, utensils, and clothes. Likewise, historians have recognized the 1740s and 1750s as favourable to growth, with expansion of both overseas trade and population.

Conclusion: the environment for growth

The evidence in this chapter demonstrates unequivocally that consumption of many household goods increased before 1725 and continued to do so afterwards. There were important changes in the late seventeenth century, especially in the increasing availability of decorative goods for use at mealtimes. In some cases expansion was very rapid indeed, especially in the wealthier London households. This leads us to one of the themes in later chapters, namely the changes in domestic behaviour to accommodate these new goods. Were people's social needs and aspirations influenced by increasing use of new tablewares like knives and forks? These questions are the specific subject of later chapters about household behaviour. Another question arising from the patterns of change in this chapter is whether the changes were evenly spread over the whole country or whether there were regional variations. It is to this problem that we now turn.

3

CONTRASTING LOCALITIES

> a regional geography worthy of exploration did actually exist....
> perhaps it still provides the only terms in which important
> problems in the empirical study of industrial as well as pre-
> industrial societies can be expressed.
>
> (Langton, 1984)[1]

Britain was, for all its relatively small size, remarkably varied, with
many distinctive economic and social landscapes, although it is in
the nature of social history to be concerned with enduring aspects
of human behaviour without much regard for geographical variations. The chapter draws on the differences in the ownership of
goods recorded in eight contrasting parts of the country and
explores their extent and meanings.

There were very considerable variations in ownership of goods
in the different parts of the country, as table 3.1 shows. They were
more commonly recorded in some localities, although no one place
was predominant for every commodity. The size of the variations
was also large, for some goods were strongly concentrated in a
few areas. There were even quite marked differences in ownership of staple goods; pewter, for instance, was recorded in nearly
every inventory from Hampshire, Durham, and Kent, but in only
four-fifths of those from northern Cumbria. Books were widely
distributed, but, even so, they were three times as common in the
London sample as in the north-east of England; clocks were five
times as common in Lancashire as in Cumbria, Hampshire, and
the north-west Midlands. The goods associated with 'front'
activities showed the largest variations, with London, Kent, and
the north-east normally, but not always, predominant, followed by
Cambridgeshire and, for some items, Lancashire. Overall the

Table 3.1 *Ownership of selected goods in a sample of inventories from eight English regions, 1675–1725*

	No. of inventories	Tables %	Cooking pots %	Sauce-pans %	Pewter %	Pewter dishes %	Pewter plates %	Earthen-ware %	Books %	Clocks %	Pictures %	Looking glasses %	Table linen %	Window curtains %	Knives and forks %	China %	Utensils for hot drinks %	Silver %
London area	367	92	80	43	91	59	53	41	30	29	37	74	67	40	13	12	15	44
North-east England[1]	325	93	76	2	95	77	37	26	10	15	25	44	55	14	3	10	3	34
East Kent	390	97	89	11	95	59	39	58	26	36	16	47	81	19	7	3	6	41
Cambridgeshire	390	96	86	6	93	72	33	32	12	14	9	27	44	9	2	3	2	15
North-west England[2]	390	83	57*	5*	92	17*	11*	75	20	33	9	31	15*	8	2	1	1	13
Hampshire[3]	260	93	73	3	97	50	20	13	24	7	3	19	35	7	2	0[3]	0[3]	27
North-west Midlands	390	87	62	13	94	42	21	17	15	7	4	14	28	3	1	0	1	8
Cumbria[2]	390	75	43*	1*	88	11*	4*	23	17	7	3	6	13*	1	1	2	0	10

Notes
See also table 3.2
1 1725 missing
2 Some goods (marked *) seem to have been badly listed in these areas. See also appendix 1 for details.
3 1715 and 1725 missing

picture is one of some complexity, and table 3.1 does not display a clear hierarchy of regions.

The substantial part of this chapter describes regional differences in patterns of ownership and also serves as an introduction to the origin of the sample of inventories. Attention is also focused on two other themes. One of these, the influence of internal trade and the convenience of local supplies, is explored with particular emphasis on the role of London as an entrepôt. The other theme is that attitudes to consumption and material goods can usefully be examined at a regional level, for in some areas people may have preferred to spend their resources on special occasions rather than in acquiring household durables.

Regional differences

Regional differences are not the same as local peculiarities, and differences between places are not necessarily suggestive of distinctive 'regional' behaviour or consciousness. A distinct geographical region is also more difficult to define than a town, especially since the geography of Britain was very varied.[2] Administrative areas, such as dioceses or counties, often have some geographical validity, even if they overlap physical and other boundaries, and this is certainly true in the coverage of the sample. Whether they cover meaningful regions of the early modern period partly depends on how we wish to define a region. It is certainly very hard to divide the country into unambiguous areas that each displayed a sense of their own identity, especially at social levels below the gentry. But cultural or political regions, even if they could be identified from the limited evidence, would not necessarily be the appropriate unit to measure aspects of material life. Likewise, farming countries, characterized according to land use or vegetation and ultimately to the underlying geology, do provide a way of examining one aspect of the economy in an area, but such divisions do not coincide with other features, such as major towns or ports or mineral resources or transport facilities, all of which influenced consumption. At the same time, the area influenced by a county town or a regional capital, or the hinterland of a port, cannot be taken as a region without regard to the agricultural and other bases of local economic life.[3]

These variations can best be appreciated as a result of complex relationships, and the possibility of an underlying regional geography

Table 3.2 *Some characteristics of inventories from eight regions of England, 1675–1725*

	No. of inventories	Mean value Whole inventory £	Mean value Household goods £	No. of inventories Urban	Yeomen	Husband-men	Craft trades	Dealers	Years sampled	Diocese
London area	367	150	30	326	19	5	65	151	1675–1725	London
North-east England	325	99	20	193	68	21	63	64	1675–1715	Durham
East Kent	390	191	38	70	132	22	75	72	1675–1725	Canterbury
Cambridgeshire	390	121	19	51	142	45	49	59	1675–1725	Ely
North-west England	390	113	23	48	139	54	80	48	1675–1725	Chester: Lancashire
Hampshire	260	204	27	54	124	15	42	24	1675–1705	Winchester
North-west Midlands	390	93	17	42	146	64	61	25	1675–1725	Lichfield: Staffordshire and Shropshire
Cumbria	390	74	11	43	182	106	24	9	1675–1725	Carlisle
All	2902	128	23	1046	952	332	459	452		

Notes
See also appendix 1, where full archive references are given. Mean values are a crude measure because the range of values is very large and the distribution skew.

behind differences shown in table 3.1 can be explored by looking at the economic and social characteristics of each area, alongside some features of the recorded ownership of goods there.[4] Table 3.2 sets out some basic distinctions between the inventories from each area. There were obvious differences between the areas sampled: Cumbrian inventories were of lower value, the area was less urbanized, and there were more husbandmen and fewer tradesmen than elsewhere; the same was true of the north-west Midlands. But the mean values of inventories in Hampshire were higher (£204) than elsewhere, whereas those in the north-east were much lower (£99), although goods were usually more frequently recorded there.

London

As London had a unique importance in the urban hierarchy, I shall begin there.[5] As a geographical region the London area was the result of a long period of human activity and, by the late seventeenth century, covered the City, Westminster, adjoining parishes to the east and west, as well as Southwark to the south of the river Thames. It was a complex metropolis, which had widespread economic, social, and political influence on the rest of the country. At least one person in six had lived there at some time in their lives, and its population accounted for about a tenth of the population of England in 1700. Its primary economic role derived from its position as a major port, as a major centre of population, and as the financial, political, and commercial centre, but it was also an important manufacturing centre as well. The wealth and occupational structure were different from that of the country as a whole, with concentrations of professionals, the better-off tradesmen, shopkeepers, and small manufacturers as well as large merchants and manufacturers. There were conspicuously wealthy people living there, with as many as 5,000 gentry families commonly in residence, apart from visitors for the season or parliament or business. Its sophistication as a region can be seen in the specialized functions of different parts, with the port and small-scale manufacturing in the east, heavy industry to the south, and more spacious dwelling to the west, although the large developments of planned squares and town houses were not built until the first half of the eighteenth century. This means that the London region was one of great complexity, and there are real problems in giving proper expression to the variety of experience to be found there. Indeed, the immense importance of London in English society is not fully apparent from this study, partly because of the nature and coverage of the sample of inventories, partly because of the nature of the subject itself.

The particular problem with the evidence used in this study is the 'match' between the variety of occupations and wealth levels in London and the limited numbers of inventories surviving. The inventories used were those from the lower courts in the diocese of London, the archdeaconry of London, and the archdeaconry of Middlesex (used for 1685). The parishes covered are exclusively those in the east of the City, together with a few parishes outside the City limits, notably Whitechapel. The diocesan records do, however, have the advantage of giving evidence about the same kinds of people covered by the records of the provincial dioceses, namely the crafts- and tradespeople below the richer merchants, but above artisans and wage-earners, as well as a few farmers. In other words, it does not tell us everything about the ownership of goods in all parts of London, and it does not tell us anything about the luxury consumption of the rich and the greater gentry, whether they lived in London or whether they were visitors. But it does enable comparisons to be made between the middling trades in London and those elsewhere, and between people of roughly similar wealth – which is advantageous in many respects. In interpreting the evidence about the role of London from the sample of inventories these limitations have to be recalled.

The inventories of middling to lower tradespeople are probably rather more representative of the whole of the London region than their relatively small numbers would suggest, for the occupational structure of the City and Westminster, at this level, was not greatly different from that of the sample. In the mid-eighteenth century the most important occupations in Westminster were those which occurred most often in inventories, namely victuallers, carpenters, chandlers, shoemakers, bakers, and butchers, although victuallers are probably over-represented and the port trades under stated. Furthermore, the Westminster inventories are similar to those from the City although they are not included in the sample. By contrast, the Orphans' Court inventories, representing the wealthier freemen of the City, were much lengthier documents and do give the quite different impression of widespread ownership of many expensive household goods.

Table 3.3 *Changing ownership of selected goods in each of eight English regions, 1675–1725*

	books (%)						earthenware (%)					
	1675	1685	1695	1705	1715	1725	1675	1685	1695	1705	1715	1725
London area	18	15	19	38	31	52	15	18	33	46	57	74
North-east England	9	9	12	8	14	–	23	18	22	28	38	–
East Kent	28	25	29	25	23	28	38	49	62	52	62	88
Cambridgeshire	11	12	6	18	14	9	11	14	28	42	43	55
North-west England	17	26	20	18	25	15	82	74	82	69	80	65
Hampshire	29	26	23	18	–	–	14	8	14	15	–	–
North-west Midlands	22	15	15	11	17	9	20	12	15	14	18	20
Cumbria	14	17	15	17	22	15	11	18	18	22	29	38

	pictures (%)						utensils for hot drinks (%)					
	1675	1685	1695	1705	1715	1725	1675	1685	1695	1705	1715	1725
London area	54	69	79	77	89	78	0	0	2	6	22	57
North-east England	26	45	42	48	58	–	0	0	5	2	9	–
East Kent	37	31	48	48	52	68	0	2	0	3	16	15
Cambridgeshire	6	18	18	42	34	45	0	0	0	2	0	12
North-west England	20	28	35	32	38	34	0	0	0	2	2	3
Hampshire	18	15	20	23	–	–	0	0	0	0	–	–
North-west Midlands	11	8	14	14	29	11	0	0	0	0	2	3
Cumbria	3	6	6	8	9	3	0	0	0	0	2	0

Notes
The number of inventories for each year for each region is 65, except for London, 1695, where only 42 were available. See appendix 1 for details. See also table 3.2.
– = no data

The expectation from much writing about London is that it would clearly predominate in the ownership of goods. But, as table 3.1 shows, while many goods were more often recorded in the London sample than elsewhere, the differences were not large, and some goods were more often recorded elsewhere. The goods in which London predominated were all associated with 'frontstage' activities, such as new eating habits, new cooking techniques, new drinks, or domestic decoration. In some cases the concentration on London was marked: there were twice as many window curtains and three times as many saucepans as elsewhere, and the new, imported goods, such as china and the utensils for hot drinks, were strongly concentrated there. The evidence from the Orphans' Court inventories shows that there were wealthier groups in London, who did more often own domestic durables.

London was, however, more important by 1725 than it had been in the late seventeenth century. Ownership of goods expanded, as table 3.3 illustrates, more rapidly than elsewhere, so that, even if London was not clearly distinct from other regions at the start of the period, it was clearly so by the end. In book ownership, for instance, London had been fourth, but was clearly ahead by 1705; in ownership of pictures, London was third in 1675 but clearly ahead by 1705. And, of course, ownership of new, imported goods expanded here more rapidly than elsewhere. Just how quickly ownership could expand among the most favourably placed in the metropolis is shown by the growth in ownership recorded in the Orphans' Court inventories. Here the new goods expanded from being virtually unknown in the 1670s to being virtually ubiquitous by 1725. This powerful growth was not confined to London, but it was an important feature of change in this region.

How far growth and concentration in London were due to different attitudes and expectations is not easy to pinpoint with any certainty. The most obvious feature of London life in this respect was that the supply of most of the domestic goods was much easier here than in most other places. There were more shops, and people had already become used to the idea of looking in them for information about what was available. New goods could be seen and appreciated more readily than in most other places. So it is important that London was a great trading centre, with 80 per cent of English imports passing throught the port and with a monopoly of trade with the Far East. London also played a central role in the inland trades: both imported and other goods were distributed to all parts of the country from London. The metropolis was, moreover, a centre for the manufacture of clocks, books, pictures, looking glasses, and earthenware. Ease of supply for the inhabitants of London could account for concentration in London inventories even at the level in society specifically examined here. London was not different in kind from other towns, but showed the same pattern in an exaggerated form.

The north-east

Examination of the north-east of England certainly warns against assuming the predominance of London in every respect, for there were some interesting concentrations in the sample from this region.[6] The north-east is one of the best-defined geographical regions of England, stretching from the river Tees in the south, and bordered by the Pennines in the west and the coast of Northumberland in the east. This region is covered by the diocese of Durham, which had jurisdiction over most of it but included a few upland parishes as well. Most of the inventories are from the coastal plain.[7]

The economy of the region was one of contrasts. Newcastle was in the vanguard of urban development, with a varied commercial and industrial basis, serving a large hinterland, and a centre for large-scale trade in coal, especially to London. Other towns in the area had similar functions on a smaller scale and, together with the county town of Durham, made a considerable urban concentration, which is given expression in the sample of inventories. On the other hand, the agricultural economy of the region as a whole was not well developed, and both the cultivated land and the grazing was often poor, even in the lowlands, although yields increased by the mid-eighteenth century. The upland and foothill farms concentrated on livestock, with crops grown for local and subsistence purposes. Holdings were small, but they were larger in the more arable lowlands, partly as a result of the actions of landlords. In southern Northumberland, for example, smaller holdings were grouped together as part of a reorganization of farming, for landlords did not allow small subsistence holdings to proliferate.[8]

Although the late seventeenth and early eighteenth centuries saw changes in farming and land ownership, especially in the lowlands, these were not fully in evidence by the time of the last decade covered by the inventories (1705–15), and from the point of view of the contrasts between urban and rural it is an interesting area, for there were notable differences between the ownership patterns in the towns and elsewhere. Table 4.3 in chapter 4 shows this; clocks, for instance, were recorded in 21 per cent of the urban inventories (not much less than in London) but in only 7 per cent of rural ones. Likewise china was recorded in 15 per cent of urban inventories here (roughly the same as in London) but in only 3 per cent of rural ones. Here too, as in London, the proportions of inventories recording the goods were increasing, although less rapidly than in the capital.

There is a certain regional unity which is explicable in terms of the constrasts between agrarian and commercial elements in the regional economy. The unifying feature of the area was the mining of coal – accounting for 40 per cent of national output in the late seventeenth century. Mining was expanding, and so too was the crucial trade in coal with London. Its importance is that there was a return trade in many household and consumer items, and this meant that such things were more readily available in this area than almost anywhere else in England. As Richard Pocock observed in a letter to his sister in 1760: 'Besides the great trade in coal ... they ... import every thing for the use of Northumberland, Durham Westmoreland and part of Cumberland so that they have great shops of all kinds.'[9]

This was of very considerable importance in the dynamics behind regional differences in the ownership of goods and is a theme that will be developed later in this chapter. It is also important in characterizing the north-east as a region with very advanced aspects in its economy, especially in the towns, alongside rather backward rural elements. Table 4.3 shows that this aspect of the regional economy did influence rural as well as urban areas, but the proportions of rural inventories in which goods were recorded were somewhere between the better-developed rural economies of Kent and the more remote places in Cumbria and the north-west Midlands.

Kent

East Kent did not have the same kind of regional identity as the north-east, for it was on the edge of the very mixed area of the north downlands and the Weald. On the other hand, north Kent was separate from the inland forest areas and, being on the coast, was also closely influenced by the London food market. In this respect, the area covered by the diocese of Canterbury can be regarded as an entity in itself but not representative of the geographical region of south-east England. This, as I shall point out in discussing attitudes to material goods, is of some significance. The area relied on mixed farming and market gardening and was much influenced by selling produce in London.[10] There were also considerable commercial, industrial, and craft developments in small towns and villages, but there were no major industrial areas based on mineral deposits or a coalfield. Rural and urban Kent as a whole was a wealthy area, with a partly landowning yeomanry and more substantial farmers and gentry than in other counties. There was a mixed occupational structure, with many shops and craftsmen, and this is reflected in the inventory sample. The area also had good communications with London, both by sea and by land, and here too there was a return trade with London in consumer items and household wares.[11]

The goods were more often recorded here than in many other places, and it was often second only to London. Table 4.3 in chapter 4 shows a major contrast with the north-east of England in that the distinctions between town and country were much less marked. Ownership of goods was more even between rural and urban areas, and ownership in the rural areas was often greater here than in other parts of the country. The regional economy was less clearly divided between an advanced urban sector and a less developed rural one. There was greater integration and similarity, with more village trades and a wider range of occupations. This too was, as table 3.3 illustrates, a growth area after 1705 for most goods, and especially the new ones. Overall it was a rather unusual area, having close links with London, an integrated urban/rural pattern, and a mixed occupational structure. The north of Kent was particularly favourable, both in terms of the supply of goods and in having the kinds of people living there who were inclined to own household utensils.

Cambridgeshire

Higher proportions of goods were often recorded in a third diocese from the east of England, Ely, which covered parts of two major geographical regions, the fenlands to the north and the East Anglian heights to the south, although most of the diocese was within the county of Cambridgeshire.[12] The county was an administrative unit and not typical of all of East Anglia, although it gives some expression to the diversity of this inland part. It was an extremely varied, but prosperous, agricultural area. After the draining of the south level of the fens in the 1650s, a wide variety of crops was possible, including hemp, flax, saffron, pulses, and grain, although the area remained liable to floods. At the same time a good deal of land remained unreclaimed and the mixed fenland economies based on grazing cattle, fishing, waterfowl, and gathering reeds continued. The inventories reflect great diversity of farming and land use, since many of them have evidence for more varied activities than in any other area examined, including small quantities of new crops, such as saffron, or water-based activities, or gardening, in addition to arable and pastoral husbandry; there were also more inventories of people called 'labourer' from this diocese than from any other.

Much consumption here was rural, but the towns predominated for some new and decorative goods, especially knives and forks, saucepans, and pictures. There was also, as table 3.3 illustrates, some rapidly expanding ownership. There were very few clocks in the area in 1675, but by 1715 they were recorded in over a quarter of the inventories; similarly, from having very small proportions of looking glasses and pictures in 1675, ownership increased notably by 1725.

This region did not rely on the London market in the same way as the two areas already discussed, for, while some of the local varied produce was sold there, there was not the same kind of bulky, water-born traffic with the possibility of a return trade in domestic goods. There were roads through the county, but communications were not particularly easy. This suggests that ownership was based on an adequate supply of goods, but more importantly on the wealth arising from agricultural improvements and diversification. The chronology of change, with expansion in ownership dating from the late seventeenth century, also points in this direction.

North-west England

Lancastria formed a fairly compact physical unit to the west of the Pennines.[13] The inventories cover the area which was to develop into the industrial region of the north-west, for only Lancashire south of the river Ribble is included. The sample does not therefore represent the whole of Lancashire and the north-west in general, but covers the most advanced parts. This was a very varied area; the uplands of the Pennines, especially Rossendale, were difficult to cross and have remained relatively remote ever since, but there were also the major urban developments around Manchester and the developing port of Liverpool, as well as a major, if as yet underdeveloped, coalfield. In this respect it was similar to, if less developed than, the north-east. The soils of the lowlands did not give rise to affluent farming (the main crops were oats and barley) but the climate and soils were best suited to a pastoral economy, so there was sheep fattening and stock rearing. In general, holdings were small and the economies of individuals were based on a mixture of activities, including arable farming for local consumption. There were improvements in drainage in the Lancashire plain in the eighteenth century and production for urban markets as the towns grew. But the most important characteristic of the area was that it was developing as a textile-producing area, based on the domestic production of linen cloth and an increasing number of other things, such as clocks, glass, earthenware, and small metalwares. Industrial crafts were already of fundamental importance in the rural economies of south Lancashire, where there was, even in the seventeenth century, a certain unity in its occupational structure. So, like the northeast, it appears as a complex region, with growing towns but with more industrial occupations in the countryside than around Newcastle. The inventories reflect this occupational structure, for there are many rural craftsmen and small farmers among them.

Ownership of goods here was generally lower than in areas already discussed, with a few important exceptions, which are in themselves indicative of the particular nature of the region and probably the whole of north-west England. Book ownership was relatively high, more so than in the north-east and even Cambridgeshire; this may have been associated with the high value that local religious dissent placed on reading the scriptures, resulting in higher general literacy. In this sense it is a reflection of regional values. Predominance of the area in the ownership of clocks and earthenware was more likely to have been associated with the fact that they were made locally and were therefore easily available. Since the supply of imported goods, or those made elsewhere, was limited, ownership of them here was less frequent.

There was some expansion at the end of the period, but there were some goods whose ownership did not increase as much here as elsewhere. Pictures, for instance, were found with about the same frequency at the beginning as at the end; earthenware even declined.

Hampshire

Central southern England as a whole has a geographical unity largely based on the geological succession of limestones, clays, chalk, and sand that underlie it. It is, however, very varied in detail because of the numerous small-scale geological and topographical differences. The inventories cover the county of Hampshire together with the Isle of Wight. Here land use was very mixed, although much of the farming depended on wheat and barley, with sheep and domestic dairies. It was primarily an agricultural area, with numerous small market towns and craft trades serving the main farming function; there were three sizeable towns, but none was expanding or prosperous at this time.[14] Hampshire was one of the most varied counties, and farming there was potentially less prosperous than further north in the region because much of the county was covered by infertile heaths and forests, notably the New Forest. But this county was typical of some of the others in the central south-west, for the geology, land form, and climate had much in common with all the counties to the west and with Sussex, although not the south-west peninsula. The inventories reflect the agricultural basis of the economy of the county, since there are many large and prosperous farmers among them, and the mean valuations of the whole inventory are substantially higher here than everywhere except Kent.

Ownership of many of the household goods and utensils measured in this study was much lower here, in some cases (earthenware, clocks, pictures, and window curtains) among the lowest proportions in the whole survey. Furthermore, there was less growth in this region before 1705 than in any other, although the last two decades are not measured here – which is unfortunate, because there was considerable expansion in some other places in the two missing decades. This pattern is unexpected in that it was an apparently favoured region. Explanation is also complicated by the fact that the inventories did list some very expensive domestic goods, especially beds and furniture; they also recorded the highest proportions of pewter. It is also less easy to argue that supply was inadequate, because Hampshire was quite near to London in the north and it had two major ports on its coast, which were connected to the capital by major roads. Earthenware was actually made in the north of the county but apparently was aimed at the London market.[15]

One possibility is that the economy of the whole region was influenced by the corn trade with London and was vulnerable to fluctuations in the price of corn, leaving even large farmers with few spare resources in cash for new consumer durables. In the 1680s cereal prices were especially low, and there were serious price fluctuations in the French wars. So, during the thirty or so years when ownership of goods was expanding in some parts of the country, in this apparently favoured area farmers did not have the money to buy utensils and consumables. But they did buy furniture, so it seems likely that, for some reason, utensils were less well regarded as household possessions here than elsewhere. Perhaps people's attitudes and values were different from those elsewhere and decorative things were not so readily acquired and valued. Likewise, none of the towns was a dynamic centre of growth. This observation will be looked at again in greater detail later in this chapter, but it is also likely that other counties in the south were similar, especially those that were not on the inland waterways to London.

The north-west Midlands

The north-west Midlands were different again, being an entirely land-locked area and covering a large part of the Midlands plain.[16] It was a pastoral region, with concentration on dairying and rearing, and little attention paid to growing cereals for the market. There was less variety both of landscape and in farming, although there were some areas of specialized industrial activities. The inventory sample is drawn from northern Shropshire and Staffordshire, neither of which was a particularly favoured area for agriculture. Much of Staffordshire was seen as barren ground or heathland in the late seventeenth century, although there were some good pastures and forests. The majority of holdings were small, and there were no major urban areas within the scope of the sample. Industrial activity was increasing in the north-east Midlands in general, for there were three areas of domestic industry and other kinds of developments, based on coalfields: in the rural areas to the south, ironwares were being made; to the north there was a growing pottery industry; and in Shropshire ironworking and other trades were already established on the coalfield.[17] Yet the region as a whole was still dominated by farming, and the occupations in the sample of inventories reflect this. It was one of the least wealthy areas and was seventh in mean valuation of the whole inventory, reflecting the small size of many holdings. Lower proportions of all goods were recorded in the inventories, the new goods were almost unknown, decorative ones were very unusual, and clocks were rare. There was little growth, with the exceptions of saucepans and clocks, which meant that by the last couple of decades the frequencies in this region were often the lowest of any, even including the geographically remote Cumbria.

Cumbria

Cumbria had a clear regional identity and covered an area stretching from Morecambe Bay to the Solway Firth and inland to the Vale of Eden in the east.[18] There are many contrasting landscapes in the area, from the central mountains of the Lake District to the coastal plain and river valleys surrounding it. The agricultural environment was, however, limited to mixed farming on the coast and fell grazing and other pasture inland. There were profound weaknesses in the regional economy in the early seventeenth century, when there had been severe famines, but the worst problems had been modified by the later part of the century through agricultural diversification and incomes from non-agricultural sources. But, although famine did not recur, the area was known for the smallness of holdings and the poverty of the freeholders and tenants throughout the eighteenth century.[19] The basic economy of the area, mixed farming for subsistence, was not transformed by the growth of industry, commerce, and trade in the Whitehaven area. It remained isolated, although some parts of the economy were altered by the increasing trade through Whitehaven with Ireland and the colonies, and with Scotland through Carlisle.

The inventories were taken from the northern part of the region, and they represent the poorer and more remote areas, rather than the whole of Cumbria. They certainly show evidence for smallness of farms and low values of estates in comparison with the other areas covered. The lowest frequencies were ⟩ recorded for virtually every item examined; for instance, there were insignificant numbers of pictures in the rural areas and even the normally ubiquitous pewter was less often recorded here than anywhere else. There were also few towns apart from Carlisle, which was itself quite small as a regional centre, although goods were more often recorded here than elsewhere in the area. Like the north-east, there were very substantial differences between rural and urban areas: clocks were twice as common in towns as in the countryside; pictures were as common in towns as they were in other regions, but virtually unknown in the rural inventories. China was as frequent in the Cumbrian towns as anywhere else, but again virtually unknown in rural inventories. There was, however, more sign of expansion in this region than in the north-west Midlands, for the ownership of most goods increased by 1715, although the absolute levels remained lower than elsewhere. It contrasts with Hampshire in that it is easier to see that sheer lack of resources were responsible for fewer people owning the goods here.

Lowland Scotland

Owing to different probate practices in Scotland, where most testaments have incomplete listings of household goods,[20] ownership patterns cannot be measured in a way that would be comparable to the method applied to the English regions. It is, however, possible to make some comparisons between Scotland and England in an informal way by using a few testaments, together with descriptions and memoirs. There are many pitfalls in doing this, not least the uncertainty in comparing English and Scottish social structures and the concentration in Scottish writing on the domestic behaviour of the upper ranks of society. Household size, structure, and function were not vastly different in Scotland, although houses were smaller, so there were none-the-less, many similarities.

One conclusion about the possible nature of consumption patterns in Scotland is possible. Lowland Scotland and Edinburgh would not, at least before 1725, emerge as one of the areas in which consumption of domestic durables was most important. Yet it would not be like the south of England, where the large farmers had very comfortably furnished houses. As will be shown in chapter 8, the farmers had basic household equipment, but their houses were smaller, and they did not have many of the goods, such as crockery or cutlery, already quite common in parts of England. Nor did they have expensive furniture or much silver. The development of consumption in Scotland came rather later than the period covered by this book; before 1725 the Scottish economy was beginning to undergo changes that were not fully visible until later in the eighteenth century. In the late seventeenth century it was economically backward, and famine was experienced, even in the Lowlands and even among respectable tenants. It is in this context that limited consumption of domestic goods (and clothing) should be seen.

Contrasting consumption

Ownership of goods was more likely in some regions than others. The metropolis stands out, followed by the north-east and Kent; these appear as the three most important areas. Cambridgeshire and north-west England were, however, important for some things, and the former is notable for some developments in rural areas. Goods were less frequently recorded in the north-west Midlands and Cumbria; in these areas there were some very sparsely furnished houses with low valuations. Lastly, in parts of the south, represented here by Hampshire, domestic durables were less often recorded, but inventories had relatively high values, and some of the houses were well provided with furniture and staple goods such as pewter. These are interesting patterns that encourage us to look at differences between different parts of the country. Many of the details also show that simplistic contrasts, such as those between north and south, agricultural and industrial, are not enough to explain the patterns. Does it help to try to understand the differences and similarities in terms of regional geography, allowing for the partial coverage of the survey evidence? This depends very much on how the impact of a 'region' on behaviour is seen. This can be looked at in four ways: the state of economic development in an area; diffusion from outside; the supply of goods; and regional differences in attitudes to consumption.

The discussion of each region covered and Scotland shows that some aspects of the economy influenced ownership. In general, in inventories from those areas that were 'backward', especially

Cumbria and the north-west Midlands, new and decorative goods were less often recorded there. Likewise, Scotland's economy was not developing rapidly at this time and there was still much subsistence agriculture and limited cash incomes. Inventories from areas with well-developed economies, like London and Kent, more often recorded a wide variety of goods. Yet, even as broad generalizations, these relationships do not explain all the patterns in the tables, and they do not necessarily explain the sparse goods found in Scotland, or why there were not more domestic durables in Hampshire, or why the north-east predominated.

Supply and trade

The variations between some parts of the country have little to do with the inner workings of the regional economy, and this can be seen in the influence of the supply of goods, whether locally made or whether bought in from elsewhere. The regional differences in the proportions of inventories with the goods suggest that supply was important. Much is explained about regional differences if trading networks are taken into account. This is especially so of goods imported from the Far East, but is also true of goods made in the provinces and sold through London, and can be illustrated in three ways: first, by looking at the return trade in domestic and other goods to some areas that provided bulky goods to the London market; second, by examining the coincidence between ownership of utensils for hot drinks and the numbers of tea and coffee dealers in an area; and, third, by considering variations in local supplies of domestic goods.

North-eastern England and Kent provided the London market with bulky goods, and the return shipping was used to carry many household and other items, whether produced in London or imported through the capital. This kind of trade accounts for similarities between these two otherwise distinct areas, as well as their predominance. The same kind of mechanism could have been at work in other places not covered by the sample of inventories; grain was traded in bulk down the Thames from Berkshire, Oxfordshire, and Wiltshire, and there may have been the same kind of return trade. There were certainly more tea and coffee dealers in these counties than in those where the bulky traffic was less in evidence, especially Dorset, Hampshire, and Sussex. This is only a partial explanation, for grain was taken coastwise

Table 3.4 *Numbers of dealers in coffee and tea in the 1730s in the counties covered by the sample of inventories, population, and the frequency of ownership of utensils for hot drinks in 1725*

	Population c.1700	No. of tea and coffee dealers, 1730s	Ratio of population to no. of dealers	Ownership of utensils, 1725 %
North-east England	131,000	67	1,955	9 (1715)
East Kent	156,000	177	881	15
Cambridgeshire	81,000	44	1,841	12
North-west England	239,000	32	7,469	3
Hampshire	108,000	20	5,400	–
North-west Midlands	241,000	40	6,025	3
Cumbria	90,000	22	4,091	2
All provincial here	1,046,000	402	2,602	7
London area	600,000	3,415	176	57
All here	1,646,000	3,817	431	15

Notes and sources
1 Phyllis Deane and W.A. Cole, *British Economic Growth, 1688–1959* (Cambridge, 1969), p. 103. These are unlikely to be totally accurate but they give a rough idea of the order of magnitude.
2 PRO, Excise and Treasury Letterbooks, CUST/48/13, p. 206, dated 17 February 1737/8.

to London from these southern coastal counties; Sussex was a 'maritime and corn county', with flour and grain taken to London, although some carriage was overland. There was a return trade in coal, salt, and manufactured goods from London.[21]

Some coincidences between supply and ownership can be shown by comparing the ownership of utensils for hot drinks and the number of tea and coffee dealers in 1736/7.[22] Table 3.4 does this, although it cannot take account of the sizes of the dealers' businesses or whether they served a very wide area or not. A ranking of regions according to the percentages with utensils for hot drinks in 1725 is virtually the same as that for the ratio between dealers and population. Kent had by far the largest number of dealers, as well as the highest proportions of inventories with utensils for hot drinks in 1725, followed by Cambridgeshire and the north-east. On the other hand, the areas where utensils were uncommon by 1725 had fewer dealers relative to the population. It also shows the dominant position of London, where many of the dealers were undoubtedly redistributing tea and coffee to the provinces as well as selling in the capital.

As manufacturing became more specialized and concentrated, some items were more easily obtained in some areas. Earthenware, for instance, was made in south Lancashire, Liverpool, and Kent, and it was recorded there with greater frequency than elsewhere; however, it was also made in both north and south Staffordshire, but was not recorded there very often. Clocks were made in many places, but there was a concentration of makers in Lancashire and London – which explains their frequency there – and they were also more common in the places that traded with London.[23] Pictures and prints were made in London and were also imported through the capital, so again the supply was concentrated, as was ownership. Some goods were more widely manufactured: pewter was made in many urban centres, and most furniture was put together locally; in these cases, both the supply and the distribution of ownership were more even.[24] Change over time was also influenced by the same kinds of factors, and growth in ownership was more rapid in some regions than in others. The newer goods (notably china, utensils for hot drinks, looking glasses, and pictures) whose supply centred on London spread, and ownership of them increased by 1715, even in the least favoured places.

Patterns of internal trade do, therefore, go some way towards showing why there were differences between the particular areas examined in this study. The networks of internal trade were part of an economic environment that extended beyond regional boundaries and, from that point of view, suggest that (while it is desirable to be aware of the distinctions between places) regional differences in themselves do not provide the only framework for discussing consumer behaviour.

Regions and attitudes

Differences in attitudes to material goods, a further aspect of consumer behaviour, can be looked at in spatial, if not strictly regional terms. There is a possibility that people were more inclined to adopt new behaviour or new goods in some areas because they were more consumer-orientated. Some societies are known to have been resistant to adopting new goods, possibly because their resources were limited, but possibly because occasional conspicuous expenditure that had little influence on everyday

Dicly

household equipment or consumption was preferred. This can be contrasted with a more 'modern' attitude to consumption, where people are prepared to own a wide variety of goods and use a wide range of services, rather than concentrate on a few symbolic or expensive occasions. Thus contrasts between 'traditional' and 'modern' can be made, constrasts that are not without foundation and meaning, especially in relation to some parts of some societies, like the Italian nobility or the Dutch peasantry.[25] But such ideas need to be treated carefully in a commercialized society such as that of most of Britain by this time. So it is not valid to examine all communities in these terms.

It is, however, difficult to find enough detail about this kind of attitude, for there is very little evidence on the subject. The diaries and memoranda used in this study often give graphic and detailed impressions of everyday routines, mealtimes, and eating habits, but they rarely make direct reference to material goods, and it is most unusual to find attitudes towards the acquisition of furniture and utensils spelt out, since such expectations were taken for granted. However, there is some evidence of a view that income had to be carefully managed and not squandered. Most of the quotations and sayings collected by Warley in the pages at the beginning and end of his account book are concerned with using money and time to best advantage and not getting into debt. Take, for instance, the caution,

Climb not too high, lest thou fall:
Creep not so low, as to be trampled on.

This does not lead us to suppose that this affluent yeoman farmer would have approved of conspicuous consumption, any more than another entry, ''tis use that sanctifies expense'.[26] But this kind of collection is unusual, and it is not possible to say from such comment whether there were different attitudes to material goods in different parts of the country.

In most parts of England middle-ranking people do not seem to have wanted to spend a disproportionate amount of their resources on a few special occasions, such as funerals, weddings, and feasts, or on items of clothing. Thus Misson, in many ways a sympathetic observer of English life, reports of christenings: 'The Custom here is not to make great feasts at the birth of their Children. They drink a glass of Wine, and eat a bit of a certain Cake, which is seldom made but upon the Occasions.' He further remarks that 'The English eat well, but are no great Feasters' and, of Presbyterian weddings, that they were 'commonly very plain and very quiet'.[27] Household routines were not systematically different in different parts of the country, although some of the details of what was eaten and how it was cooked did vary. The implication of this is that the 'sober and industrious' households of the middling ranks spent only modestly on family and other rituals. They did not behave in a manner characterized as typical of 'traditional' societies, where relatively large sums were spent on a feast or celebration and limitations in the availability of attractive consumer goods meant that people were unable to spend any surplus resources on them. It is therefore often taken as an essential step in the growth of a consumer-orientated society that people should devote resources to rather ordinary clothes and manufactured things, rather than to a few large-scale occasions or purchases. One way of discovering whether there were different perceptions in some regions is to look for any evidence for this kind of expenditure in some of them.

The only evidence about celebrations in the diaries used here is from Sussex, an area represented by the inventory sample from Hampshire. Burrell's diary shows that he received many presents during the year, mostly of game, food, and wine – evidently part of a mutual interchange with his neighbours. Christmas was celebrated on a large scale, and after 1691 he invited his humbler neighbours to dine at New Year; in that year he had thirty of them, with their wives. The implication is that hospitality continued on this scale every year until 1711, when he invited the humbler people to dine on Sundays in groups of two or three instead. The menus were lavish and the entertainment hospitable. He also spent a large sum, £35, on his sister's funeral in 1708. This could partly have been a mark of his social position, for he was a lawyer, but, since he claimed his income at about £300 a year, he was not exceptionally wealthy, although well above most middle-ranking people. The diary does not give details of his regular domestic expenses or what kinds of furniture he had, so whether his hospitality was related to limited expenditure on domestic goods is not known. He mentioned the new hot drinks only twice, once as a gift and once when he drank chocolate in London.[28] The other Sussex diarist, Marchant, also mentions a number of gifts and also feasted his workmen at Christmas; in 1727 he recorded that seven roasting pigs were used when 'our workmen dined here as usual'. He also frequently gave and received mourning rings and gloves.[29] This was not lavish expenditure, but there are no similar references in the diaries from other places, where Christmas often passed without notice and weddings, baptisms, and funerals were mentioned more as occasions for visits than for expenditure.

Silver was the only household item selected here that might be considered as representative of 'conspicuous' consumption, and it was recorded in about a quarter of the inventories. Among the middle ranks it does not seem to have been used in a conspicuous way; households usually had a few pieces of useful silver, such as tankards, silver spoons, or porringers. The silver owned by Allen Wyat, glazier of Newmarket, in 1675 was typical; his household goods consisted of the usual furniture, bedding, and utensils, but he did have a clock.[30]

	£	s	d
Item 3 silver boules 12 silver spoones 1 silver salt 2 silver wine cupps	13	10	0

This does not suggest that silver was a 'conspicuous' possession, although it was much more frequently owned by those of highest status, the gentry (61 per cent), than by others. It was more often recorded in inventories of professional people (55 per cent) and dealing tradesmen (43 per cent) than in those of yeomen (13 per cent) and husbandmen (2 per cent). It was associated with wealth and was recorded in virtually every inventory (94 per cent) from the Orphans' Court sample and in most inventories with a total valuation over £500. Yet it also seems to have been a staple, even traditional, material, for there was little change in the proportions of households owning it from 1675 to 1725, although rather more recorded it in 1715 than usual (29 per cent). It was also concentrated in the three most advanced areas (London 44 per cent, the north-east 34 per cent, Kent 41 per cent) and, with one exception, was recorded in about a tenth of inventories in other places. The exception was Hampshire (27 per cent), an area in which there is some other evidence that people might have used their resources for traditional things rather than consumer durables. They may also have invested in silver rather than in other items – which suggests that there were different attitudes in parts of the south.

The evidence from Scotland is clearer, for here there is some commentary from the Lowlands suggestive of some kinds of 'conspicuous' expenditure. The writers of the later eighteenth and early nineteenth centuries who looked back over the changes in Scottish society make several comments about the importance that was attached to feasting and to rather elaborate clothes. Dress, it was recalled, 'was in general plain and frugal, but upon great occasions they scrupled no expense.'[31] It was also remarked: 'Then the heads were all dress'd in laces from Flanders; ... the price of those was high, but two suit would serve for life.'[32] And another writer observed: 'The dress of both men and women alike in the middle and higher ranks exhibited by turns the extremes of gaudy ostentation and disgusting slovenliness.'[33] This implies there was normal expenditure at a low level on consumer goods (in this case clothing), but combined with some apparently excessive expenditure for particular occasions. Such a contrast is also shown in these comments:

> In their general habits the husbandmen [the writer meant farmers here] of those days were a sober, a frugal, and an industrious race. Though not averse to indulge occasionally in convivial sociality with their friends and neighbours, yet the leading tendency of their minds was parsimony and thrift.[34]

> Though our gentry lived plainly and frugally in common, yet upon certain occasions they wished to make a show. ... It was at marriages, christenings, and burials, particularly the last, that country gentlemen were wont to exceed the bounds of moderation.[35]

Ramsey comments on the 'old hospitality so much boasted of in Britain', which involved eating a great deal of food and pressing guests to do the same, which became 'troublesome and disgusting'.[36] Here surplus was consumed in excessive food and drink on a few occasions, rather than on durable goods or even clothing, again characteristic of a 'traditional' attitude to consumption. All writers record that such behaviour had changed since the mid-eighteenth century; Somerville recorded that 'A taste for amusements and festivities has rather declined, particularly among the middle and lower classes'; he specifically made the link between this and increased consumption of ordinary things, for he emphasizes that people were better fed, clothed, and housed than before.[37] This too was characteristic of a society which valued some kinds of celebrations over domestic goods and even clothing. By the time these commentators wrote, things had changed, and people's expectations were different. It is hard to be sure that they were not giving an exaggerated account, in order to stress improvements in Scottish society by emphasizing some old-fashioned aspects of its past.

The idea of conspicuous occasions was, however, evidently appealing to Scottish taste, for there are illustrations of wedding feasts and dancing. These too presented an image of what viewers wanted to believe about their society, rather than an accurate record of social mores, but perhaps this in itself suggests that certain kinds of apparently lavish expenditure were acceptable on some occasions. David Allan based his dancing figures in the *Penny Wedding* and other paintings on styles that he had seen and developed while he was in Italy, but his work, if not accurate in detail, serves to illustrate feasting and celebration as people wanted to see it, even in the late eighteenth century. The images in these illustrations and in the memoirs contrast with descriptions of English life, where there is not the same kind of interest in stressing lavish or conspicuous behaviour.

Plate 5   Penny Wedding, David Allan, 1785 (National Galleries of Scotland, Edinburgh). The style of the dancers was based on Allan's Italian experience, but the scene as a whole gives an evocative impression of feasting, drinking, and celebration.

There were considerable differences between different parts of the country. These are partly explicable in terms of an area's general economic development, but the availability of new goods was uneven. Transport links with London were important in making goods available. So too was the extent of urbanization, and it is to this that we now turn in the next chapter.

4

THE INFLUENCE OF TOWNS

The towns are so many electric transformers.

(Braudel)[1]

The role of the town must be severely curtailed.

(Daunton)[2]

Towns are often taken to have played a crucial role in modifications to consumer behaviour throughout the pre-industrial era, acting as 'electric transformers' on national or regional economies.[3] London has also been identified as a centre of consumption, and the growth of facilities in provincial spas and resorts has been taken as an indicator of changing consumption of material goods and leisure.[4] Thus towns have been established as important elements, possibly even the most important element, in changing consumer tastes and behaviour. Even Daunton, in questioning the role of towns in economic change as a whole in the eighteenth century, confirms that they were the location of new consumption patters.[5] This chapter considers the influence of towns by making comparisons between goods recorded in urban and rural inventories and follows three interrelated but rather different themes. First, were towns different? Second, what was distinctive about town life? Third, it asks what part provincial towns played in expanding consumption and altering consumer behaviour, a question that is logically different from the first two in that it deals with changing patterns and diffusion, not with static comparisons.

Towns and culture

Why were towns given a role in consumer behaviour distinct from that of the country? Towns were not just collections of buildings grouped together with populations of various sizes in them, providing various services. They were, and were felt to be, different *kinds* of communities: not only did they look and smell different, but people in them behaved differently and valued different things. They were seen at the time, as they have been since, as representing something distinctive about civilized human behaviour and experience. In the seventeenth century it was taken for granted that towns were not merely social and economic centres, but essential manifestations of political civilization and of a well-ordered state. That this was so can be seen from the confusion that visitors felt when they went to Virginia or Maryland, where there were no urban developments until much later. Settlement there was in widely dispersed plantations of various sizes, with the marketing, administrative, and other functions of towns also widely distributed. Social and commercial life functioned in an orderly and sophisiticated way, but visitors, government officials, clergymen, and others condemned the lack of towns and villages as fundamentally detrimental to life and morals; it hindered the proper government, and it led to a fear that there could be a mass reversion to savagery, for it was thought that the very nature of man required settled communities, in which natural, sinful instincts could be controlled and civilized. Thus there were many comments on the 'barbarism' of scattered dwellings, and officials held that towns were desirable both for people's behaviour and for trade.[6] The attitudes expressed in this physical and cultural environment, different from Europe in many ways, are revealing, since they show that towns were believed at the time to have an important role in cultural experience and that an area lacking in them was seen as devoid of important elements of civilization.

Town life has been seen as intrinsically different from life in the country; our image of urban life is that it was aesthetically, psychologically, and economically more advanced than life in the country. This does reflect contemporary perceptions and descriptions; the overall impression given by Defoe and Fiennes, for instance, is that towns were worth visiting, that something interesting would be seen in them, and that they were busy centres of local life.[7] The plays and poetry of the period give an impression of the sophistication of towns and their inhabitants, although they were written for an urban audience and it is easy to be over-influenced by these accounts into thinking that they represented everyone's views and experience.[8] In addition, towns have often been seen as a vital force in breaking down 'traditional' patterns of behaviour and consumption and as the places in which new ideas and new ways of life are first introduced. For all these reasons we might expect differences in the material lives of townspeople and consequently different patterns of ownership in town and country.

The sample of inventories was not stratified to include a balanced sample of urban inventories, but urban and rural probate practices were sufficiently similar for many urban inventories to have entered the selection along with those from villages and the countryside. The importance of towns is not unequivocal when the ownership of goods is taken as an indicator of consumer behaviour there. Table 4.1 gives the proportions of inventories in urban and rural places in which the goods were recorded, and it does show that higher proportions of inventories from towns recorded the goods. The apparently simple patterns of the table become more complex when it is evaluated in more detail. Interpretation of the patterns depends on what parts of town life are examined and how nearly the sample of inventories can be taken as representative of those parts of urban life in general. In particular, there is an obvious distinction between people's domestic lives, with household goods and durables used within the home, and, on the other hand, life outside the home, where dress or community experiences were important.

One problem in dealing with urban experience is that of deciding what kind of town to examine. By the late seventeenth century there was considerable diversity in town life, most notably between small markets and the great cities, or between the atmosphere of the developing industrial towns and the resort towns. Between such contrasting places we might expect as much diversity as between town and country. Urban networks and functions were becoming increasingly complex, and there was no neat urban hierarchy ranging from the prinvincial capitals down through market towns to lesser towns and villages. Comparisons with the countryside are also inhibited by the fact that small towns and large villages were not clearly distinct, although a higher density of dwellings and a mixed occupational structure usually distinguished a small town from a large village.

Complexity of function is usually associated with the size of population, although there is no absolute agreement about the minimum population necessary for urban functions and status. Gregory King included small settlements and assumed that the minimum size for market towns was about 500 people. There is much to be said for taking a contemporary view into account, and many places with some urban functions had quite small populations in the late seventeenth century. There were perhaps 500 market centres, with spheres of influence of only a few miles, with populations between about 500 and 1,500.[9] These small places were local centres with craft and other tradespeople serving a restricted population, but they were distinct from the dispersed settlement in the countryside because the majority of people who lived in them did not farm the land, although some did. Their function was largely to provide services for the local population and to process and market agricultural products, so they were integrated into the local farming economy as an essential part of it. On the other hand, the more sophisticated economic and social characteristics of town life were not fully developed in settlements as small as this, and some urban historians have argued that the smaller places should not be taken into account in considering the extent of urbanization.[10] There were only forty or fifty towns with populations between 2,000 and 5,000, and only twenty-four had populations over 5,000, so these were exceptional places in the English urban hierarchy; the seven towns with over 10,000 people were even more so. London towered over the rest with a population of about half a million in 1700, nineteen times as large as the next biggest city, Norwich. It contained a tenth of the population of England and accounted for two-thirds of the urban population in towns over 5,000 people.

England had a relatively large urban population in 1700, although the exact proportion counted as urban depends on whether the smaller towns are included or not. In 1700 about 16 per cent of the population lived in towns with over 5,000 inhabitants and a further 7 per cent in the smaller towns.[11] This means that between a quarter and a fifth of the population lived in urban communities of some kind, and of these between a third and a half lived in London. By 1750 towns had grown relative to the whole population, and by then over a quarter of the people lived in towns. This is a relatively high proportion, although not by the standards of present-day industrial countries.[12] From the point of view of this study, there is advantage in taking as towns any settlements with mixed and non-agrarian functions with over 500 inhabitants, for many places that served some urban functions had quite small populations in the late seventeenth century, but care is needed in specifying the kinds of town discussed and the types of urban experiences that might be specific to some kinds of town. This is true both when examining generalized comments based on travellers' or visitors' reports, and when matching the towns covered by the inventory sample with urban experience in general.

The urban inventories

The sample of inventories encapsulates some elements of urban experience and has the advantage that comparisons can be made from the same kind of document. The proportions of urban inventories obtained is not out of keeping with the proportions of urban dwellers in the country as a whole, since 18 per cent of the inventories were from provincial towns and in only one diocese (Durham) was the proportion out of keeping, where it was rather high. Secondly, some recognition of the urban hierarchy is possible by dividing provincial towns according to whether they were regional or county centres, or whether they served less central functions or were very small in size. So inventories were coded according to the kind of community from which they came, based on the parish of residence. It is rarely possible to tell exactly where someone lived and impossible to distinguish village dwellers from those in dispersed farms and hamlets. The distinctions made here between rural and urban are therefore generalized, with an attempt to acknowledge different types of town by distinguishing major centres from other towns. This distinction is based on a combination of size and importance; Carlisle, for instance, was quite small, with about 3,000–4,000 people, but it was the economic and political centre for an extensive hinterland in Cumbria. The major towns are listed in the notes to table 4.1. These cover, and thus represent, large developing centres, such as Liverpool and Newcastle, as well as towns with less dynamic economies, like Shrewsbury and Winchester. The other towns include medium to small market towns and other small places with a variety of functions, but there are none from the developing spas and leisure centres. It is gratifying that a few errors in definition would make little difference to the overall totals, because there are so few cases from each town.

The sample from London does not cover the whole of the metropolis, for it is largely from the City parishes to the east, together with Whitechapel; it does not include Westminster, the West End, and the growing suburbs to the south; nor does it include the richest inhabitants. The London sample amounts to 11 per cent of the total, so is not out of keeping with the proportion of Londoners in the population as a whole, although this part of the sample does need to be treated with caution. The inventories of the London freemen from the Court of Orphans have also been used to illustrate comparisons between conclusions based on the main sample and those more relevant to the upper middle ranks, but the role of London as a region in its own right has already been considered in the previous chapter.

The sample does not therefore cover all towns or even all towns in each of the dioceses examined, and it does not include all types of town, but it does give expression to experiences in many towns in many areas. The strength of the conclusions that can be drawn from it are greater than the coverage might at first suggest because they have not been selected from places where unusual facilities were becoming available. They draw upon evidence from ordinary towns and they are also comparable with the rural areas. This is important because much of the evidence quoted by urban historians in support of a view that town life encouraged consumption is drawn from visitors' impressions or the behaviour of the gentry and aspiring gentry on holiday in Bath, Tunbridge Wells, and other resorts and spas.[13] Such evidence refers to public occasions, rather than to household behaviour in many market towns, ports, or centres of commerce or manufacturing. There was more to town life than leisure and luxury, and the evidence from inventories has the advantage of drawing attention to this.

Comparisons between town and country

Table 4.1 can now be looked at with some confidence that it provides grounds for comparisons between town and country and between major and other towns. The goods were generally more frequently recorded in urban inventories, but there are distinctions between different types of goods. There were few differences

Table 4.1 Frequencies of ownership of selected goods in towns and country areas in a sample of English inventories, 1675–1725

	No. of inventories	Mean value of inventory £	Tables %	Cooking pots %	Sauce-pans %	Pewter %	Pewter dishes %	Pewter plates %	Earthen-ware %	Books %	Clocks %	Pictures %	Looking glasses %	Table linen %	Window curtains %	Knives and forks %	China %	Utensils for hot drinks %	Silver %
London	319	153	92	81	46	92	58	54	42	31	29	41	77	66	43	14	13	16	46
Major town	217	97	91	72	11	93	67	46	45	21	18	41	58	55	27	6	8	6	44
Other town	291	135	92	70	10	94	56	37	39	23	20	23	50	55	15	4	7	3	37
Villages & rural	2,075	126	88	69	5	93	43	20	35	17	17	5	21	35	6	2	1	2	16
All	2,902	128	89	70	11	93	48	27	37	19	19	37	33	42	13	4	4	4	23

Notes
Definitions of town and country are discussed in the text.
The major towns included are: Durham, Newcastle, Berwick, Carlisle, Southampton, Winchester, Canterbury, Cambridge, Shrewsbury, Liverpool, and Manchester.
See chapter 1 and appendix 1 for a discussion of the sample.

between the provincial towns and rural areas in the ownership of staple goods, used alike for essential purposes in town and country. On the other hand, saucepans, associated with cookery on enclosed stoves, were four times as common in London as in other towns; they were twice as frequent in the provincial towns as they were in the countryside, where only about one in twenty households owned them. Earthenware, although used in farming as well as in households, was more common in London and provincial towns. Although people in towns are usually thought of as being more conscious of clock time and more literate, there were no significant differences between rural and provincial towns in ownership of clocks and books; however, the higher proportion in London inventories is in keeping with this view.

The decorative and new goods were generally much more common in towns, and a few were virtually confined to them. Pictures and window curtains, both with largely decorative functions, were extremely scarce in rural areas but were quite common in London, with moderate frequency in provincial towns. Looking glasses were more widely distributed but they were found three times as frequently in London as in rural areas, and were twice as common in provincial towns. The indicators of new modes of eating and drinking were virtually unknown in the countryside and in the lesser towns, but were more common in the major centres and London. Taken together, the goods indicative of 'frontstage' activity were more common in towns than elsewhere, they were more common in the major centres than in the others, and they were more common in London than elsewhere.

A hierarchy of place, from rural through provincial towns to London, is not unexpected in that towns have been associated with consumerism and with encouraging a demand for services and goods. On the other hand, it is unsatisfactory to leave it at that, for the urban hierarchy was more complex than the simple subdivisions in the tables allow, and we need further examination of the meanings of ownership of some of the goods in an urban context. What was it about the experience of living in a town that led to these kinds of differences? One possibility is that the differences shown in table 4.1 are reflections not of the experience of urban life but rather of the occupational structure of towns. All urban areas had more varied trades than rural ones, with concentrations of manufacturing, crafts, dealers, and services. We will see in chapter 8 that tradespeople, especially dealers and retailers, were more likely to own all kinds of goods than those in

Table 4.2 Frequencies of ownership of selected goods in farmers' and tradesmen's inventories, in town and country, 1675–1725

Occupation		No. of inventories	Mean values of inventory	Tables %	Cooking pots %	Sauce-pans %	Pewter %	Pewter dishes %	Pewter plates %	Earthenware %	Books %	Clocks %	Pictures %	Looking glasses %	Table linen %	Window curtains %	Knives and forks %	China %	Utensils for hot drinks %	Silver or gold %
London	All trades	199	177	93	80	45	91	61	58	48	31	30	43	78	68	44	16	14	17	42
	Farmers	7	103	100	86	57	100	100	100	43	14	43	43	86	71	43	0	14	14	43
Major town	All trades	125	109	94	70	14	95	72	49	51	22	20	43	63	58	30	7	10	9	46
	Farmers	10	106	80	90	0	100	70	40	30	0	20	30	40	40	10	0	10	0	40
Other town	All trades	144	137	97	74	9	97	62	42	39	19	20	26	53	65	14	3	8	3	40
	Farmers	43	118	93	65	9	95	33	23	37	12	16	5	30	35	7	2	5	0	9
Rural or village	All trades	443	109	93	74	8	96	52	28	46	19	22	9	29	46	9	3	3	3	22
	Farmers	1,224	132	89	66	3	94	38	16	31	14	15	2	17	30	4	1	1	1	10
All	All trades	911	128	92	75	17	95	58	40	46	22	23	24	48	55	21	6	7	7	3
	Farmers	1,284	131	89	66	4	94	47	17	32	14	15	3	18	30	4	1	1	1	10

Notes
See table 4.1. Occupations are discussed in chapter 8 and appendix 2.

agricultural occupations and even than the lesser gentry. Table 4.2 cross-tabulates the proportions of inventories with the goods in a more complex way by distinguishing all trades from all farmers in each kind of place.

There are two features showing that both occupation and locality influenced ownership. The influence of place can be seen by comparing the tradesmen in different kinds of places. Here the same kind of hierarchy can be seen, with tradesmen living in towns more likely to own most of the goods than tradesmen living in rural places. There were exceptions; clocks and books appeared as frequently in rural as in urban trade inventories. Some goods were as common in the rural trades as in the lesser towns, but were more common in major towns and London. The influence of occupation can be seen in outline by comparing trades and farmers in the different places, allowing for the small numbers of these in the major towns and London. Farmers in the urban parishes were more likely (again with the exception of clocks and books) to own the goods than the ones in the rural sample. The same proportions of farmers and tradesmen in the London area had pictures and china, whereas these were virtually unknown among farmers in the lesser towns and in rural places. Looking glasses occurred twice as frequently among farmers in the parishes of provincial towns as among those in rural places.

It is the meanings of these patterns that are important, both in what they tell us about urban life and culture, and in what they reveal about the impetus behind consumer behaviour, changing or not. Urban areas could be integrated to a greater or lesser extent into the local and regional economies, and a further perspective on the likely importance of towns can be gained by observing the proportions of goods recorded in urban and rural inventories from the eight regions of the country from which the sample was taken. Table 4.3, which distinguishes urban from rural, shows that there were considerable differences between town and country in each region, as well as between the regions themselves. In particular, there were greater differences between town and country in some regions than in others, and this reflects the differences in regional development examined in the previous chapter.

Urban experience and material life

Why should living in a town result in a greater likelihood of owning domestic goods? One explanation that has been found attractive is

Table 4.3 Frequencies of ownership of selected goods in a sample of inventories in towns and country areas in eight regions of England, 1675–1725

Place		No. of inventories	Tables %	Cooking pots %	Sauce-pans %	Pewter %	Pewter dishes %	Pewter plates %	Earthen-ware %	Books %	Clocks %	Pictures %	Looking glasses %	Table linen %	Window curtains %	Knives and forks %	China %	Utensils for hot drinks %	Silver %
London area	Urban	326	92	81	46	91	58	54	42	31	30	40	77	67	43	14	13	16	47
	Rural	41	90	78	15	90	71	49	32	17	27	12	51	66	17	5	0	7	27
North-east England	Urban	193	94	72	3	94	80	49	34	14	21	37	56	64	21	5	15	5	46
	Rural	132	92	83	81	96	72	20	14	5	7	7	25	42	5	2	3	1	15
East Kent	Urban	70	99	91	20	93	67	57	66	40	33	43	71	81	31	10	4	9	50
	Rural	320	97	89	8	96	57	36	57	23	37	11	42	80	17	6	3	6	39
Cambridgeshire	Urban	51	94	75	22	86	53	43	37	16	6	25	57	53	27	8	2	4	31
	Rural	339	96	88	3	94	75	32	31	11	15	6	23	43	6	1	3	2	12
North-west England	Urban	48	88	62	13	90	35	32	63	27	33	31	63	29	15	6	2	4	29
	Rural	342	82	56	4	92	14	8	74	19	33	6	27	13	8	1	1	1	11
Hampshire	Urban	54	94	67	7	98	48	30	24	19	7	7	93	37	17	2	0	0	35
	Rural	206	92	74	2	96	50	17	10	26	7	2	14	34	4	1	0	0	24
North-west Midlands	Urban	42	86	60	19	98	48	31	26	36	10	17	38	36	12	2	2	2	24
	Rural	348	87	63	12	94	41	20	16	12	6	2	11	28	1	1	0	1	6
Cumbria	Urban	43	77	58	2	98	30	12	30	21	12	23	23	37	5	5	7	2	37
	Rural	349	75	41	0	87	8	3	22	16	7	1	4	10	1	1	1	0	6

Note
See table 4.1 and a discussion of regions in chapter 3, especially table 3.2.

that urban life and culture focused on display and on the concentration of leisure and other facilities for people to meet each other.[14] Public and civic rituals certainly celebrated (in a number of symbolic ways) the life of the town as a unit and the political and social authority of its leaders. It is interesting to be able to show that urban community feeling was expressed in ways that distinguished one town from another and from the countryside, but it does not tell us why ownership of household goods should be different. Public occasions were *public* expressions of civic values, and did not influence private, household consumption and behaviour. There was more to individual consumption than social competition, fashion, and emulation, and there was more to individual consumption in towns than public competitive displays of personal wealth and status. Display of fine clothing in public places was not necessarily motivated in the same way as behaviour within the houses of middle-ranking people, and it is important not to conflate descriptions of entertainments with domestic material life and needs.

Yet it is appropriate to enquire whether the experience of living in a town could have contributed to a greater tendency towards ownership of household goods. One possibility arising out of a central theme in this study is that personal and household behaviour influenced material life. Did something about the way people lived in towns lead them more frequently to own goods? Some of the goods most strongly associated with a concern for the ambiance of the domestic environment, especially pictures, looking glasses, and curtains, were certainly more common in towns. One aspect of the whole urban environment and of the psychology of living in towns, which could have influenced people's attitudes towards their domestic movables, was that people lived there in closer proximity to one another than they did in villages or in dispersed settlements. Illustrations show visual images of this different density, and one of the Portsmouth area shows a compact town and open countryside. But would this have influenced what people did inside their homes? Dwellings were closer together, sometimes the buildings were built to accommodate more than one household, and buildings often abutted and were overlooked by other buildings.[15] People are remarkably adaptable, but observations of modern communities have revealed that close proximity is stressful, even if the degree of overcrowding does not approach that in later tenements. In households that were not forced by poverty into overcrowding, one response to living near

Plate 6   Covent Garden, London, J. Van Aken, *c*.1720 (Museum of London).
A town. A high density of people, market stalls, shops, and large buildings.
Could these give a greater opportunity for consumption?

Plate 7   Dixton Manor House, eighteenth-century British school (Art Gallery
and Museum, Cheltenham). The countryside. A low density of people and
fewer close daily contacts than in a town. Did this matter?

other people could have been a greater desire to look inwardly to the living space and to make this as aesthetically pleasing and comforting as possible through the addition of furnishings and goods. Window curtains, very strongly concentrated in towns, could be regarded as giving greater privacy to households living close to one another, as well as dampening noise and adding a softer texture to the décor of rooms. The new and decorative goods associated with eating and drinking were also markers of people's concern that the material goods used in 'frontstage' activities should be attractive in appearance. Material goods could compensate for some of the inconveniences of town life.

In some other ways, town life does not seem to have been markedly different. There is no evidence that the fundamental roles and activities of households were different in urban areas. The household still provided shelter, food, security, warmth, and a basis for full participation in a social life. The practical physical circumstances in which this happened were different, and there were more occasions when people met together, performing day-to-day activities, such as collecting water, buying bread or ale, or doing washing, than there were in the country. People did meet one another in the country; the difference lay in the numbers of people at an urban centre. The distinctions between town and country were not hard and fast, for a few country dwellers owned the new goods. Books and clocks were almost as common in rural areas and in some parts of the country they were more so. Likewise, there were many households with just basic utensils and furniture in both kinds of place. Three urban tradesmen's inventories show this kind of variation. In the inventory of a potter in Burslem (a small industrial town of about 1,000 people) in 1714, basic equipment is listed, as well as decorative things:[16]

	£	s	d
In the house place Eleven pewter dishes 2 dozen of plates 8 small dishes	1	10	0
Two Little kettles, 2 potts one Warming pan one ffurnace one bakestone 9 small iron Things in the Chimney Place 15 white Earthen plates	1	2	0
2 small tables & 6 chairs 2 spinning wheels 3 looking glasses	0	15	0

For a weaver in Wellington in 1711 the inventory contains just ordinary furniture:[17]

	£	s	d

In the Kitchen
one ovall Table; one Short Skreene; one Grate, ffire
Shovell & Tongues & other Iron ware; one old
dishing bench & 3 pewter dishes & other old pewter
& 3 old Segg Chaires; ffoure Stooles & one warming
pan & Six Candlesticks   1 0 0

A blacksmith in a village (Dawley, Shropshire) in 1725 had very
few domestic goods:[18]

	£	s	d
In the Housplass			
It. one Tabell Bord and one form	0	8	0
It. one Brass pan one Brass Keettell and a Brass pot	0	12	0
It. one old Cobort	0	5	0
It. Eight Small Poutter Disshess	0	5	0
It. one Iarn pot and a Keettell	0	4	0
It. one Geen [?] Cheers and other Lumber Goods	0	5	0

Furthermore, a distinctive urban domestic culture is not apparent in contemporary commentaries by the diarists and travellers.
William Stout, for instance, lived in Lancaster from his teens,
although his family were yeomen farmers. His values and daily
behaviour do not seem different in kind from those of the other
tradesmen diarists, who were less obviously urban. He certainly
had his peculiarities, but these seem more a result of his own
personality and experience than a reflection of 'urban' values. He
did not approve of anything that seemed consumerist, especially
in other people's behaviour, and the values he expresses of hard
work and sobriety would not have seemed out of place to people
living in the country.

Supply and the inland trades

There were other circumstances leading to some goods being
common in towns. Many manufactured and most imported goods
were more readily available in towns, for they often had markets
and were at the nodes of transport networks. Images of town life
often focus on the busy market, and even a rather pastoral scene
of Henley-on-Thames shows the barges linking this area with

London. The marketing function of towns is the one characteristic of urban life that unequivocally distinguished town from
country. Even the smallest towns were centres for the distribution
of various kinds of goods. The retail and wholesale trades in
consumer goods were not as sophisticated in the early eighteenth
century as they were to become in the later part of the century,
and this is one of the least-explored aspects of commercial
change, partly because the evidence either does not exist at all or
is very scattered. Studies of retail networks and itinerant dealers
necessitate fitting together a complex jigsaw of scattered references. When this is done, it is apparent that there were coherent
networks, flexible enough to expand and include new goods when
necessary.[19] They were also normally centred on towns and
especially on the more important regional centres, where virtually
every kind of household equipment and furniture was available,
while many goods could easily be obtained in the smaller towns.
In Cheshire, for instance, Chester was the largest town and had a
market area that stretched beyond the county boundaries. It had
shops able to supply many goods, and traders came from many
parts of northern England and from London to display goods at
the fair in the town. Travelling retailers also used inns. Other,
smaller towns in the county had weekly markets, annual fairs, and
a few shops.[20] An engraving of the market square in St Andrews
in the late eighteenth century presents an image of how a fair or
market was seen as providing many kinds of goods. Urban dwellers, and especially those in the larger centres, had easier access to
consumer durables, and especially to new goods, than people
living outside the towns. In particular, townspeople could learn
about new goods or appreciate the potential attractiveness of
established things by seeing them at fairs or markets or in the
shops where goods were displayed. This kind of mechanism had
more to do with the towns' role in the distributive trades and in
the concentration of customers and facilities than with some
abstract notion of consumerism inherent in the psychology of
urban living. It is therefore worth exploring further.

One of the problems in demonstrating relationships between
the ease of supply and ownership of goods in towns is how to
discover the distribution networks for domestic goods at this early
date. Evidence from newspaper advertisements or trade direc-
tories are, for instance, extremely useful in enabling trading networks in particular commodities to be traced, but these sources
are not widely available before about 1750. However, patterns of

trade in china, earthenware, and pictures illustrate how certain goods could be more readily available in some places than in others.[21]

The trade in chinaware is a useful measure of the influence of distribution networks on patterns of ownership.[22] All of it was imported from the Far East before the 1740s, and it entered the British markets through auction sales at the East India Company's warehouse in London. Here it was bought in large lots by specialist dealers, who came to be known as 'chinamen'. These dealers, in turn, sold it to others, both in London and elsewhere; in so doing they played an important part in the development of the sales network in the trade. Chinese porcelain had long been imported in small amounts, but, owing to reorganization of the trade in China itself in the late seventeenth century, large quantities began to be imported in the 1680s; the import trade reached (with many annual fluctuations) a peak between the 1720s and 1740s. The main mechanism of distribution from London was for the chinamen to sell to wholesalers in the provincial centres, who resold to other dealers. Other dealers in London also bought from the chinamen, who also themselves had retail outlets in the City and West End. This means that stunningly attractive, decorated, useful china was available at modest cost in London and in certain provincial centres before it was widely known elsewhere. Inventories of shops selling glass and earthenware in Stamford (1721) and Abingdon (1696) show varied stocks of many kinds of pottery, but no significant amounts of chinaware.[23] Details of the activities of the chinamen and dealers are obscured through lack of records, and only three of the forty-five merchants making purchases at the East India Company sales in the 1720s can be traced in other sources, two as chinamen in the 1730s and the other in a trading partnership with Ireland, having formerly been involved in making stonewares in Vauxhall and in an experimental factory in North Staffordshire.[24] In Norwich, auction sales were held in inns in the early eighteenth century, and this was probably true of other centres. There were probably dealers in Liverpool, for Blundell was able to buy china there in 1719, having previously bought some from an itinerant dealer in 1710.[25] By the 1760s, when the trade was much more clearly visible from many kinds of evidence, it is evident that the trade in china and earthenware was centred on London (where 153 dealers can be traced before 1780), but there were concentrations in Newcastle, Liverpool, and Bristol of twenty, twenty-eight, and thirty-two dealers respectively. By this time there were dealers in most of the major and many of the minor provincial towns.[26]

Ownership patterns for china before 1725 are in keeping with a developing distribution network, centred on London and some main towns, but barely extended as yet to other places. Ownership was strongly concentrated in London, with forty-four out of 109 references to it there. The next largest concentration was in north-east England, with twenty-eight references in towns and a further four in rural places. These followed trade routes, and in the north-east differences between town and country were more pronounced than in some other areas, notably Cambridgeshire and Kent. These reflect differences in economic development at a regional level.

The importance of urban centres in the internal trading networks can also be seen by considering patterns of ownership in earthenware. China and earthenware were commercially different, for earthenware was made in many centres, such as London, Staffordshire, north Devon, Lancashire, Bristol, and parts of Yorkshire. There was a sophisticated distribution network, especially for decorated wares and the new stonewares. There were dealers in many places, and distribution was not centred on major towns or London. Ownership patterns too were less strongly concentrated on towns, although there were slight differences between rural areas and major urban centres.

On this basis we might expect that new goods imported through London, such as hot drinks or pictures (many of which were imported), would be more strongly concentrated there, and in other towns, than items, like pewter, that were more widely available. Towns were important as centres of distribution, and this influenced the patterns of ownership of some goods with strongly concentrated sources of supply. It does not account for all the differences but was an important factor in some cases, as it was in the regional differences.

Diffusion from town to country

If urban life gave opportunities for acquiring household goods – for whatever reason – did the process start there and diffuse into the countryside? Evidence from inventories and elsewhere shows differences between town and country, but it also shows that these were complex and were not great enough to suggest that towns

Table 4.4 Changing frequencies of ownership of selected goods in towns and country areas, 1675–1725

Saucepans (%)

	1675	1685	1695	1705	1715	1725
London	11	36	43	57	55	73
Major town	3	3	8	10	13	35
Other town	2	7	5	8	31	37
Rural/village	1	2	5	5	9	12

Earthenware (%)

	1675	1685	1695	1705	1715	1725
London	14	19	33	52	59	75
Major town	37	26	39	44	54	74
Other town	36	38	35	26	54	74
Rural/village	26	26	34	34	43	51

Books (%)

	1675	1685	1695	1705	1715	1725
London	18	17	19	41	34	56
Major town	23	23	16	13	23	30
Other town	18	22	24	23	23	42
Rural/village	18	18	16	16	17	13

Clocks (%)

	1675	1685	1695	1705	1715	1725
London	11	15	19	24	52	51
Major town	7	3	8	28	33	26
Other town	17	16	19	15	31	43
Rural/village	8	8	13	19	29	31

Pictures (%)

	1675	1685	1695	1705	1715	1725
London	9	26	21	57	60	60
Major town	30	20	32	49	60	48
Other town	21	24	21	6	43	47
Rural/village	2	3	3	5	9	10

Looking glasses (%)

	1675	1685	1695	1705	1715	1725
London	58	74	79	81	91	80
Major town	50	59	47	67	62	61
Other town	36	45	49	51	69	74
Rural/village	11	16	20	25	30	28

Window curtains (%)

	1675	1685	1695	1705	1715	1725
London	23	30	43	39	60	62
Major town	20	20	13	31	33	52
Other town	6	13	17	11	29	26
Rural/village	4	5	5	6	7	10

China (%)

	1675	1685	1695	1705	1715	1725
London	0	0	0	7	33	35
Major town	0	0	11	13	13	9
Other town	0	7	8	8	17	11
Rural/village	0	1	1	2	2	4

Utensils for hot drinks (%)

	1675	1685	1695	1705	1715	1725
London	0	0	2	7	22	60
Major town	0	0	3	3	12	22
Other town	0	0	2	0	17	16
Rural/village	0	0	0	1	3	6

Notes
See table 4.1. Changing ownership is discussed in chapter 2.

were islands of active consumption surrounded by 'traditional' values in the countryside. On the other hand, table 4.4 shows changes in the frequencies with which some of the goods were recorded in the different kinds of places. This suggests that diffusion from town to country was taking place, especially for some of the newer goods. In most cases higher proportions of inventories recorded the goods in 1725 than previously, but the highest frequencies were in London or in major towns in 1715 and 1725. In some cases, such as utensils for hot drinks, this is a very clear pattern. Clocks and books show a more uneven pattern, and the established goods record smaller differences.

This discussion shows that there was a closer integration of town and country than the polarity of the words suggests. From the practical point of view of how people acquired goods, visits to towns were frequent enough for country dwellers to see new things and buy them if they wanted to. Markets, shops, and fairs were visited regularly, even by those with few resources, or those living at a considerable distance from them. The diarists frequently refer to visits to towns in order to buy things; Rachael Pengelly made monthly visits to London, where she visited and bought clothes, groceries, and other things. This suggests that there could be close relationships between town and country and that the functions of towns as service and provisioning centres for a hinterland meant that goods were, if required, rapidly diffused to country dwellers.

This returns the argument again to the nature of town life itself. Was there something particular about living in towns that led people to develop a slightly different material culture within their households? That there is not one answer is apparent from the scope of this chapter, and it is important to stress that the exact influence of life in towns on people's behaviour and needs is elusive. It is one thing to feel that town life gave different opportunities; it is another to demonstrate exactly what was distinctive, especially since there was not one urban experience but many.

The differences are best seen in terms of the more complex personal contacts possible in towns. People were liable to meet others and to learn about consumption and to have the opportunity to present themselves in a variety of different situations. This does not exclude the idea that some towns encouraged the display of wealth and status, but this was not the only motivation for owning household goods or decorating a living space. Thus the influence of towns can be seen in the same kind of way as the influence of status: just as emulation and conspicuous consumption were not the prime movers behind the differences between people of different occupation and status, a desire to display wealth was not a prime mover behind urban domestic consumption. This evidence also supports the view that England was not a dual urban/rural economy, but that the towns and the countryside were integrated at many levels.[27] However, this chapter focuses on the middle ranks in both town and country, and community of interest and behavioural similarities between tradespeople or farmers in the towns and country are more apparent than between wage-earners in agriculture and those in the urban trades. Perhaps the dualism was greater for those with few resources, and so this evidence about the middle ranks does not reveal everything about the influence of town life and its part in altering attitudes towards leisure and consumption at a lower level in society. In any case, it is also clear that the regional economy of the localities surrounding the towns was significant.

Part 2

THE HOUSEHOLD

5

FINANCING THE HOUSEHOLD: INCOME, WEALTH, AND PRICES

A man he was to all the country dear,
And passing rich at forty pounds a year.
(Of the village preacher; Oliver Goldsmith, 1770)[1]

The final chapters take a different perspective on consumer behaviour, with the main focus on the economic and social behaviour in individual households. This enables us to examine what it was about everyday life that led to consumption of domestic goods. Consumption patterns are the aggregates of individual decisions, and the 'unit of consumption' was the household. It is therefore essential to have some perception of domestic behaviour to understand consumption, just as it is necessary to understand the firm in order to understand production.

Four aspects of the relationships between domestic experience and consumer behaviour are outlined. First, the income of households is examined, for it was through their cash incomes that people were able to buy goods and services. Second, expenditure patterns are examined, since these give some indications of priorities and suggest that domestic goods were only one small part of the outgoings from middling households. Third, the social and expressive roles of households, and specifically the utilization of domestic space, are outlined by descriptions of the main activities of households. Finally, the relationships between ownership of selected goods and social position are discussed; in doing this the argument returns again to general problems about the relationships between economic change and social structures.

Household size and composition

First of all we need to understand what households were like.[2] They were of modest size: most early modern households in England and Scotland had between four and seven people living in them, and the houses for which there is evidence surviving contained between three and seven rooms.[3] In some places households were larger: the London listings of the 1690s record an average of as high as seven in one parish, whereas in Cambridge the average was four. Likewise the households of the middle ranks were larger than those of labourers: yeomen households in the English listings had an average of almost six people, but those of labourers had just over four; the same was true in Scotland.[4]

The shelter and nurture that these household gave was on a small scale in comparison with the establishments of the wealthy gentry. It is essential to emphasize this because many accounts of the domestic economy of early modern households are based on evidence from large establishments.[5] On the other hand, the stress and impoverished material culture arising from one-room living does not apply to the majority of the middle-ranking households either. Life within the household was based on interactions between a small group of people who were well known to each other and who cared about each other, but each household was also a dynamic entity, with various phases in its life-cycle and many possibilities for change. Analysis of particular households and of the relationships that could arise when widows or widowers remarried show that these could become complex. The physical environment, especially in the established households that are the inevitable focus of historical study, had a certain continuity independent of the comings and goings of individual household members.

All studies of household composition in England and Scotland show that most of them were headed by a married couple (70 per cent in the English listings) and most of the rest (18 per cent) by a widow or widower. Most had children (74 per cent), and just over a quarter had at least one living-in servant or apprentice. Yet there was plenty of scope, within this basic structure, for variation according to individual circumstances. Diaries enable the family lives of individuals to be traced; the household of Ralph Josselin, for instance, consisted of Josselin, his wife, a servant, and at least one child from 1642 to 1677. Ten children were born between 1642 and 1664, but only five lived in the household at any time, and its maximum size was eight for a few years in the 1660s; with the departure of children, the household became smaller again and contained three adults after 1678. The diary does not say anything about the changing material life of the household, but it is evident that there were continuities, in that it stayed in the same place and retained the same functions, although there were changes in the numbers of people to be cared for.[6] The same was true of the Lancashire yeoman, Richard Latham, who was far less well off than Josselin, and employed a servant only for a couple of months after each of his children were born. It is possible to trace some of the changes in consumer behaviour of this household through Latham's carefully kept notebook of accounts; these show that expenditure on domestic durables, clothing, and books was greater at the beginning (before children) and at the end, when the children had grown up – an observation commented on more fully in chapter 6.[7]

There were other kinds of household. Those of unmarried men and women were more likely to change in composition than in size. Some instance of this is shown in two autobiographies of unmarried tradesmen, William Stout and James Fretwell. Unmarried men had the choice of 'housekeeping' for themselves, in the sense of having their own household with a housekeeper, but both Stout and Fretwell recorded that they were not comfortable living with servants – itself an interesting comment on their expectations of domestic life. They could board and lodge with someone else, to whom they made payments for a room and meals. Fretwell gave up housekeeping in 1735, 'being weary of living with servants only since my sister left me', but being a boarder was not always a good solution. Stout recorded of the few years (1735–9) in which he 'gave over housekeeping and borded with my nephew' that he 'was not easy there'.[8] The preferred solution was to have a female relative, preferably an unmarried sister, to keep house; Stout lived with his sister from 1691 until her death in 1725. After her death he normally lived with one or other of his nieces until they left to marry.

Incomes

The financing of households of middle rank enables us to understand the economic basis of consumption, although less is known about the salaries and incomes of the middling ranks than about wage rates. Income is obviously important to any understanding of the role of economic factors in consumer behaviour, for it was mainly through spending income that people could acquire consumer goods. Income and wealth are not the same thing, since wealth could take many forms not immediately relevant to the acquisition of household goods. In a later section of this chapter the wealth of the middling ranks is briefly discussed; it is demonstrated that inventories do give some measure of movable wealth and cross-tabulations show strong relationships between ownership of goods and the values of goods contained within inventories. This is followed by a discussion of another aspect of economic constraints on the ownership of goods, namely the prices of individual items. These were generally quite modest, and there is little evidence for price reductions at this time. This leads to expenditure patterns, which is the subject of the next chapter.

Measurement of the incomes of the middle ranks presents considerable conceptual and methodological difficulties. It is best to take income to mean all kinds of input into households from all sources, whether formal cash payments, household labour, or informal rights and non-cash receipts. There is a serious lack of well-recorded evidence about incomes seen in this way, for, even if people kept accounts, they did not write down everything they received.[9] Nor did they look at their composite income in the same way that we need to do in assessing the financial status of households, for garden produce, customary rights, and many things produced within the household were never (quite reasonably) valued by them in cash terms. Even cash incomes are hard to trace because the middling ranks did not receive regular sums in cash, so there is not even a source of evidence comparable to wage rates for labourers. The mixed nature of incomes causes very real difficulties in making generalizations about the sums of money that they might have had at their disposal.[10] This is unfortunate, because it makes regional differences and differences between individuals difficult to quantify. The evidence does not show whether the incomes of people of middle rank were changing and whether they went up at the same time as increases in the ownership of goods. They were undoubtedly liable to short-term fluctuations, and people's perceptions of them were liable to have constrained, or encouraged, expenditure. In examining the resources that went into households of middle rank we have to be aware that the situation was complex and the evidence sparce.

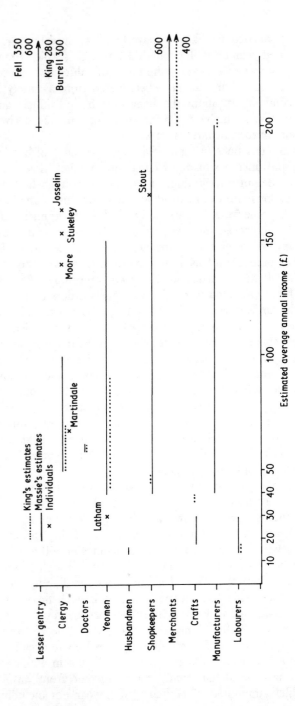

Figure 5.1 To illustrate the range of incomes available to households of middle rank

The range of incomes likely to have been received by clergy, tradesmen, and yeomen is illustrated in figure 5.1, which draws on a variety of evidence to show the range of values that household incomes had. This can be substantiated from a variety of scattered commentary about the behaviour of individuals and their expectations, which emphasizes that income was derived from various sources, in various ways.

The continuous lines in figure 5.1 show estimates of 'family' (i.e. household) incomes made by King and Massie.[11] There are many difficulties in interpreting, or even having much faith in, these calculations and the revisions of them that historians have suggested. In some ways they are vague, both in the annual totals suggested for the social and occupational subdivisions and in the fact that they do not give any indication of the complexity of the sources of incomes from fees, rents, investments, land, trade, and farming. Nor do the estimates link easily with other ways of seeing the social hierarchy. However, they do suggest orders of magnitude and the kinds of relationships that might be worth exploring further; they also have a certain internal consistency. Individual experiences, some of which are also shown in the diagram, could be anywhere within the suggested range, and even outside it. Figure 5.1 therefore gives a generalized overview of incomes and shows that they fell within the range £40 to £200 a year, and only the lesser gentry and the wealthier tradesmen received incomes of much over £200 a year. The overlaps in the incomes of yeomen, shopkeepers, and manufacturers are also worth noting, in view of the differences between their lifestyles and, as chapter 8 will show, ownership of household goods.

The diagram suggests that the incomes of middle-ranking households were normally over £40 a year. There is some other evidence which supports a view that £40 a year from all sources was a minimum amount for maintaining a 'middling' lifestyle. Very ordinary yeomen were said to have incomes of £40 to £50 a year in the first half of the seventeenth century.[12] Ralph Josselin commented in 1648 that his ecclesiastical income of about £50 a year was not adequate to maintain himself, his wife, three children, and a maid 'in a very low manner' – which again points to a limit of around £40 for a smaller household.[13] The recurrent theme in Adam Martindale's autobiography is how to procure a basic income, especially after the loss of his living in 1662. He claimed to have 'lived handsomly' on an income from various sources which amounted to perhaps £60 a year not including produce from his tenement.[14] In the mid-seventeenth century £50 a year was thought capable of supporting a minister and his family.[15]

William Stout's commentaries about his family's finances and prospects are particularly revealing in indicating a lower boundary, because one of the themes in his autobiography is the problem of how people became established in farming or a trade and the need for hard work to do so. His comments, smug though they are on occasions, also point towards £40 to £50 a year as the kind of income that he, as a member of a yeoman/tradesman family, would expect if he was to support a household. His family farm was worth £40 a year. He offered to buy his nephew, John, an estate of £40 a year for farming; John refused and became a draper. His dealings with his nephew, William, are revealing in this context; after he took over Stout's business he was not successful as a shopkeeper. Eventually, having subsidized him and paid off his debts, Stout made him an allowance of £40 a year to live on in 1739, which was increased to £50 in 1742. Stout comments (with some relish) that his nephew William's family were able to 'subsist' on this with 'great care', a subsistence which included food, fuel, malt, meal, and clothing, but little beyond, as Stout put it, 'plain fare'.[16]

A general 'average' household income does, of course, ignore annual and other fluctuations. Tradesmen or farmers could make net losses for some time without having to go out of business or even without recognizing that they were falling behind. Shopkeepers and traders are reported by Stout as having given up because the enterprise did not 'answer' after a few years, and Stout was especially keen on relating these incidents. Stout himself went for a number of years (1698–1704) without doing more than covering his household and personal expenses when he traded as an overseas merchant from Lancaster. From 1697 to 1703 he estimated that his estate 'went down by £140' (or 10 per cent), although it recovered rapidly when he took up dealing as a wholesale grocer.[17] So that in any year, or even for several years, a household could receive less than usual and still be of middle rank.

Several different occupational and status groups had incomes around the lower limits suggested in figure 5.1. This has importance for the study of expenditure and consumption patterns because the sources of these incomes were different; the lesser yeomen derived income largely from farming, including a large 'subsistence' or non-cash element which could not be used for acquiring consumer goods. Some craftsmen, small manufacturers, and shopkeepers were also at the bottom end of the scale, although, since they received more of their income in cash, they had a choice about buying goods and clothing. The least well-paid schoolmasters and clergy, especially if they had no income beyond their fees and stipends, were also at the bottom end of the scale, but professional families were usually better off because they received incomes from many different sources and did not rely on one salary or set of fees.

Aside from annual fluctuations and individual variations there were two groups with incomes consistently below £40. The lowest estimate, apart from labourers and servants, was made by Massie for the husbandmen, although King had not distinguished different kinds of farmer. Massie was probably not considering the same people as those called 'husbandmen' in probate records, and he made little distinction between them and labourers in estimating income; but in any case this points towards a group of small farmers with fewer resources than yeomen.

Understanding the position of the craft trades is crucial to appreciating the limits to the middle ranks, just as it is to appreciating their position in the status hierarchy. The crafts and manufactures were not clearly defined in King's tables; they were probably underestimated by King and included several different kinds of people. There is considerable difficulty in defining these groups, since the terms used for many crafts could include people of different wealth and status, from manufacturers on a large scale to wage-earners. For example, the term 'potter' was used in many parts of the Midlands to denote several kinds of person, whose potential income, family connections, and life experience were radically different. A potter could be an employee, for potteries usually had several workers in them at this time.[18] Such potters could earn as much as 10s. a week if they were in the skilled parts of the trade, such as throwing and turning. They probably worked most of the year, so their annual income could have been as much as £20, to which must be added food production and anything earned or produced by other members of the household. Such potters were not of middle rank but they were obviously better off than labourers and unskilled workers, also called 'potters' on occasions, who received lower wages of perhaps 6s. a week. Within the middle ranks were the small master potters, and some have left probate papers showing that they had estates comparable in size with those of yeoman; they sometimes had an income from land ownership, either in rents or, more commonly, through farming it themselves, or keeping a few animals. They had possibly received an apprenticeship, and a retrospective estimate of the financing of a small pottery suggests that they got about £20 a year for their labour and a further £20 a year in profit if they were making ordinary earthenware. Finally, there were a few larger-scale manufacturers of earthen- and stonewares by the 1730s, especially in North Staffordshire, and there were a few large manufacturers of delftware in Bristol and London. These people had substantial investments in the fixed capital needed for a pottery of some size, as well as in circulating capital in the form of money owed to them by dealers. This could amount to several hundred pounds, and the scale of these enterprises suggests that these 'potters' were of higher status, with greater incomes than the others received.[19] Even in the terminology of this one trade there were people called the same thing but with very different incomes.

The same was true of other crafts; there were different kinds of weavers, from small independent masters to out-workers. Blacksmiths and ironworkers varied from owners of large wholesale concerns to workers in the iron trades; builders could be employees or substantial entrepreneurs – differences in scale that were reflected in different incomes. That this is less true of some trades like shoemakers, leather-workers, or brewers does not affect the overall conclusion that the craft trades could include people ranging from out-workers to substantial owners. Revisions to King's and Massie's statistics do try to take account of this in that the crafts and artisans are separated from the master manufacturers, but this can only be a crude way of acknowledging the variations within the same craft.

Figure 5.1 also illustrates that the incomes of the better-off among the middling ranks were very much higher than £40, and, not surprisingly, much of the evidence about individuals falls within the upper part of the ranges of incomes. Many yeomen seem to have received up to £150 a year, although individual incomes are not easily traced.[20] Professional people are better documented, and their incomes seem often to have exceeded £100 a year from different sources. Ralph Josselin's income has been estimated at about £150–160 a year after 1660.[21] Giles Moore valued the tithes of his living in Sussex at £131 a year, although he may not have collected the full sum. He also had £8 a year from the rent of a piece of land, as well as the produce of his gardens and fishponds.[22] William Stukeley reckoned his two livings in London were worth £150 together.[23] The incomes of the other professions are not so fully listed because they were made up of many fees which are not recorded. James Yonge, who was a successful doctor, by the 1680s was getting a fairly high income from fees and other sources, although he had begun modestly in the 1660s. He numbered his patients at about 400 in 1703, but he evidently did not know what he had received in fees, for he never filled in the space in his diary saying how much they paid him. He did record £60–70 a year from being the surgeon in the docks in Plymouth, and he records getting £80 in a year from one family, so his total income was probably several hundred pounds a year.[24] Teaching was less remunerative, although it was often done alongside something else or by a young person just beginning to work. Martindale quotes 15s. a week as the usual rate for tutoring mathematics in a household of the gentry.[25]

Some shopkeepers could make a good living; Stout seems to have made, after his household expenses were covered, between £100 and £150 a year from 1690 to 1715, increasing to over £200 in the early 1720s, although he actually lost £300 between 1698 and 1705 when he traded as a merchant in Lancaster.[26] The Pengelly household received at least £200 a year in the 1690s, and probably a lot more, because only the expenses of the household are documented.[27] King estimated his own household expenses at £152 a year, but he does not include anything for rent and financial transactions of various kinds.[28]

More is known of the incomes of the lesser gentry, partly because they are better documented as a group and partly as a result of studies of gentry families in the mid-seventeenth century. In Lancashire most of them had incomes of less than £250 a year in the mid-seventeenth century, although the wealthy gentry households that are outside the scope of this study had very high incomes; in Lancashire 32 out of 774 identified gentry had over £1,000 a year. Individual experience here varied a lot, but the incomes of the gentry diarists used in this study were in the middle of the range. Timothy Burrell recorded his expenditure in 1686–8 at around £300 a year. Sarah Fell's accounts show expenditure of about £350 a year, but the income of the whole household was undoutedly greater.[29]

Sources of income

Income was made up of a number of components from a number of different sources, some of which are very occasionally valued in money terms in the rare accounts of expenditure. The important distinction is between income received in cash, which could be spent on anything, and that which was less readily exchanged for goods and services. Concepts about occupation and work derived from a less flexible view of industrial societies should not be applied to the more fluid conditions of the early modern era.

Most households produced some goods and food for their own use, and this is the most difficult part of household income to discover much about in detail, for garden produce, milk, hens, and so forth, are not valued in accounts and commentary. It is clear that most of the diarists had productive gardens with fruit and vegetables, as did Richard Latham, and these could have produced a large part of the non-staple food requirements of the household, whatever its status and occupation.[30] Many farmers were able to retain some staple foods, but farms were not normally intending to be self-sufficient. The smaller farmers and husband-men were likely to have derived a larger part of their needs from the farm, but even Latham bought a surpising amount of staple food, such as cheap cuts of meat, bread, and grain for bread. Thus households of middle rank, while not self-sufficient in food, could often produce a great deal themselves, and this gave them a certain independence from conditions elsewhere. The extent of this varied; town dwellers had less ready access to land and large gardens but more ready access to shops and markets. Similarly, some occupations, especially those with flexible work schedules like the clergy or doctors, were more suited to combination with other activities like gardening and farming. It was more difficult to combine farming with a craft or with dealing.

Cash incomes were varied and complex, for one individual could receive fees, stipends, salaries, profits, rents, investments, gifts, and inheritance. It is rare to gain enough detail to recon-struct the proportions of income that came from each source, so that the one full attempt to do this for the Essex clergyman, Ralph Josselin, is all the more valuable. This shows that three compo-nents, which varied over his lifetime, were of greatest importance. After 1650 his annual income was about £150, with a peak in the 1650s of about £200 a year. Of this, £60 a year came from his ecclesiastical living, which rose to £80 a year after 1659. In the

1650s he also got about £65 a year as the schoolmaster in Earls Colne. His third major source was from the rent, profits, and produce from land, which he gradually acquired after 1659, some with the salary from his teaching. From 1659 until his death in 1683 he received about £80 a year from it.[31]

Varied sources of income can be seen in a more general way in some other diaries, although these do not give enough detail for us to reconstruct the sums involved. Benjamin Rogers, for instance, nowhere says what he received, but it is clear from his diary that he farmed the glebe and ran a productive garden. He also did a considerable number of other things, such as making wills, giving advice, and acting as a doctor, for which he was presumably paid some fees; he also owned two houses in Bedford. Even so, having a large family, he once commented that he did not find his income adequate, had debts of £200 in 1729 and recorded resentment on 5 May 1732 that his mother did not leave him anything at her death, or only £20 which he claimed was his anyway.[32]

Others had less varied sources of income. Craftsmen, manufacturers, and dealers probably concentrated on their trade in order to survive, and many trades needed a great deal of commercial know-how or technical dexterity which were not readily combined with any other activity. In this respect, Stout seems representative of shopkeepers and wholesalers, and his experiences exemplify those of many other dealers and tradespeople. His main source of income was derived from running a shop (before 1698) and then a wholesale grocer's and a shop after 1705, with a few intervening years in which he was a merchant and traded in other ways. His commentary suggests that he worked at these most of the time but he also did other things, although there is no indication of how much, if any, income he derived from them. He had a garden, and he gave legal and other advice to people, for which he could have been paid in some way. He also owned houses in Lancaster, and he may have had a small legacy from his family.[33] His sister contributed to the shop by working in it and overseeing apprentices.

Multiple occupations and varied sources of income were also possible for rural households, for there were different kinds of farming and a widening variety of crafts. In northern Cambridgeshire and the fens in general, for instance, the inventories show that income was to be derived from several sources, such as a cash crop like saffron or flax, from a smallholding, from spinning, or from activities such as that of waterman. In the West Midlands and West Yorkshire the combination of iron or textile working and small-scale farming are well known, but the incomes derived from each component are not documented. Richard Latham likewise seems to have derived most of his income from the farm, but his family also spun flax, wool, and cotton.[34]

The income of the whole household was even more complex than that of its head, and this is extremely hard to trace because the work was often informally organized and casual. It is becoming clear from hints and references in many sources that the work of women and children could be significant, even if the sums involved were relatively small. Thus Martindale felt that 'my wife being willing to keep a little stock of kine, as she had done formerly' contributed markedly to the family's economic security.[35] Historians of women's work have been especially interested in the informal work and incomes available to women and are gradually piecing together evidence that confirms that, although the main sources of income into a household derived from the occupation of the head of the household, the labour of women and children could give flexibility and contribute to the living standards of the whole.[36] Latham's accounts show that small sums could be involved in domestic handicrafts, and the small income derived from them could extend the range of goods, clothing, and food purchased. Here the patterns of expenditure became more varied in the 1730s when the household contained several daughters, and there is evidence for more activity in textile production than formerly. It is thus essential to take note of the income of the whole household, especially if some of it was received in cash.

Wealth and consumption

The relationship between incomes and the ownership of goods cannot be derived from the probate inventory sample. On the basis of this discussion of the sources of income it can be suggested that people with a cash element in their incomes would be more likely to be able to buy a wider variety of household goods, and, from this point of view, it mattered whether income was from many sources and that some was available in cash. It is, however, possible to show relationships between the ownership of goods and the movable wealth of households, and it is to this that I now turn.

Wealth and income are not the same thing, although they are not unrelated. In this context, wealth can be taken to include all the accumulated resources of an individual or a household. It had two distinct components, akin to the capital employed in a manufacturing enterprise. Wealth was made up of fixed items like land and buildings, and movables of many kinds, including cash and credits. In addition, a useful distinction can be made between wealth that generated income or further wealth (such as rent from land or produce from agricultural equipment) and that which did not (such as dwelling houses, food, or consumer goods).

Probate inventories list only movable goods, livestock, and debts *owing to* the deceased, so the total value gives only a partial account of an individual's total accumulated resources. In particular, it omits real estate and debts *owed by* the deceased. In the case of traders receiving and granting credit (which was an acceptable and normal business practice at this time), the omission of their debts gives an inflated impression of their total 'wealth'. Someone owning land or properties rather than movable goods appears to have had fewer resources than someone whose wealth consisted of movable goods or investments. People may have had access to vastly different resources during their lifetimes, although their movable estates were of similar value. As far as the use of probate inventories is concerned, it is virtually impossible to do anything about this because the relevant information is not normally recorded elsewhere.[37] In addition, the total value of the inventory measures different kinds of things for different kinds of estates, and in particular the inventories of farmers and tradesmen did not record the same kinds of assets. Normally a farmer's inventory listed a greater value in producer goods because the livestock, most of the crops, and any money owing for things sold were included. A tradesman's did usually list producer goods, that is to say tools, materials, and stock, but these often had a low value relative to the income that was derived from them and they were less valuable than the farmer's capital goods. As a result, inventories of tradesmen and farmers with the same total valuation show a different balance between the values of the goods recorded, and smaller proportions of farmers' estates were recorded in household goods. The average total value of yeomen estates was £165, much the same as that of the dealers at £162, but the yeomen had lower valuations of their household goods, at £23 in comparison to £33 for the dealers. The mean value of household goods in yeomen's inventories was one-seventh of the total value, but was one-fifth in all tradesmen's inventories.

Table 5.1 Percentages of a sample of inventories with selected household goods in wealth groups defined by the value of the inventory

Total inventory valuation £	No. of inventories	Tables %	Cooking pots %	Sauce-pans %	Pewter %	Pewter dishes %	Pewter plates %	Earthen-ware %	Books %	Clocks %	Pictures %	Looking glasses %	Table linen %	Window curtains %	Knives and forks %	China %	Utensils for hot drinks %	Silver %
1–5	84	80	52	7	76	50	20	17	6	0	5	14	19	0	2	1	1	0
6–10	150	81	67	7	86	50	17	28	7	4	9	20	28	6	1	3	3	5
11–25	500	86	67	7	89	48	22	31	11	6	9	27	35	8	1	2	1	11
26–50	552	87	64	10	93	47	23	34	12	11	12	28	39	10	3	3	3	19
51–100	628	90	69	9	93	43	24	39	19	18	11	28	40	11	3	3	4	21
101–250	627	93	78	13	97	49	34	43	26	28	14	41	48	17	5	6	5	31
251–500	234	94	81	15	97	53	38	42	33	44	23	50	60	21	9	7	6	44
Over 500	127	95	85	18	98	50	45	44	46	51	39	61	65	29	15	9	10	67

Sources and notes
The sample is discussed in chapter 1 and appendix 1, where there are also details of the calculations and significance.

Table 5.2 Percentages of a sample of inventories with selected household goods divided according to the value of household goods

Value of household goods £	No. of inventories	Tables %	Cooking pots %	Sauce-pans %	Pewter %	Pewter dishes %	Pewter plates %	Earthen-ware %	Books %	Clocks %	Pictures %	Looking glasses %	Table linen %	Window curtains %	Knives and forks %	China %	Utensils for hot drinks %	Silver %
1–2	107	61	54	0	66	28	6	23	3	0	0	5	7	0	0	1	0	0
3–5	343	76	56	5	83	38	11	22	7	1	3	10	15	1	1	1	1	2
6–10	598	85	63	5	94	47	18	28	8	6	7	16	29	5	1	2	1	6
11–15	435	92	68	9	94	46	25	38	14	13	7	29	40	9	2	1	1	13
16–25	571	94	73	10	95	50	28	36	18	20	12	31	46	9	2	2	2	23
26–100	772	97	82	18	98	53	42	50	35	39	26	58	64	26	9	8	8	50
Over 100	76	100	91	33	99	59	63	59	3	67	50	84	74	57	29	26	22	84

Sources and notes
The sample is discussed in chapter 1 and appendix 1, where there are also details of the calculations and significance.

Table 5.1 shows the proportions of inventories in different 'wealth' groups, defined according to valuations derived from the whole inventory; table 5.2 shows the same information according to the value of household goods. In both, the goods were more likely to be recorded in inventories of higher value, and the relationship is stronger for household goods. These patterns are indicators of stocks of movable goods accumulated over a period of time, and the tables express relationships that cannot take account of many of the details of wealth, or of changing resources over a life cycle, although they do show that economic resources were important. The patterns in tables 5.1 and 5.2 show that higher proportions of inventories recorded goods in the groups with higher valuations. In every case there is a general tendency for ownership to increase as the recorded values become greater. The progression is also a fairly smooth one. There is more even distribution among the well-established goods, especially pewter, tables, and cooking pots, although the estates of lower value were less likely to own even these common goods. Clocks were individually expensive and barely occur at all in the inventories of lowest value. Of the other goods, only looking glasses and table linen were frequently recorded in the inventories with totals valued under £25 and the new goods were rare, occurring in few inventories with household goods valued at under £25, roughly the mean value for household goods in the sample as a whole.[38]

Costs and prices

Another way of looking at ownership of goods in economic terms is to examine their costs and prices. There is scattered information on the values of individual goods in inventories as well as the prices paid in household accounts. Table 5.3 lists the ranges of values commonly assigned to the goods examined in detail. There is a reasonable consistency in the values given to most items, and for the purposes of suggesting orders of magnitude there is no need to be over-concerned about the criteria that appraisers used. (They were supposed to value at what they might reasonably expect to sell them for, rather than a new price.) There were no systematic changes in valuations within the sample, so the table covers all areas and dates of the survey.

The values of the household goods have some bearing on the realtionships between wealth and ownership, and are also

Table 5.3   *Ranges of values given to selected goods in inventories*

Goods	Range of values for the piece or item	Comment
Pewter	1s. to 2s.	Frequently valued by the piece
Pewter dishes	1s.6d. to 3s.	
Pewter plates	6d. to 2s.	
Tables	3s. to 4s.	Not often valued separately
Large tables	10s. to 22s.	
Brass pots	5s. to 25s.	Rarely valued individually
Iron pots	1s. to 4s.	
Coarse earthenware	1d. to 2d.	Rarely listed individually
Other earthenware	2d. to 1s.	
Wooden plates	½d. to 1d.	See also Latham, 'Account book'
Books	6d. to 4s.	Very varied
Clocks	£1 to £2 10s.	Often valued separately; some under £1 in Lancashire
Pictures	2d. to 9s.; usually 6d.	Very wide range; rarely valued alone
Looking glasses	1s. to 5s.	Rarely valued alone
Large looking glasses	20s. to 25s.	
Tablecloths	about 3s.	The quality varied considerably
Napkins	3d. to 2s.	
Curtains	1s. to 4s.	
Knives and forks	6d. to 8d. each	Not often valued separately
China	2d. to 6d.	

suggestive of the ways in which choices were made. Materials used for tableware and drinking vessels are instructive as examples here. Ownership of tableware, drinking vessels, and other utensils of different materials is illustrative of the complexities of relating prices to consumption in this period. Earthenware cost very much less per piece than pewter: typically an ordinary earthenware utensil that might be used at table cost about 2d., whereas pewter cost at least a shilling and normally 2–3s. for a dish and rather less for a plate. However, pewter was actually better value because it retained its monetary value, with old vessels valued at about two-thirds of the new cost, and they could also be part exchanged for new.[39] Secondly, pewter was not liable to break, and a potter suggested in the 1690s that if the price of delftware (a white decorated form of earthenware, with a very fragile surface) went up it would not sell: 'other vessels of Pewter, Tin etc. would have been used, rather than Pots, because of their being very liable to break.'[40] China was newly available in reasonable quantities in the early eighteenth century, and was most commonly used for new purposes, notably for hot drinks and for decoration, so it was not in competition with pewter. At about 6*d.* a piece it was much more expensive than pewter because it was more fragile; although the initial price of pewter was greater, it wore well and retained part of its value. It was not until much later in the eighteenth century that earthenware became stronger and more aesthetically attractive than pewter, which was then gradually superseded by crockery as we know it. Even so, Cobbett was still fighting a rearguard action against crockery in the 1820s as being too costly for labourers' families; he argued (somewhat unreasonably) that they would be best served by pewter because of its durability.

Another problem in specifying economic relationships is that some of the relatively new goods, whose ownership was expanding markedly in the early eighteenth century, were not individually very costly. Pictures and prints, for instance, varied a great deal in price, but many were valued at less than a shilling each; small looking glasses were a few shillings each; a knife-and-fork set was about a shilling. The highest-quality pieces of these goods were more expensive, but what matters here is that they could be acquired for what seem to be fairly modest sums in comparison to the incomes of families of middle rank or even the total value of their household goods. This requires another way of looking at the domestic economy of middle-ranking households, namely their expenditure patterns on all kinds of goods and services, and this is the subject of the next chapter.

6

FINANCING THE HOUSEHOLD: EXPENDITURE AND PRIORITIES

Look about your houses, in every degree:
And as your Gettings are, so let your Spendings be.
(Kentish yeoman in the 1760s)[1]

Expenditure patterns can tell many things about spending priorities and the contexts in which household durables were acquired. Household expenditure by people of middle rank is unfortunately difficult to trace and analyse, for comprehensive household accounts are rare, even for the more literate and self-aware professional people and the lesser gentry. Furthermore, those that do survive are extremely awkward to analyse because they contain so many detailed entries. They do, however, give a more eloquent view of the economic life of a household than can be seen by looking at income alone. They also enable us to place expenditure on household durables within the context of expenditures on many other things needed to maintain the household, for household goods were not the most expensive things bought and they were often acquired in an erratic and irregular way. In examining household expenditure patterns, we are getting close to consumption, as opposed to ownership. It is not possible to take account of enough households to enable the kinds of regional and other distinctions that have been made using inventories to be maintained. Instead, the accounts used here can be taken as exemplifying broad trends.

Three accounts are used here in order to convey something of the many ways in which households could use their resources and spend their incomes.[2] These three are not necessarily representative of all households; they just happen to have survived. Their value is that they contain a great deal of detailed evidence about the ways in which households were financed and goods acquired. They are, fortunately, from different types of household – one of a small farmer in a simple nuclear family in south Lancashire; one of a merchant's wife (later a widow) in Finchley, near London; and the other of lesser gentry status in north Lancashire. Detailed breakdowns of expenditure from these accounts over a number of years are shown in tables 6.1 to 6.3. In conjunction with these, an analysis of expenditure by an aristrocratic family in Edinburgh and a budget by Gregory King of the costs of running his own household in London in the 1690s are outlined in table 6.4.[3]

The tables subdivide the expenditure of these households under headings that distinguish food, clothing, household maintenance, furnishings, miscellaneous spending, and financial affairs. This book focuses on furnishings and equipment, which normally amounted to only a few per cent of domestic spending. This chapter therefore places these things in the context of total expenditure, and thus of household consumption. In trying to observe people's outgoings and expenditures from household accounts, there is a temptation to try to ask rather modern kinds of questions which would asume that all (or most) things that were used or eaten were bought with cash. This temptation is reinforced by King's analysis of his own household, which is firmly based on the assumption of cash expenditures. There is also an opposite temptation to imagine that the households with which this study is primarily concerned dealt 'in kind' and that it is therefore not possible to know much about them and their outgoings. It may even be inappropriate to think in terms of 'expenditure' at all. These are important points about the meanings behind the documents, and there is no single answer to the issues that this raises. One approach lies in trying to be sensitive to the particular household economy represented by each account, and to take notice of this before endeavouring to answer wider questions about the proportions of expenditure on food, clothes, entertainment, and domestic goods.

As has already been noted in discussing people's incomes, the inputs into most households of middle rank were by no means simple and were not always in cash; the same is true of expenditure. In addition, the documents themselves are not always clear about the exact purpose of every payment; whether grain was for seed or for consumption; whether flax was to be spun for cloth and clothing for household use, or whether the yarn was to be sold (or both); whether a servant worked on the land or in the house; whether milk was sold or consumed in the household. Thus our perfectly reasonable and proper desire for clear answers to questions about how much was spent on food or clothing is easily thwarted by the fact that the documents themselves are reflections of a complex domestic economy based on different kinds of input and output. In addition, there are obvious problems in knowing how accurately the account was kept, what was left out, and how to allow for this. As we do not know anything about what is not there, the discussion is based on what is in the accounts but with some regard to the possibility that explanations for curious patterns are due to omissions of various kinds. The rewards of observing expenditure from an individual account, as well as some of the problems of doing so, can clearly be seen from the account book of Richard Latham of Scarisbrick in Lancashire, which he began in the year of his marriage, 1724.

Richard Latham

Richard Latham's account book is unusually detailed, with sums recorded for many small items as well as a large payment of £40 for renewing his lease in 1728, a sum that was more than twice his normal annual expenditure. In table 6.1 each entry was categorized under headings which try to do justice to the complexity of his outgoings and to the fact that entries about his household and farm were made alongside one another, sometimes on the same line, even if each was valued separately.[4] Typical of many entries are these from 1735:[5]

	s	d
garden seeds.5d: treakel.4½d: pease2d	0	0	11½
Plowing in midle filde ye 5 of April	0	1	8

It is clear that some of the expenses must have generated income, although the accounts do not show this, for he does not note money that he received. Here he is recording the purchase of flax, but what happened to it is not noted, except that no payments are to be found for weaving or anything that might suggest that it was spun for use in the household. It is most likely to have been sold as yarn.

	s	d
for 2 stone of flax at Kirkam.10s. dressing of it.6d.		
14 pound to ye stone.ye 23 of November	0	10	6

This intermingling of expenses connected with household consumption and with production makes it meaningless to analyse Latham's affairs in as simple terms as those that might be used for a household whose economy relied mainly on cash income and cash outgoings. So the table distinguishes expenditure associated with production from that associated with consumption, in so far as this is possible, for an unknown amount of the produce of the farm and garden were consumed by the household. There were also unpaid labour inputs by the household into brewing, making clothes, washing, and cleaning.

The part played by each outgoing can best be seen by examining expenditure on different things separately, except for one general observation, which is that there were remarkable variations from year to year, quite apart from the evolution of the household from one containing a newly married couple without servants, to one with up to five children, still without servants, and indeed very little paid domestic help, except for washing, and household help when Nany Latham was giving birth to children and once when she was ill. The average expenditure shown in the table (excluding the first year because of unusual purchases of livestock, furniture, and utensils when the household was set up) on most items gives only a generalized impression of expenditure in any one year. Payments in connection with farming and livestock were as low as £1. 8s. 9d. and as high as £9. 4s. 8d., with a mean of £5. 2s. 4d. Equally, whereas about half as much was expended on average on food as on the farm and garden, in some years the differences were much greater and in others the amounts were similar. Household maintenance was the most steady, at about 12s. 5d. a year, but even here there were some years in which the sums were much lower. Expenditure on furniture and utensils was the most liable to wide fluctuations, with virtually no purchases made in many years, but with unusually large sums laid out in the first year. Such annual variations (unless they were the result of poor record-keeping, which is always possible and should not be over-looked, even though these accounts seem particularly detailed) may have been characteristic of a household of restricted means. Expenditure would be made on those things which were the most urgent in the circumstances of any one year, circumstances which the accounts do not enable us to reconstruct but which were related to many factors, such as harvests, illness, childbirth, the need to pay debts, to renew a lease, or to support additional people in a household. Thus it is notable that expenditure

Table 6.1 Household and other expenditure of Richard Latham of Scarisbrick, Lancashire, 1724–1740

	Farm and food production				Food				Clothing				Raw materials		
	Farm	Live-stock	Garden	All	Staple	Sugar, groceries	Brewing	All	Clothes	Cloth	Trim-mings	All	Wool, flax, cotton	Yarn	All
1724	91	366	16	473	84	5	–	89	4	10	1	15	24	2	26
1725	67	21	2	90	67	8	–	76	6	7	*	13	11	1	12
1726	70	64	*	134	69	12	5	86	6	4	2	12	10	–	10
1727	64	75	1	140	64	12	50	126	18	9	3	30	7	2	9
1728	46	136	3	185	46	10	2	58	4	7	*	11	3	1	4
1729	45	66	*	112	45	10	10	65	4	2	3	8	5	–	5
1730	8	73	*	81	8	6	*	14	6	5	1	12	17	*	17
1731	29	30	1	61	29	7	*	36	9	8	2	19	22	3	25
1732	33	15	2	50	33	7	–	40	14	14	1	28	16	–	16
1733	33	37	1	72	27	6	5	38	23	12	2	37	2	–	2
1734	53	121	2	177	53	9	*	62	16	10	2	28	12	–	12
1735	72	91	7	170	69	7	4	79	23	3	*	26	7	–	7
1736	49	12	4	64	42	8	–	51	21	19	2	41	19	5	24
1737	24	3	1	28	23	7	4	34	17	11	1	29	11	2	13
1738	21	30	1	52	19	6	2	26	23	20	2	44	15	1	17
1739	33	88	1	122	33	7	4	36	37	11	1	49	17	1	18
1740	79	11	7	97	79	11	2	92	15	8	1	24	18	–	18

Source
'Account book of Richard Latham of Scarisbrick, Lancashire, 1723–1767', Lancashire Record Office, DP 385.

Notes
All figures apart from the last column are amounts calculated to the nearest shilling.
See also text and notes 2 and 3.
* = amount less than 6d.
– = no data

Table 6.1 Cont. Household and other expenditure of Richard Latham of Scarisbrick, Lancashire, 1724–1740

Maintaining household			Furnishings and utensils			Miscellaneous					Non-finance expenditure	Financial			Total recorded			
Heat and light	Cleaning, washing	All	Furniture	Utensils	All	Medical	Books	Education	Services	Travel, etc.	Total	Lease	Interest repayments	Tax, misc.	Shillings	£	s.	d.
16	*	16	45	37	82	2	–	–	3	2	708	–	17	4	729	36	9	8
5	2	7	5	7	12	3	1	–	–	3	217	–	43	1	261	12	16	8
15	3	18	1	1	2	4	1	–	6	1	274	–	84	3	361	17	19	8
10	3	13	–	11	11	4	1	–	–	2	336	803	–	1	337	16	5	10
13	3	16	–	2	2	1	*	–	–	1	278	–	34	2	1117	55	15	9
8	3	11	–	1	1	3	1	–	4	1	211	–	29	*	240	12	0	2
12	2	14	–	2	2	*	1	–	–	1	142	–	68	4	214	10	11	11
10	2	12	–	1	1	4	*	–	8	–	166	–	28	1	195	9	12	7
3	2	5	*	*	*	*	–	–	4	1	139	–	358	2	499	24	19	10
13	2	15	–	1	1	2	1	–	4	1	173	–	224	3	400	19	19	0
8	2	10	–	1	1	*	–	6	–	1	297	–	151	1	449	22	8	11
9	3	12	2	2	4	3	1	2	5	1	309	–	207	1	517	25	15	4
17	2	19	4	2	6	1	1	–	–	31	238	–	6	3	247	12	5	11
7	2	9	2	3	5	3	*	5	3	1	130	–	61	1	192	9	10	6
14	2	16	–	5	5	*	2	–	–	1	163	–	42	81	286	14	6	9
14	2	16	*	6	6	1	–	–	–	1	248	–	210	1	459	22	19	0
17	3	20	–	3	3	1	*	4	–	*	259	–	195	4	458	22	16	11

on food and clothes was lower than usual for several years after the lease was renewed in 1728 and did not return to previous levels for five or six years. On the other hand, the years after about 1735, when the household seems to have done more spinning of cotton and flax, saw greater expenditure on furniture, equipment, books, and clothing. A household of this kind needed to be extremely sensitive to maintaining the balance between income and urgent outgoings in order to survive, as this one clearly did most successfully. The result was that in some years the balance between expenditure on different things varied markedly from 'normal'.

In most years, production and purchase of food accounted for a very high proportion of recorded expenditure, but we cannot know how much of the produce of the farm was sold because the accounts do not record receipts, though some of it undoubtedly was sold. Income was thus generated to pay for other things and also to pay off Latham's lease and loans over a reasonable number of years. The farm was a mixed one; normally he kept about four cows with a pig and some hens, and these were numerous enough to have produced milk, milk products, and young animals beyond the needs of the small family and therefore to have generated income. He grew a remarkable variety of crops, to judge from the seeds purchased, including the staple grains, wheat and oats, potatoes, cabbages, peas, carrots, onions, clover, other garden vegetables, and fruit. Some could have been retained for household use and some sold, but the accounts do not say which. The farm and garden alone produced such a wide variety of food that, if it was eaten by the family in reasonable quantities, it amounted to a very adequate, mixed diet.

Food was purchased as well as grown, and about the same was spent on staple foods as was spent on the farm or on the livestock separately, again with notable annual variations. The staple foods included bread, oatmeal, and cheap kinds of meat, notably the hearts and plucks of sheep and the heads of sheep and calves. A further few shillings a year were spent on sugar, dried fruit, pepper and spices, and these added variety to the diet that could have been had from the farm and garden alone. This shows that a farm, even if a wide variety of field and garden crops were grown and livestock kept, was not necessarily 'self-sufficient' in the sense that it produced all the food that was needed. Here meat and grains were purchased as well as things that could not be grown locally. This should be seen as adding variety and security to food supplies, rather than as making up deficiencies.[6]

Food was of central importance to such a household of small means, although this is rather difficult to demonstrate purely in terms of the proportions of expenditure devoted to food production and purchase. Table 6.1 shows that the proportions varied from year to year, but, even if we take the mean of the years after the first, the proportions also depend on whether the financial affairs of the household are included or not. As a proportion of expenditure on consumables, bought food accounted for 26 per cent of expenditure and all farming and food production (some of which was sold) for 46 per cent, making a total of 72 per cent. If the percentage is calculated on the basis of total outgoings, then only 17 per cent was spent on food and 30 per cent on food production, including that for market – a total of 47 per cent. Both are shown in the table for comparison with other accounts or budgets, but, either way, no other single kind of purchase was of such great importance.

A second basic need, that for clothing, shoes, and other miscellaneous items of dress, is also listed in some detail in the accounts, and here too a distinction is apparent between purchases of wool, flax, and (after 1736) cotton on the one hand and other items of clothing and cloth on the other. The raw materials do not seem to have been purchased to make clothes for members of the household, for there are no records of payments for weaving, and they do not seem to have had a loom themselves. They bought flax in order to spin it into yarn for sale, so that purchases of raw materials, equipment for spinning, and several pairs of knitting needles were part of the productive activities of the household. Table 6.1 distinguishes these two kinds of purchase and shows that the production of yarn or knitted goods was variable and on a modest scale at less than £1 a year, although in the 1730s this accounted for about a tenth of outgoings. This does not mean that the cash income from this was unimportant to the household, especially since the work could have been done by the daughters, the eldest born in 1725.

Clothing itself was the second largest single expenditure on the people in the household, and in some years its cost was similar to that of staple food. The purchase of clothing was very varied, and different things were acquired in different ways. The main garments were made up from cloth bought specially for particular items and made up by a tailor, who was paid at a daily rate. These kinds of entries are illustrated by this extract, from August 1737:

	s	d
dicy new shoon.2d: & Ann. new shoon.	3	3
....		
cloath dicy 3qs. 1.7d: searg. Alice new gown 1 yard & h.	1	9
lin & wool Ann & kerch.	5	5
dicy new hatt.11d: silk tape. 4 yards.8d: sop.1d.	1	8
....		
Taylors work. ye 16.17.18.19. of August	4	0½
bety.dicy.Rachael new clogs. 8d: bacon.4d	1	0½

There are no references to yarn being woven, either in the household or by a weaver. Clogs were made up in a series of steps; the wooden soles were bought, someone was then paid to shape them, leather and nails were bought, and they were presumably made into clogs in the household. Some smaller or specialized things were bought ready-made, including aprons and scarves, shoes, stays, and hats. There was therefore a mixture of different ways of acquiring items of dress and of using household labour to make much, but not all, of what was needed – a characteristic pattern for purchases of clothes in other households.[7]

Heating (by coal and peat bought a few times a year), lighting (by candle), and washing (soap, starch, and cleaning utensils bought frequently in small amounts) accounted for much less than was spent on food, but it was still an important part of the expenses of the household. These were important to the well-being and comfort of people living in the house, and expenditure on them was more regular than on some other things.

On the other hand, furniture and utensils were not recorded regularly, and many years went by without any purchases recorded. In the first year of the accounts, the year in which Latham married and set up the household, the relatively large sum of £4.2s. was spent on utensils and furniture, but after this only a few shillings a year went to buy utensils such as cups, plates, and dairy equipment or to mend metalwares, and this gives the impression that the household did not seek to expand or improve its equipment, although the sums increased a little in the late 1730s. This was due to purchases of dairying vessels and to some replacements of basic equipment, such as a fire grate, rack, and pothook, costing 2s. 3d. in 1737. None of the new or unusual goods that have been observed from inventories were recorded, although a few books were bought, as in 1733:

	s	d
spend 4d: salme book new & horn book 6d	0	10
version by N. tate & brady		

There were also payments for the repair of a clock.

There were a large number of very small payments for numerous other purposes, and these are shown separately in the table because they are indicative that even a household of rather small means had interests other than day-to-day physical survival and did maintain some contact with the outside world. As a proportion of total expenditure these were trivial, but they may well not have been trivial in relation to how the family behaved and saw itself. Thus a few shillings were spent on 'school wages' for sending children to school and on books for them in the 1730s. In 1735, 'new teastament. 1.1d. ... for betty to learn in', and in 1738, 'new psalme book.10d: & childs guide: 1.1d'. Such purchases distinguished this from many illiterate households. A few pence were spent each year in travelling to the local market, in visits, and at the fair – as in 1740, 'Nany going to her sister Alise ye 26 Feburary 1d'. At the birth of each child, a midwife was paid and a payment made, usually to a relative, for someone to look after the house for a few weeks, as in 1731:

	s	d
the midwifs office at ye birth of ye child	1	6
Ann Prescot ye 13 day of July. Margaret bigins	3	0
....		
wages for 3 weeks to Ann Culshow tenting my wife	4	6
Ann my wife returning thanks after child bearing	0	6

The other medical expenses were small, usually herbs, oils, or 'physick', but, while small, the sums spent were important at crucial times and therefore in prolonging the life of the household. In 1735:

	s	d
sirups of march malo 2 ounces.5d. ... for fisick when		
nany my wife was ill ye 11th day of november	1	6
....		
wages to bety Latham 1 week nany was lame	1	0

Likewise there were a few sums for special occasions, such as a funeral in 1735: 'for funeral expenses for the child the 7 day of may £1 10s 0d'.

The financial affairs of households are always the most obscurely documented and difficult to understand from accounts, but they were obviously crucial. The largest single payment, of £40, was for a new lease in 1728:

	£	s	d
Paid to Mr Scarisbrick ye 16 day of April 1728 in part for a new lease	20	0	0
Paid the other part the 26 day of April	20	0	0
for parchment writing ye lease & giving possession 26th day of April	1	10	0

The accounts do not indicate how this was paid, but in every year there were payments for the 'use' of money as well as some large sums repaid to various individuals. It seems that part of the money for the lease was borrowed and repaid during the 1730s, mostly before 1735. But the accounts do not say for what purpose the money had been borrowed, and it is also likely that small sums were borrowed for other purchases and repaid quite quickly. However, repayments and interest accounted for a notable proportion of the annual cash expenditure of the household, and they were undoubtedly essential for family security and well-being.

Overall, Latham's accounts show a number of features of the way in which households were financed and the place of consumer goods in their expenditure patterns. One is the importance of financing the three basic needs of households – for food, clothes, and shelter – and these accounted for most of the cash recorded here. Among these payments are those for new foods, notably sugar. They also include payments for clothing in much larger amounts than those for household equipment. The second is that very little was spent on utensils after the household was initially equipped, and this is what might be expected. However, this should not lead us to conclude that such expenditure was not important, either to the household or an an indicator of the consumption of domestic equipment and furniture. Domestic utensils were accumulated and not immediately consumed like food, so the small sums spent in some years do not mean that they were not important. Likewise, while only minute sums were spent on many miscellaneous things, these were not as trivial as they might at first seem, for they enhanced the lives of people in the family. Something *was* spent on services, the fair, books, and education, all of which contributed towards a cultural life that involved contact with the world outside the household. This was, of course, an unusual household in that the head of it kept such detailed accounts; it is difficult to know how typical it was of other small farming households, and we cannot say how other yeomen and tradesmen behaved on the basis of this set of accounts by themselves. It does, however, have certain things in common with other households and shows the importance of expenditure on growing and purchasing food, and in the provision of clothes and warmth.

Rachael Pengelly

Can the same be said of other households? Let us look in detail at another, which was very different in its structure, age, wealth, and location. The accounts kept by Rachael Pengelly began two years before her husband's death in January 1695/6 and continued until just before her own death in 1709. Changes in the size and especially in the structure of the household had some obvious influences over expenditure patterns, so table 6.2 (showing the same kind of information as given for Latham) is divided into three phases. From 1694 to 1696 it contained Rachael and her husband, Thomas (a merchant, according to the catalogue of the document in the British Museum), and two servants, together with some other people in the household for part of the time. Their son may have lived there at the beginning but was living in chambers in London by May 1696. Three other people, Cousin Dyer, her maid, and a Mr Clarke, also lived there for all or part of the time. In January 1695/6 Thomas Pengelly died, but Rachael's mother then visited with her servant, and stayed until her death in December 1697, paying for her board. So in the first phase of the accounts the household was quite complex, with a married couple (then a widow), co-resident relatives, and servants; this kind of complexity was not uncommon. In the next three years the household continued in the same kind of way, with Rachael Pengelly at its head, although the boarders seem to have left. Betty Alldersey, who was Rachael's sister's daughter (probably in her teens), and whose father had died in January 1698/9, joined the household in 1699 and stayed until 1708; many payments in the accounts after 1700 were made on her behalf. The third phase, which continued until the accounts ended in 1709, began when, for some reason not apparent, there was some change in the way in which the household was financed. After 1700, quarterly payments were

Table 6.2 Household and other expenditure of Rachael Pengelly of Finchley, 1694–1708

	Food production			Food				Clothing				Maintaining household		
	Live-stock	Garden	All	Staple	Sugar, etc.	Brew-ing	All	Clothes	Cloth	Trim-mings	All	Heat and light	Cleaning and washing	All
1694	169	34	203	201	96	224	521	216	164	25	405	320	48	368
1695	160	19	179	213	134	218	565	183	47	32	262	251	26	277
1696	253	43	296	219	40	145	404	24	12	21	57	133	21	154
1697	171	33	204	769	53	274	1094	43	27	4	74	423	36	459
1698	70	19	89	600	35	109	744	16	75	9	100	145	30	175
1699	85	21	106	532	98	135	765	20	106	20	146	186	29	215
1700	8	10	18	173	31	53	262	71	23	11	105	268	32	300
1701	6	6	12	67	60	54	181	150	62	18	230	188	15	203
1702	3	–	3	77	45	77	199	155	46	25	226	160	25	185
1703	–	2	2	102	67	73	242	58	57	13	128	180	2	182
1704	16	3	19	51	69	78	198	55	142	16	213	198	18	216
1705	11	1	12	48	85	84	217	32	26	16	74	47	10	57
1706	21	1	22	23	116	73	212	57	256	14	327	79	8	87
1707	23	–	23	53	88	101	242	8	46	2	56	26	21	47
1708	22	1	23	91	71	133	295	50	19	–	69	16	23	39

Source
Rachael Pengelly, 'Household accounts, 1693–1709', BM Add. MS 32, 456.

Notes
All figures are amounts calculated to the nearest shilling. – = no data.
See also text and notes 2 and 3.

Table 6.2 Cont. Household and other expenditure of Rachael Pengelly of Finchley, 1694–1708

Furnishings and utensils			Miscellaneous					Non-finance expenditure	Financial			Total recorded		
Furni-ture	Utensils	All	Medi-cal	Books	Educa-tion	Services	Travel	Total	Rent, repairs	Gifts, repay-ments	Tax, poor	Shillings	£	s.
44	61	105	83	16	–	275	26	2002	236	1921	137	4296	214	16
68	47	115	51	13	–	196	14	1672	203	1261	108	3244	162	4
12	43	55	45	1	–	156	89	1257	113	3638	176	5184	259	4
–	14	14	4	5	–	346	165	2367	183	240	241	3031	151	11
–	8	8	87	–	–	228	19	1450	249	1182	133	3014	150	14
6	15	21	18	2	–	177	50	1500	358	150	226	2254	111	14
–	20	20	2	3	–	152	28	890	104	185	86	1265	63	5
–	21	21	16	–	–	98	29	790	2125	64	18	2997	149	17
–	4	4	19	3	–	231	12	882	103	61	42	1088	54	8
–	19	19	10	–	–	129	12	724	115	94	28	961	48	1
15	9	24	3	2	1	226	18	920	151	98	44	1213	60	13
–	4	4	–	2	–	206	15	587	121	145	32	885	44	5
57	5	62	12	1	–	218	19	960	179	64	39	1242	62	2
47	12	59	7	–	–	195	5	634	166	58	24	882	44	2
34	4	38	21	–	–	212	14	711	27	89	25	852	42	12

made to 'Cousin Ottway' of about £1.10s., with a payment of £100 to him in 1701. After this many household items continued to be recorded, but no basic food like grains or meat; payments for heating, lighting, furniture, utensils, her servants, and personal things such as travel and clothing continued to be recorded. In this respect, the last nine years were different from the first six, and this is reflected in the patterns of household expenditure.

As might be expected in a household which spent ten times as much, or more, in a year than Latham's, the proportions spent on food were much lower, amounting to 30 per cent of total expenditure on consumer items, or 12 per cent if financial payments are taken into account. Food was, however, the most important single item. But, except for small amounts of tea and coffee, this larger and wealthier establishment did not buy different kinds of food from the type bought by Latham, although the quality was certainly higher. They even had a garden and kept a few livestock, and some of the milk and milk products were sold. After Thomas's death about twice as much was spent on food, which then amounted to a higher proportion of consumer spending, at 49 per cent. The household seems to have reduced its own food production at the same time, for little was spent on the garden, and fewer animals were kept. In the last phase, much less was spent on food, especially on staple food, although brewing and purchases of sugar, dried fruit, and hot drinks continued. This is interesting in showing how the same household, under different circumstances, could record very different patterns of expenditure, even on such a major item as food.

Expenditure on clothing was proportionately less important for most of the time than it was for Latham. The sums could be quite large: in 1695 damask for a mantua, silk, and lining cost 18s. 6d., with a further 5s. 0d. to make it up. In 1693, 4½ yards of cloth 'for Tomme' cost £4. Before Thomas's death as much was spent on clothing as on heating, lighting, and washing, largely because the cloth and clothing bought was mainly for him. Thereafter less was usually spent on it in a year than on heating, lighting, and so on, and many purchases in the 1700s were for Betty. Running the household was proportionately more important than for the Lathams – not surprisingly, in view of its larger size and greater resources. Rachael Pengelly continued to spend similar sums on heating, lighting, cleaning, and washing for many years after her husband's death, and the reasons for the reductions after 1705 are not immediately apparent.

Furniture and utensils were bought irregularly and in relatively small amounts, just as they were in Latham's household. For many years after Thomas's death only very minor purchases were made and things bought were normally replacements for ordinary utensils, even if they cost quite large sums, as in 1693 when a brass kettle cost £1. 10s. 0d. and an iron one 5s. 0d. Decorative items were rare. A few furnishings were bought in 1706–8, but the amounts never reached the sums spent in the first two years of the accounts. They included things like linen, white earthenware, brewing tubs, and a few cooking utensils. This is most important in showing, in conjunction with the irregularity in Latham's accounts, that household durables and especially furniture were not necessarily (then as now) bought with any regularity, for they were relatively enduring and there was little need to do more than replace minor items for many years.

The greater resources available to this household also meant that proportionately more was spent on servants, tips, and small payments for services of many kinds, as well as for travel and for the services of apothecary and doctors. One of the last entries is for 13s. for 'my doctor for things he gave me to take'. Rachael herself went to London using a coach at the cost of around 3s. 6d. about every other month to visit relatives, to attend 'the meeting', and to go to the shops, where she bought groceries, clothes, and many miscellaneous personal items. Expenditure on books and papers ended with Thomas's death, although small payments were recorded for ink and paper, and Rachel could write very clearly and kept her accounts for many years, so was clearly not illiterate.

The largest payments recorded here are the sums of money paid to relatives and others for no stated purposes, and these represent aspects of the financial affairs of the household. Some could have been for money previously borrowed: thus she paid £87. 14s. and then £5 to Allwin 'upon morguage' in May 1694; she also recorded at the same time £100 as 'money received and borrowed from my mother for repayment of Allwin's morguage'. But it is rare for her to be so specific or for the sums to be so large, although as much as £100 a year could be spent in this way. The other rather odd set of payments are those to 'Cousin Ottway' for lodging, because they seem rather small for herself, her niece, and two servants at 30s. a quarter, although she did pay a lump sum of £100 to Ottway in 1701. Her accounts do record less food after this date, but the rest of her domestic payments continued.

Moreover, it was not unusual for single people and widows to board with others, or even to live separately and eat their meals with another household.

These rather variable sums spent on essentially financial affairs stress again that a household's expenditure cannot easily be distinguished from its productive function and from how it was financed. It is also notable that there are considerable similarities between these two rather different households, and I shall return to the significance of this after a brief review of a third household, that of Swarthmoor Hall in Furness for the years 1675 and 1676.

Sarah Fell

The household account or, more accurately, the cash book kept by Sarah Fell relates to a complex set of family property and relationships. Sarah was the daughter of Margaret and Thomas Fell (d. 1658), who had six other daughters and a son (d. 1670). At the time of the accounts, Margaret had married again to George Fox, well known as a founder of the Society of Friends, and she continued to run Swarthmoor Hall, which she had inherited from her first marriage. She also had other property, including Marsh Grange where one of her married daughters, Mary Lower, lived. Four daughters had married and three were living at Swarthmoor, together with their mother, George Fox (from June 1675, when he was newly released from prison in Worcester), and three servants. It was one of the largest houses in the area, with thirteen hearths in 1673. The accounts are complex because they record many payments other than for the running of Swarthmoor. There are a few references to other properties, especially Marsh Grange; there are many purchases on behalf of the married sisters; there are a few for ironworking, amounting to £3. 10s. in 1676; there are some in connection with the Society of Friends; there are many letters which were probably received in this connection as well. At the same time, there seem to be gaps, so that there is one small reference to hops but none to the other materials used in brewing, apart from yeast, which can also be used for bread. Likewise, although this was a mixed farm, seeds were bought for the staple crops, but no bulls or cows were recorded; pasture was rented in 1675 but not in the next year. An additional factor is numerous sums varying from a few shillings to over £100 recorded as repayment of borrowed money, money lent

Table 6.3 *Household and other expenditure of Sarah Fell of Swarthmoor Hall in 1675 and 1676*

| | Farm and food production | | | | Food | | | | Clothing | | | | Raw materials | | |
| | Live-stock | | | | | | | | | | | | | | |
	Farm	stock	Garden	All	Staple	Sugar, etc.	Brewing	All	Clothes	Cloth	Trim-mings	All	Wool, flax	Yarn	All
1675	912	73	19	1004	136	7	17	160	13	67	8	88	1	17	18
1676	462	683	6	1151	431	125	–	556	119	125	4	258	1	24	25

Source
The Household Account Book of Sarah Fell of Swarthmoor Hall, ed. N. Penney (Cambridge, 1920).

Notes
All figures are amounts calculated to the nearest shilling. – = no data.
See also text and notes 2 and 3.

Table 6.3 Cont.   Household and other expenditure of Sarah Fell of Swarthmoor Hall in 1675–1676

Maintaining household			Furnishings and utensils			Miscellaneous					Non-finance expenditure	Financial		Misc., tax, poor	Total recorded		
Heat and light	Cleaning, washing	All	Furniture	Utensils	All	Medical	Books	Education	Services	Travel	Total	Lease, rent, repairs	Money		Shillings	£	s.
59	13	72	22	6	28	3	40	5	134	112	1664	119	5183	148	7114	355	14
90	44	134	57	52	109	62	100	–	138	239	2772	32	3749	402	6955	347	15

(sometimes for only a few days or weeks), interest on borrowed money, and other financial transactions, the details of which are not specified. As table 6.3 shows, these amounted to rather more than half the total value of outgoings, at about £225 a year, out of about £350.

Table 6.3 includes all the entries in the cash book, even when they appear obscure or to relate to other properties. The totals are not just for the running of one simple household, but include a number of people and properties. Even so, food predominated, and expenditure on livestock and farming was high. How much of the produce of the farm was sold, and how much was consumed at Swarthmoor, is not recorded, but, taken together, over half of the expenditure (excluding the financial transactions) went on food production and purchase. One difference between this and the much smaller one of the Lathams fifty years later was that sugar and other groceries were not regularly recorded, and most of the entries shown in the table arose from a payment 'to David Poole of Preston for sugr bought of him' for £4. 10s. This is partly a reflection of the increased availability of such items by the 1720s rather than the remote location of Swarthmoor, for other things were bought in Lancaster and even Newcastle, and 1d. was spent on 'chocoleta' in November 1675.[8] Most of the staple food purchased consisted of meat, eggs, cheese, and fish, and a few shillings were spent on white bread but grains were not otherwise recorded.

Expenditure on clothing was also important, but the patterns of purchasing were slightly different from those already noted in the other households, since more working of raw materials is implied by payments made for spinning, weaving, and dyeing. Entries such as these were quite frequent (January 1674/5):

pd Alis Atkinson for spininge 7: hankes of hempe
tow   2s   4d

(Alis was possibly the daughter of a local shopkeeper, whose wife is also recorded as spinning for the Fells.) The yarn may have been sold, but this cash book, unlike Latham's accounts, records payments to weavers, usually for household linens, as in May 1675:

	s	d
Geo ffell wever for workinge 24: ells, of teare of hempe	4	6

	s	d
whiteninge 30 yrds of teare of hempe and 19 yrds huggabacke	1	10½.

Some cloth was bought for particular people and garments, and made up by a tailor, with shoes and other accessories bought ready-made. Thus in October 1676 Scotch cloth was bought for the three sisters and their mother, and a tailor was then paid to work on this for each of them separately. How much spinning, weaving, or making of clothes was done by the three sisters is not, of course, recorded in the accounts, which are even silent on purchases of trimmings that might be suggestive of remaking of clothes, but they may well have done so without leaving a record of it in the accounts; needles and spindles were recorded once or twice.

About the same was spent on household maintenance, furniture, and utensils as was spent on clothes – possibly a reflection of the large size of the house. This was normally for the replacement of miscellaneous things, but in November 1675 several pieces of furniture were bought at 'John Cowell's sale', including a chair for 1s. 2d., a little table for 1s. 4d., and 'A great backe Chaire' for 4s. 6d.

Where this account does differ from the others is in the amount spent on other things, especially those associated with frequent and varied connections with the outside world. Almost £7 was spent on incoming letters, apart from tips and gifts to the people who brought them or took messages. Likewise expenditure on travel, mostly by horseback, to local meetings of the Friends and to visit people was large, even in comparison with Rachael Pengelly's coaches to London. This was partly because the household contained five adults all spending money in this way, and because there were relatives living close enough for frequent visits, as well as the fact that contacts were maintained with local market centres and with Lancaster. But it was largely the result of the correspondence that Fox maintained on behalf of the Society of Friends, although the sums here do not include any of Fox's journeys on behalf of the Friends or the costs of his return from Worcester. This is particularly interesting in showing how the expectations and status of a household influenced the minutiae of its expenditure, just as it influenced its possessions.

Table 6.4 *Household and personal expenditure in several households as a proportion of recorded annual expenses*

Date	Household	Food production %	Food bought %	Clothing %	Raw materials %	Heating and washing %	Furniture and utensils %	Medical %	Books %	Education %	Servants %	Travel %	Total Values All purchases and services £	All expenses £
1690s	Gregory King (estimate)	–	46	14	–	5	7	–	3	–	12	12	147	154
1693–1714	Lady Griselle Baillie (20 years' av.)	–	45	16	–	with food	11	3	–	–	9	16	392	630
1675–6	Sarah Fell (2 years' av.)	49	16	8	–	5	4	2	4	–	6	8	111	352
1724–40	Richard Latham (16 years' av.)	46	26	11	5	4	2	1	neg.	neg.	1	1	11	17
1694–6	Rachael Pengelly (3 years' av.)	13	30	15	–	16	6	4	$\frac{1}{2}$	–	12	2	82	212
1697–9	Rachael Pengelly (3 years' av.)	8	48	6	–	16	1	2	–	–	3	4	89	138
1700–8	Rachael Pengelly (9 years' av.)	2	28	15	–	18	3	1	–	–	23	3	40	63

Sources and notes
See notes to tables 6.1, 6.2, and 6.3, as well as notes 2 and 3.

Expenditure patterns and consumption

Table 6.4 juxtaposes summaries from these three accounts, Gregory King's budget for his own household, and summaries from that of Lady Griselle Baillie in Edinburgh. This adds a further perspective to the households already looked at, one being much wealthier and the other based on different assumptions about how a household might be financed. King's budget portrays a household in which no expenses were allowed for the production of food or clothing, even on a very small scale. This should not be seen as another instance of King's tendency to do inappropriate calculations with a great air of authority. It rather presents a different kind of household, with its expenditures being made more clearly in cash, and it reveals King's urban and professional expectations that a money value would be placed on expenditure in this way. In making a budget for the purpose of drawing conclusions about household incomes in general, he is obviously measuring something different from expenditure actually made. He is also expressing a way of providing for a household that is different from the methods indicated in the accounts, for he is seeking to quantify possible costs of living solely in money terms.

The table and the comparisons in it summarize much that has been said already. There were some ways in which the households were remarkably similar, for food and clothing accounted for the highest proportions of expenditure in all cases. The differences arose out of the particular circumstances of individuals, with some spending much more on travel, servants or letter-writing. Likewise, the proportions of expenditure on utensils varied from household to household, as well as from year to year in the same household.

We now need to move beyond observations of how much people spent on what, to possible ways of interpreting expenditure patterns within the contexts of this study. How was the financing of a household likely to have influenced the ownership of furniture, domestic textiles, and utensils? For one thing, it does not appear that goods were bought only when other 'needs' had been met. Even the Lathams bought books and spent a small proportion of their outgoings on domestic equipment. The other households, with greater resources, did spend relatively larger sums on these things, but the proportions were only slightly greater. In the accounts examined here, there was very little outlay on new kinds of goods.

Something is also suggested about people's general priorities, in that food was the most important single item in every one of these different households. As we would expect, the highest proportions were found in the poorest household, where food purchases and production (including some for the market) accounted for 72 per cent of recorded outgoings on average. The lowest proportions were recorded in the unusual circumstances of Rachael Pengelly at the end of her life, although even then 30 per cent of her household outgoings were spent on it, more than on any other item in the accounts. King's budget is of particular interest because this recorded the highest proportion on food alone, and, according to King's own comment, the household intended to live in comfort. This, and the kinds of food bought by Pengelly, suggests that additional spending on more or better food was a high priority for a modest household in comfortable circumstances. It suggests that food was not a kind of fixed 'given' in expenditure, at some adequate but simple level, but was something that people were prepared to spend more money on if they had it, then as now.

Another way of looking at priorities is to see what other items of expenditure feature in King's budget more strongly than in the accounts of the other households. Enduring priorities, regardless of total resources, were to be found in clothing, heating, lighting, and washing, for the amounts spent on these were much the same as a proportion of household expenses in King's budget as in the other accounts. On the other hand, the budget allows for a higher proportion to be spent on many of the miscellaneous things, like services, travel, or entertainment. Even the Fells, with their considerable contacts with the outside world through the Quakers, did not spend as high a proportion as that in King's estimate – 18 per cent as against 27 per cent. The Lathams spent minute sums in this way, amounting to about 2 per cent of household outgoings, although it is worthy of note that they spent anything at all. This kind of personal expenditure was possible with increasing resources.

The environment of the household, judged by expenditure on domestic goods, was seen by King as more important, for he allows for a higher proportion to be spent on repairs to furniture and for buying equipment than any of the accounts. This difference is even more marked if utensils for use in the dairy and the like were excluded from the farming households. This may partly be because budgets often allow more generously for items of this kind than is spent on them in practice, but apart from this it might also be taken as an indication of the expectations that a household such as King's (concerned to live well and spending a largely cash income) intended to devote a regular part of its resources to the domestic environment, even if this was small in comparison to expenditure on food and clothes. The Pengelly household was not dissimilar in the first few years of the accounts, in that it had access to consumer items in London and was the kind of household (that of a merchant) inclined to higher ownership of many goods. By contrast, although the Lathams and Fells bought some domestic utensils and textiles, these were less important to them, just as they appear less frequently in the inventories of these kinds of rural household.[9]

That there was some flexibility in these totals is important, for it was the position of domestic goods in household expenditure that made it possible for new things to be adopted very quickly, if people chose to do so. Furniture, linen, equipment, and household goods were purchased in an erratic way. Many things were bought, or otherwise acquired, only once or twice in a lifetime. In aggregate, households spent relatively small sums on them in comparison with regular expenditure on items for immediate consumption or that wore out rapidly (like clothes and shoes). Some food was needed every day, a new cooking pot perhaps every five years, new pewter every seven years, new furniture every ten or fifteen years. Some consumer durables were less durable, among them pottery and china, teawares, and mirrors. Yet these relatively small sums in comparison with total outgoings on food and farming, together with relative infrequency of purchase, does not mean that these things were not important. Expenditure on them was part of a wider economic strategy adopted by a household in order that it could survive, and this gave high priority (as it even does in a consumer society) to food, clothing, and shelter. What is of significance is that there was scope, within the expenditure patterns discussed here in some detail, for middle-ranking households to have spent a little more on domestic goods if they chose to do so.

Why they chose to do so leads to the question of what roles goods and services played in people's lives. The answers are complex, and it is to these that I now turn in the next chapter.

7

THE DOMESTIC ENVIRONMENT

Some respite to husbands the weather may send,
But huswives affaires have never an end.
(Thomas Tusser, *Five Hundred Points of Good Husbandry* 1580)[1]

Households were complex social institutions in which most people's psychological, physical, and emotional needs were met. The processes of providing food, shelter, clothing, income, and nurture were the main preoccupation of most people of middle rank. Activities such as cooking, eating, drinking, bringing up children, visiting, and reading had a profound influence on the material life and culture of households. Space was used in coherent ways, with appropriate furniture and utensils for public and private activities. Some, notably eating and drinking, were the occasion of valued social contacts. This value is reflected in the utensils used and the introduction of new decorated tablewares, changes in eating and drinking habits, and, in the wealthier households, separately furnished rooms for eating. Yet this was only one area of activity, and in order to view domestic possessions comprehensively it is necessary to observe all domestic activities. It then becomes apparent that there were many levels of inter-connection between domestic organization and domestic goods and chattels.

The context: women, work, and servants

Everyone in a household was involved in maintaining it, although the more strictly housekeeping activities were seen as the respon-sibility of women. The distinction was clearly stated at the time between the man's role, 'whose Office and imployments are ever for the most part abroad, or removed from the house', and that of the woman, 'who ... hath her most general imployments within the house'.[2] This responsibility can also be seen in the more limited education available for women, based on the assumption that they would be keeping a house rather than learning a trade.[3] Virtually all diarists and autobiographers took it for granted that women did the housekeeping, although this accepted role did not mean that men were never involved or that women never did anything else.[4] Men certainly took an interest in household affairs, and conduct books advise that the husband should control the money and be generally responsible for obtaining household goods, although the day-to-day running of the house should be left to the wife.[5] Comments in men's diaries about household matters are frequent and often show an active interest in the smooth running of the house, if not in the details of domestic routine. This commentary, together with advice in conduct books, enables us almost to observe many daily routines and how tasks were done, although meals, visits, and some work tasks tend to be more fully recorded than activities such as washing and cleaning.

An enormous amount of sheer hard work was required in feeding, clearing up, and providing clothes, shelter, and nurture for all members of a household. Some impression of this emerges from a very cursory glance at books of advice or cookery books, although it must be recalled that these were addressed to the wealthier farmers, merchants, and gentry, and they tend to be about catering on a scale larger than that in the normal middling household. Even so, there are many overlaps, and Markham's list of the virtues 'which ought to be in a Compleat Woman' is a schedule of considerable length, including cookery, making cloth, malting, brewing, baking, 'and all other things belonging to an Household'. He also lists activities that we would not expect of a small household, such as 'chirurgery', ordering great feasts, banqueting, distilling, perfumery, and preserving.[6]

The need for hard work is often referred to in diaries and autobiographies, usually as a retrospective comment of some kind. Fretwell wrote of his mother:

> she spent the remainder of her days in a great variety of usefulness, and not a more serviceable person ever came to Thorp in the memory of man than she has been. ... She was a prudent manager of her family affairs, and a true pattern of a

good housewife; ... as great an enemy to idleness (which is an enemy to all that is good) as most I ever see, for she was rarely to be seen without her hands at work about her lawful business. ... She had a numerous family for many years, for which she provided in a most decent, orderly manner.[7]

Stout reported of his parents, 'my father and mother were very industrious in their children's infancy'.[8] Defoe, as ever, is prepared to pontificate on the behaviour of tradesmen, and argued that servants were needed so that the wife of a tradesman did not need to do the 'drudgery' of housework and 'might be useful in the Shop'.[9] Even among the better-off, considerable effort was needed, and Elizabeth Pepys occasionally spent a very long time cooking and shopping, as when 'my wife was making her tarts and larding her pullets till 11 a-clock'.[10]

There are not many paintings or engravings that show what hard work housekeeping could be, for domestic scenes do not include the more arduous activities, but rather seek to present an idealized image of domesticity in which dirt and hard labour have no place. The most frequently depicted task is cookery, perhaps because the cook could be presented in a calm pose if she were seated or tending a pot. *High Life Below Stairs* by John Collett has many levels of meaning, but the washerwoman here is one of the few images of the misery of domestic work. The servants or cooks in many pictures (especially the Dutch and Flemish ones) are intended to convey the moral value of domestic life, and in looking at these pictures we have to remember that they were not painted to show physical labour. From this point of view, Sandby's drawings are perhaps the most evocative; they do not overstress the miseries but convey the feeling of the tasks being done.

Servants were a necessity in maintaining the household of middle rank without excessive toil.[11] They were not a luxury or a form of conspicuous consumption; they were a fundamental part of domestic life. Stout, for instance, was hardworking himself and expected others to be so as well. For much of his life (1691–1725), his sister, Ellin, kept house for him, and 'she did it without a servant, but got one to wash and dress the house once a week'. After her death, 'I was sencible that my home and shop was not taken care of as formerly'.[12] He then had several young nieces to housekeep for him; they too did most of it themselves but had the help of servants who came in to do the heavier tasks of cleaning and washing. If one man, living in a few rooms with a shop,

Plate 8 (above)   High Life Below Stairs, John Collett, *c.*1750s (British Museum). The young women enjoy themselves and the child copies, but there is real drudgery for the older washerwoman. A rare picture of the hard work of housework.

Plate 9 (facing page, above)   Kitchen scene: women washing, Paul Sandby, 1765 (Royal Library, Windsor Castle). Washing here is a more relaxed task, but still not without physical work.

needed a housekeeper and some help from servants, then a family with children and another adult to care for certainly required several people's labour to maintain the kind of standards that Stout claims was appropriate. Some commentary in diaries suggests that overwork arose from the stress on domestic organization caused by childbirth or illness. Elizabeth Newcome felt to be overworked with two servants and needed another; she was six months pregnant at the time.[13] Latham employed someone to live in and do domestic work when the children were born, although

Plate 10 (facing page, below)   A kitchen at Steeple, Isle of Wight, anon., no date (Carisbrooke Castle, Isle of Wight). Books and other oddments are high on shelves. There is the clutter of everyday life and the ubiquitous pot over the fire.

the family did not normally pay for domestic help except for a washerwoman.[14]

There is not a great deal of comment on the standards that people expected. It is unfair to quote travellers' criticisms of household affairs because they often comment on situations from the outside and from the standpoint of different conventions, but clearly houses were not always clean and well organized. Brereton's famous diatribes against conditions in Edinburgh do suggest that the tasks could be overwhelming. For example:

> their chambers, vessel, linen and meat, nothing neat, but very slovenly. . . . The people here are slothful . . . their houses, halls, and kitchens, have such a noisesome taste . . . as it doth offend you as soon as you come within their walls. . . . Their pewter, I am confident, is never scoured. . . . To come into their kitchen . . . will take off the edge of your stomach.[15]

We do not, of course, know how the people responsible for housekeeping in the places that Brereton visited saw their attempts, but it was probably extremely difficult to clean and carry water in overcrowded tenements. They could well have felt overwhelmed by the physical labour involved.

Domestic schedules and the time spent on them

How individuals managed to do all the tasks they had to do and how they saw the pressure of work on their lives is not directly documented; it is only when someone was unsure what to do and wrote introspectively that anything of this kind is revealed. The comments in the diary of Richard Kay are interesting here, because in 1737 and 1738 (he was born in 1716) he was uncertain what employment to take up, although he helped his father with his medical practice and later became a doctor himself. He lived with his parents, and in 1737 (30 April) he recorded: 'I see Persons employed, and therefore I think it my Duty to be employed also'. For several years he spent his time in a number of ways, 'attending on Father in his Business' or with 'my closet duties' or 'in Husbandry' or 'about the Carpenters' or 'some concerns about the house' or 'in Domestic Affairs'. On 11 October 1738 he recorded that he wished to spend some time writing about his religious meditations and spiritual exercises, which he had previously begun to write down, but he was clearly worried that he would not have the time.

Table 7.1   *Household activities: estimates of time spent doing them*

	Daily hours	Weekly hours	Irregular days per year
Production			
Farming			
Trade	10		
Profession	8		
Gardening	1		
Animals	2		1
Milk			
Making clothing/cloth	2		
Furniture			2
Household and personal maintenance			
Meals, preparation	3–4		
Baking		3	
Brewing		3	
Getting food and water	1	1	
Preserving food			2
Keeping fire in	1		
Cleaning the house	2		
Washing		4	2
Eating	2		
Sleeping	8		
Leisure: reading	0–2		
spiritual	0–4		
Child care: play	1		
education	2		
feeding/suckling	1		
Shopping			12
Visiting		4	

Notes and sources
As explained in the text, this draws on many diaries and similar sources, largely those referred to in the notes to this chapter and in the Bibliography. The times are impressions based on these.

I find it will be difficult to get Time to do it, my Attendence and Assistance in other Matters being so often call'd for; ... I resolve to spend my vacant Time Morning and Evening in the doing of it ... let me ever remember I've no Time to lose.[16]

In fact he did complete his manuscript and presented it to his parents on 11 April 1740. The interesting thing about this is that Kay was a dependent member of the household, who was not fully responsible for its running or maintenance, yet even he could feel a lack of time for something he felt 'a Duty' because of the pressure of the necessary activities of the household.[17]

Commentary in diaries and elsewhere on daily routines is

patchy, yet frequent enough to enable some rough estimates to be made of the time spent in maintaining a household. These are listed in table 7.1. In the first place, and not unreasonably, some household members spent most of their time in making a living. Working patterns in the early modern period, whether of self-employed craftsmen, tradesmen, farmers, or wage-earners, are not well understood; it is part of the received historical wisdom that trades could be done 'in the home', but it is not clear what this meant in practice, even for trades where the workshop or shop was adjacent to the dwelling house. When any trade is examined in detail, it is apparent that the workplace was distinct from the living space; the requirements of a craft or trade were such that work tasks must also have been separated from tasks which maintained the household.[18] Among the craftsmen that left inventories it is most unusual to find working tools, looms, or anything connected with the trade in the main living area.[19] Again, some of the pictures of domestic interiors, especially Flemish ones showing tradesmen working in the living room, are misleading, not so much because no one ever worked like this but because they are not portraying the kind of society with which this study is primarily concerned. Nor do the spinners in the background of David Allan's domestic scenes give an image of behaviour applicable to English middle-ranking households. This does not mean that weavers or other textile workers never had their looms and equipment in the living room, but better-off ones did not. Activities associated with trades, crafts, the professions, or shop-keeping took place in separate parts of the house, in outbuildings, or out of doors.

The routines of the people responsible for trade or husbandry were important to the way in which the household's day was planned. Shops and warehouses were separate from the living area, and work here involved long hours and attention to detail. Stout gives a graphic impression of the kinds of tasks and working hours involved when he had taken a shop and cellar of his own. He boarded next door; 'But lodged in the shop, so was seldom in the house, which was adjoining to my shop ... were frequently caled up at altimes of the night to serve customers [which] obliged us to have a bed in the shop.' He opened the shop about an hour after sunrise and shut by 9 o'clock in the evening: 'I was much confined and imployed in keeping accounts and making up goods ready for market.'[20] In this situation, domestic life would receive little time and require little space. On the other hand, some occupations (and specifically the professions) did not necessitate a closely confined working life, and such people led more varied lives, requiring more varied domestic space.

Varied amounts of time were spent on making things for household consumption. Gardening was often done by one of the dependent members of the household, according to need and interest; Kay spent many days 'employ'd in Husbandry', which included gardening and care of animals.[21] Benjamin Rogers, rector of Carlton in Bedfordshire, had a vegetable and flower garden; the work in it was done by a gardener paid one shilling a day. He bought seeds and plants, and he also farmed. John Salusbury, a bachelor living with a maid and a boy, had a very substantial vegetable garden.[22] Spinning yarn for domestic use was a common routine, signs of which are to be seen in household accounts and many diaries. Cloth and clothing were made in various ways, often at odd times of the day by dependent members of the household. Stapley records the making of a bed in 1694. He bought 11 pounds of flax which his mother (with whom he lived, for he was not married) spun into yarn; the cloth was woven by the weaver and made into a bed by the tailor; they then filled it with feathers at home.[23] Richard Latham records buying cloth, which was made into clothing by a tailor. He and his wife also bought wool and flax, which was spun, but sold, rather than woven for use by his family.[24] The same applied to furniture, and Roger Lowe bought some ash wood 'to be two chears'.[25]

The social meanings of the productive activities of households were associated more with the values that the communities placed on particular kinds of work than with material goods or with how households sought to present themselves to others. Most production was done outside the main living space and was often out of sight, 'backstage'. There were, however, other activities that enabled households to be seen, and some of the most interesting changes in utensils and some of the most valuable goods were associated with 'frontstage' activities, especially eating, drinking, and leisure. By contrast, many ordinary utensils were associated with 'backstage' activities, especially cookery, cleaning, and food preservation.

Feeding the household: cookery

Cookery and eating were regular, time-consuming activities, although some tasks, like baking bread or brewing, were not

undertaken in every household. The variability here was considerable, with some households having a dairy, buttery, or bakery
for large-scale food preparation and others apparently devoting
little space and time to them. Cookery and food preparation took
up several hours of the day, allowing for cooking meat, preparation of vegetables, and maintaining the fire. Many households
spent a couple of hours a day eating, and on a few special
occasions dinner lasted well into the afternoon.

Cookery had a central role, for it fulfilled essential physical and
symbolic needs. The equipment used was functional and, except
for saucepans, well established. It was not a public or status-
orientated activity, although its importance in maintaining health
and comfort was recognized, as Markham said about the skills
of housewives: 'I hold that the first and most principal to be,
a perfect skill and knowledge in Cookery'.[26] There was a
consciousness that poor cookery was undesirable, even in the
preparation of staple food. Celia Fiennes commented:

> Here it was I saw the oat Clap bread made ... it will bake and
> be as crisp and pleasant to eate as any thing you can imagine;
> but as we say of all sorts of bread there is a vast deal of
> difference in what is housewifely made and what is ill made.[27]

Some commentary was undoubtedly a result of a gradual per-
meation of awareness of other ways of eating. In particular, the
contrast was often made between 'French' habits, where food was
presented in 'made' dishes, whereas '*English* eat every thing that is
produced naturally. ... I say *naturally* in Opposition to the infinite
Multitude of our made Dishes; for they dress their Meat much
plainer than we do'.[28] This contrast was also good ammunition for
moralists, who could contrast honest food (representing decent
behaviour) with 'made' dishes (representing degeneracy and
deceit). Newcome made the analogy between excessive recreation
and 'a French feast', which he contrasted with 'Good meat',
representing work and action, with the implication that you cannot
live on '10 dishes of sauce for one of Good meat'.[29]

In general people in the middle ranks approved of eating food
that had been well, but simply, cooked, and all illustrations of
meals have simple food on the table. Few households had the time
or the facilities to produce the elaborate sauces, pies, and con-
fections found in recipes and cookery books.[30] Misson, of 'the
middling Sort of People', said:

The *English* eat a great deal at Dinner ... they chew meat by whole Mouthfuls ... they have ten or twelve Sorts of common Meats, which infallibly take their turns at their Tables, and two Dishes are their Dinners; a Pudding, for instance, and a piece of roast Beef.[31]

It is unlikely that people in general always ate as much meat as this French visitor says, but it was expected, at least among the middle ranks, that some cooked meat would be available at meals, together with bread and vegetables. King's comment on his calculations of meat consumption suggests that middle-ranking families expected to eat meat almost every day.[32]

The activity of cooking itself was varied and depended on the fuel, fireplace, food, and time available, and on the skill of the cook, but it influenced the material culture of the household because it could be done in any room and required some utensils. An open fire, frequently in the main room of the house, was the most common means of providing heat for cookery. Several of the illustrations in this book include some impression of the act of cookery, although in some the ubiquitous pot over the fire is intended more to convey an image of domestic life than a realistic picture of how cookery was actually done. Cooking of meat by roasting or boiling was, as Hannah Glasse put it, 'the most necessary Part of it; and few Servants there are that know how to Roast and Boil to Perfection'.[33] Considerable skill and experience were needed in spit roasting, since the fire had to be at the right temperature and the spit turned at the right time and speed. Some households had jacks, driven by clockwork or weights, but they were not essential, for spits could be propped in front of the fire and the cook had to turn them by hand. Roasting was done quite quickly once the fire was properly made (it had to be at the right temperature and had to glow hot, rather than burn with flames); Hannah Glasse advises one and half hours for 10 lb of beef and one hour for a leg of mutton weighing 6 lb, 'at a quick fire'.[34]

Food could be boiled in a pot over a fire, and this is shown in many pictures of domestic interiors. It was extremely convenient, for the pot could be used over any kind of fire and in any room. If nothing went wrong (pots could boil over), it was a clean and economical way of providing large amounts of hot food. Puddings and vegetables could be cooked alongside the meat in a large pot. Cooking pots and kettles were ubiquitous household equipment, found in all parts of the country, although there were local

Plate 11   Making Pies, Paul Sandby, *c.*1765 (Royal Library, Windsor
Castle). Such specialized kitchens and cookery were rare in middle-ranking
homes. This one even has a water pump indoors.

variations in shape, and iron ones were cheaper than brass. In
Scotland, the central and open hearths were particularly well
suited to this kind of cookery, with the pot suspended over the
fire, as the scenes of domestic life by David Allan so well show.
Open fires were also used in other ways, especially for toasting,
frying, and baking various kinds of flat breads. Oatcakes of
different kinds were cooked on bakestones or girdle pans; these

were common in the north of England and were the most
common form of bread in Scotland.

Other cookery was more specialized. Most bread was cooked in
an oven, which was often part of the chimney of the house itself,
but ovens could be made out of doors or built in an outbuilding.
They represent fixed investment in cookery on a much larger
scale than a hearth, but they could be used for all kinds of other
dishes and preserves, especially when they had cooled from the
hottest bread temperatures. Bread baking also required considerable skill and experience, for the dough had to be correctly
prepared and the oven heated to the right temperature. Kitchen
ranges considerably simplified this task, but they were only just
beginning to be installed in the wealthier household by 1700 and
were still uncommon in 1730.[35] Similarly, cookery of pies, such as
that shown in the drawing by Paul Sandby, was probably confined
to larger households.

Larger households also had the facilities for storing and preserving food. Smoking bacon and ham was commonest, but beef
was salted, and various fruit preserves were possible with the
increasing availability of sugar. It is something of a problem to
know how much food preservation was done in middling households and what happened if supplies were not laid up every year.[36]
But many smaller households, and those in the towns, did not
have the facilities for storage and large-scale preservation of food.
In Latham's accounts, food storage is not immediately apparent,
but since fruit was grown and he bought sugar he could have
preserved fruit, and since animals were killed and he records
purchases of salt some meat could have been preserved.

Part of the social meaning of food preparation can be discovered
from the fact that it was generally the responsibility of the wife or
housekeeper rather than the servants. Women, even among the
gentry, were expected to be able to cook, even if they did not
always do so. Rebecca Price, for instance, who married a man of
some substance and lived the life of a country gentlewoman in
Bedfordshire, started to collect recipes while she was at school
(where she was apparently taught cookery), and she seems to have
continued to collect and try them throughout her life.[37] Elizabeth
Pepys evidently cooked quite complex things, and she normally
cooked the meals.[38] Stout's sister clearly did the cookery, for her
domestic help was with the heavy tasks of cleaning and washing.[39]
Cookery was not a low-status household activity, as were washing
and cleaning. It confirmed the role of women in giving care and

nurture to household members, and in this way it was as important in household cohesion as it was in satisfying the physical need for food. Rather later, in 1747, Hannah Glasse claimed, in her introduction to *The Art of Cookery made Plain and Easy*, that she was attempting something new in trying to offer instructions in cookery to 'every Servant who can but read' and that her intention was 'to improve the Servants, and save the Ladies a great deal of Trouble'.[40] This implies that even women of some social position did the cookery and that it was not easy to replace them with servants.

Complex attitudes to cookery can be seen from the fact that it was done both in general living rooms and in parts of the house otherwise devoted to 'backstage' activities. In Norwich, for instance, most cookery (over 90 per cent by 1680) was done in kitchens, a few butteries, and wash-houses. Kitchens became of greater importance there in the late seventeenth century and were integrated into the main part of the building, but they were not used for formal dining or for sleeping; by contrast, halls and parlours were no longer used for cookery from the middle of the seventeenth century, and in the eighteenth century the halls were furnished as entrances to the larger houses.[41] Norwich was, however, a large town, and in rural areas kitchens were less common and were not always used for cookery alone but were either living rooms or used for miscellaneous storage, rather like a later scullery. In Van Aken's *Grace before a Meal*, the meal is evidently taking place in a living room, but there is a jack over the fireplace. In North Shropshire, kitchens were less common, and two-thirds of the houses recorded cookery in the houseplace, with only a third in the kitchen, but there were slow changes towards a more specialized use of space after 1700, when about a half of the kitchens were used for cookery, although such changes were gradual and otherwise unremarked.[42]

Most houses had a living room, variously called the houseplace, hall, or house, in which the family lived and often cooked, but the evidence about room use in inventories does not, of course, tell us if people tried to use a separate room if they could. There were many reasons for not using a separate room, and cookery was certainly done in the houseplace, even when there were outhouses. It was a central activity in practical and symbolic terms, and cooking in a general living room was convenient. On the other hand, no unusual or lavish equipment was associated with it, although the wealthier households had an impressive battery of

practical utensils, pots, dripping pans, and the like. Cookery does
not feature in English art, but there are some Dutch and Flemish
interiors in which it does – usually the making of pancakes or the
tending of a pot. The Allan domestic scenes show the pot over the
fire with someone in charge of it, but these are depicting the
centrality of the hearth and the warmth it offered in a rather
self-conscious way in the changing society of eighteenth-century
Scotland, and are not necessarily accurate representations of the
activity of cooking itself.

Maintaining the household: cleaning

Cleaning was more varied than cookery, for it was not confined to
any one part of the building and it could be done at any time 'as
need doth require', as a contemporary ballad put it.[43] The main
tasks were to keep utensils clean, to wash clothes and linen, and to
'dress the house' (to use Stout's words). This too involved a great
deal of hard work and took a long time, while the results of poor
cleaning could be immediately apparent, especially to travellers,
whose unkindly critical reactions were often based on their own
different standards and expectations. Celia Fiennes, for instance,
makes many disparaging comments about the dirt and discomfort
of homes in the Scottish borders.[44]

Cleaning was important in terms of the energy expended in a
house, but it is not well documented, except in symbolic terms. It
was widely held to be a moral duty because of the association
between virtue and cleanliness. It is clear that some of the impact
of the Dutch domestic scenes of the time lay in their calm and
polish, but there are few references to the specific work tasks
associated with cleaning and washing. Many were confined to
'backstage' areas of the house, such as wash-houses or outbuildings. It is notable, however, that servants were employed to
clean and to do washing, even when a household used little other
domestic help. Utensils bought for cleaning and washing, such as
besoms and washtubs, were part of the clutter of the house, but
they were not elaborate pieces of equipment.

Mealtimes

The utensils and equipment used at meals were of particular
significance in the material culture of households. Meals were

'frontstage' activities, even when eating and cookery took place in the same room and even if no visitors were present.[45] People were certainly aware of the atmosphere in which meals were served and they wished to feel comfortable when they ate. Celia Fiennes, for instance, was so repelled by the smoky atmosphere of a house she was to have stayed in on her travels that 'I could have no stomach to eate any of the food they should order', although the food itself was 'a good dish of fish' with butter and clap bread. This kind of revulsion is, of course, more likely from a traveller in a strange country (in this case the borders with Scotland) than within a household, but it illustrates the non-verbal communication of atmosphere, for the food itself was perfectly wholesome, and Fiennes got round the problem by having the fish cooked else-where.[46] This kind of reaction means that we should expect care to have been taken with the presentation of meals and the use of utensils. This can be seen by examining the way in which food was served and the values that were attached to meals.

The main meal (dinner) was eaten at midday by virtually every-one in the seventeenth century, although it became later among the upper ranks in the early eighteenth century. It had a central position in the day, just as it had a central position in the social life of the household. The food itself was prepared quite simply, and so was the table. Hannah Glasse, writing in 1747 about the layout of the table, said that it was up to each household to set its meal as it thought fit: 'Nor shall I take it upon me to direct to a Lady how to set out her Table. ... Nor indeed do I think it would be pretty to see a Lady's Table set out after the Directions of a Book.'[47]

According to the 'traditional' way of serving a meal, whether for the family or for a feast, all the dishes were placed on the table at once, but if there were many dishes some were removed and replaced with others that were similar in food content. There are fewer descriptions of simple family meals than of feasts or special occasions, but it seems that most families had one or two dishes on the table, appropriate to the size and status of the meal. Celia Fiennes, for instance, normally had meat or fish, bread, and beer served to her on her travels.[48] This tradition of serving the main meal was retained into the eighteenth century, and the division of a meal into courses was a novelty in the later seventeenth century, confined for many decades to the households of the fashionable élite.

When eating the meal, people each had their own dish, plate, or trencher on to which they carved or helped themselves from the serving dishes. Food was eaten with a knife and fingers, except for pottage, which was eaten with a spoon. With some kinds of food, and in some households, the food was taken directly from a large vessel and not served on to a person's own plate at all. Of mid-eighteenth century Scotland, one observer recalled later that 'it was the custom with the gentry, as it still is with our substantial tenants, for the whole company to eat broth out of one large plate.'[49] The few pictures of meals painted in England evoke something of their atmosphere and something of table layouts. That by Van Aken is of special interest. The table, which probably folds away, is very simply laid; the dishes and plates are pewter; and there are no forks for personal use. Other pictures of meals show similar things, and all convey, perhaps deliberately, a certain family intimacy.[50]

Other meals were eaten in a similar way, although the meals were differently regarded. Misson observed: 'The *English* eat a great deal at Dinner; ... Their Supper is moderate: Gluttons at Noon, and abstinent at Night.'[51] Supper was eaten at some time in the evening; it was less formal than dinner, consisting of pottage or meat or cheese and bread and ale or other drink, all of which were relatively easy to serve. Supper was often eaten in company with friends or visitors; people went out to supper, so that it could serve a function similar to that of dinner, but was less formal. People could even snatch a snack, as depicted in the domestic scene by David Allan.

There were changes during the late seventeenth and early eighteenth centuries in the behaviour expected at meals, although these were so gradual that they are extremely difficult to trace, and even those obsessed with recording meals rarely describe how they ate. There were also gradual changes in utensils and cutlery. Changes in the way in which food was conveyed from the plate to the mouth occurred as knives and forks gradually came into use at table in the first half of the eighteenth century. The possibility of using a fork was known in the seventeenth century, but it was not until the eighteenth that knives and forks became common. It seems that the change was so slow that there was little comment at the time, but they were still infrequently recorded in inventories by 1725. Other changes altered the appearance of the table rather than the way in which meals were eaten, but decorated crockery was uncommon before the 1760s, and undecorated pewter continued well into the eighteenth century. New ways of serving and cooking became better known but were not adopted by the

Plate 12   A domestic scene by David Allan, *c.*1780 (Glasgow Art Gallery and Museum). A Scottish scene. Play, sociability, cooking, and eating are portrayed together.

middle ranks until they gradually infiltrated into English traditions in the nineteenth century. These differences did have the important social implication that later dinners and meals served in a succession of courses became associated with an upper-class lifestyle, differentiating the lower and middle from the upper ranks, rather than to providing a model of behaviour for everyone.[52] The period covered by this book was one in which new forms of behaviour were developing and being tried in some households, but at the same time the old ways continued with no rapid acceptance of change. The interesting question, examined in the next chapter, is which households adopted new behaviour and used new equipment.

Meals were orderly and valued occasions. Many contemporary accounts give the impression that behaviour could easily deteriorate; in particular, conduct books anxiously warn the young and unwary against all sorts of rather nasty-sounding things, like wiping hands on the hair or putting scraps on the floor.[53] There were many conventions about the proper way to carve, how to serve and be served, and how to eat with the fingers. We must not assume that shared utensils and the lack of cutlery as we know it resulted in indelicate and unmannerly behaviour. Even eating from a common dish with a spoon and pieces of bread could be done neatly, although changes in behaviour at table in the later eighteenth century led many of the old mores to be associated with poor manners and the lowest ranks in society. The general pattern seems to have been for people either to carve meat for themselves or to be helped by someone else, according to personal taste rather than the status of the meal. Conduct books (really aimed at the gentry and aspiring gentry) suggest that you accept what is offered to you (out of politeness), that you do not take the best pieces but carve or serve yourself from the bit closest to you. Whether such formality and politeness were to be found at family meals is not known, but, then as now, it probably varied.

The urge to behave in a proper way and take account of accepted conventions confirms that meals were occasions on which people presented themselves to others. Meals were served in 'front areas' in a house, and the surroundings and material culture were influenced by a desire (albeit subconscious) to convey an appropriate image of the household, whatever that may have been. The larger houses had separate space for eating, although meals were normally taken in the houseplace (or whatever the main living room was called); thus two-thirds of the inventories from Telford (1670–1729) list the main table as in the houseplace, only five dining rooms were listed in 123 inventories, and about a third of the parlours were also used for meals.[54] In Norwich too there were only a few rooms used exclusively for eating.[55] In illustrations the tables are shown in general living rooms, rather than in specialized dining rooms. It is notable that the larger households did differentiate between rooms for eating and those for other purposes, and the possession of a separate room enabled a more elaborate 'front' to be constructed. In the smaller houses this had to be established alongside other activities in the living areas.

The equipment used at mealtimes had a singular importance in the material culture of middling households in two ways. In the first place, some of the most valuable and attractive items (sometimes displayed on shelves) were associated with meals. Secondly, some of the most visible changes in domestic equipment in the early eighteenth century were associated with eating and drinking, and many of the goods examined in detail in this book were intended for use at the table.

The most basic requirements for eating meals were very simple: a knife and a platter were enough, with a spoon and a serving dish. Meals could even be eaten without a table. However, most middle-ranking households had a good deal more than this, with specialized furniture, linen, and equipment. Table linen, if it was used at all, could be simple, but it could enhance the layout of the table. Pepys, for instance, commented that he was so pleased with how the 'fellow' had laid the cloth and folded the napkins for a special dinner that 'I am resolved to give him 40s to teach my wife to do it'.[56] Pewter was the normal material used for dishes, plates, and miscellaneous objects like salt containers, although wooden platters were probably widely used for ordinary meals. The overall effect of these was plain in colour, but the better-quality pewter could be burnished and the shapes were aesthetically pleasing, for the design of pewter in the late seventeenth century was of high quality.[57] Later commentary on the replacement of pewter by crockery tends to leave the impression that people were surrounded by rather dull and uninteresting things, and that pewter was overdue for replacement with something better. For example: 'among all the improvements made in the household furniture and utensilry, the greatest about this time was the introduction of a new species of dishes from England, instead of ... the more ancient pewter plates.'[58] Commentary of this kind does not do justice to the virtues of the traditional materials, which were long retained.

There is no one single way of interpreting the role of mealtime activities, but their central importance is shown by the amount of time and space that they occupied and the number of utensils they used. They were an important element in maintaining the household as a psychological and social entity; members met together and shared their food in a more or less intimate way and controlled their behaviour according to accepted mores. Friends and family from outside the household were also given meals, either in a formal way or more casually. In this respect, meals were 'front' activities, in which the resources and appearance of the household were open to people from outside – the more so on special occasions and in the houses which had separate places for dining. From this point of view, the location of the meal in a room used for other activities (even cookery) points to the complex interrelations of private and public functions in a household. This could account for the apparently special symbolic role of meals and gradual changes in behaviour and the environments associated with them.

Drinking and material culture

Drinking, like eating, took time, but it was a more sociable activity, whether or not the drinks were alcoholic or whether or not they were consumed in public places. Public drinking was common, especially by men, and was often associated with other activities, such as reading or business. Misson reports of London coffee houses, 'You have all Manner of News there: You have a good Fire ... You have a Dish of Coffee, you meet your Friends, for the Transaction of Business and all for a Penny'.[59] This kind of public entertainment was limited to a few places, and to the upper ranks, but in the late seventeenth century some towns were beginning to cater for entertainments of this kind. The drinking and sociability to be found in taverns and alehouses was much more widespread and of longstanding importance; the facilities here improved in the late seventeenth and early eighteenth centuries, in response to rising expectations of customers. The furnishings were of a rather better quality than those found in many private houses, and utensils, such as china, made a rapid appearance in taverns and even in the more humble alehouses, so that drinking in these establishments (and in inns) was not necessarily disreputable, although not without danger. A wide range of drink was available, together with simple food, and sometimes books and newspapers, meetings, and games.[60]

From the point of view of the material culture of households, drinking with friends and relatives at home was of greater importance. Many of the visits reported in diaries refer to drinking of some kind, and there seems to have been a very close association between visiting and refreshments, the more so when tea became available and a visit could be described as 'taking tea' or 'drinking tea' with someone. Sometimes drinking was excessive. Giles Moore records occasions on which he drank too much: 'This evening, ... when I had began prayers with my family, I was so overpowered with the effects of some perry which I had taken, not knowing how strong that liquor was, that I was obliged to break off abruptly.' A certain shame at this is suggested by the fact that the entry was in Latin.[61] Some men went out to drink in the evening;

Plate 13   An English Family at Tea, J. Van Aken, *c*.1720 (Tate Gallery, London). An upper-class lifestyle against an unreal background. But the utensils and tea-table give a realistic impression of a formal occasion.

Marchant too makes many references to drinking and a few to having drunk too much: 'I went to Danny [the local big house]. ... I got drunk – fie upon it.'[62] The vessels used for alcoholic drinks were often valuable, especially if they were silver or pewter. Here too an essentially sociable activity engendered an identifiable material culture.

So too did drinking tea and other hot drinks. Tea was becoming familiar to many people of middle rank in the late seventeenth century, even if it had not completely entered into daily routines.[63] Massive increases in imports of tea and coffee date from the 1710s, and by the mid-eighteenth century to drink tea was an expected part of the behaviour of people of middle rank. The circumstances of tea drinking were different from those of alcohol, and it appealed to people who wanted light refreshment during the day or in the evening. In some households it became something of a ceremony, with expensive equipment. John Thomlinson, reporting on a clergyman's family in County Durham, wrote: 'Aunt would have 50L to furnish her drawing room. ie, 20L for silver tea-kettle, lamp and table'.[64] Not everyone had utensils which cost as much as this; tea was usually made in a more modest way. Conversation pieces of family groups drinking tea, in spite of a rather odd formality, give an impression of something of the atmosphere of an occasion, with pretty utensils laid out on a table. Van Aken's is especially interesting because the realism of the utensils and the people drinking contrast with a rather curious, classical, and unreal background. But, whether tea was taken with ceremony or not, it influenced the appearance of the household through the variety of utensils associated with making and drinking it. Some of the most dramatic visual changes in material culture resulted from the influx of decorated, functional utensils for drinking the new hot drinks. Blue and white china is stunningly different in style and colour from any other domestic utensils of the time – an impact lost on us because we have become accustomed to decorated china and crockery. Yet china, at about 6d. a piece, was not expensive in comparison with silver and other attractive items, although it did cost a great deal more than durable materials like wooden vessels, at perhaps a halfpenny each.

Sleep and rest

The household provided a secure environment for other physiologically necessary things, notably sleep and rest. These too influenced the organization of space in the house and the material goods associated with them. The length of time that people spent asleep varied, but the diarists who recorded this kind of detail usually spent eight or nine hours in bed, getting up between 6 and 8 a.m. There were rooms, even in the smaller houses and usually on the upper floors, devoted largely to sleep. In Norwich, for instance, over half the garret and parlour chambers had beds in them, and chambers for sleeping were common in all urban and rural houses. The rooms used for sleeping depended to some extent on the size of the house and the numbers of people in it. Norwich was an advanced area in this respect, for only about a fifth of the parlours contained beds, whereas this room was more often used for sleeping in other, especially rural, areas, and about half the parlours in Telford contained beds.[65] In most of England the houseplace did not contain beds and bedding, but an enclosed bed was a feature of Scottish living rooms and kitchens.[66] By the late seventeenth century, sleep was considered to be a private activity, and adults were expected to sleep in their own beds; in Norwich the number of bedsteads per household (at about three in the late seventeenth century) suggests that few people other than married couples and small children shared beds.[67] Books on behaviour certainly assume that it was not proper to share a bed, although in the sixteenth century it had evidently been considered not so much improper as inconvenient.[68]

The furniture and textiles associated with sleep were of evident importance and were often among the most valuable and elaborate household goods. In some households they made up as much as half of the total value of the household goods and an even greater proportion of some smaller households. The furniture necessary for sleeping could quite simply be a mattress, some kind of bedstead, and several covers. At its most basic, a bed and bedding could be made from rough material and filled with chaff or flock; covers could be simple and the overall valuation low. Take, for instance, George Cleaton's bed in 1724:[69]

	£	s	d
In the roome over the house			
one flock bed and bedding	0	10	0
One little Chest a box two small Chaires 2 coffers			
and a table	0	12	0

By contrast, a house could have more rooms and more beds; the wealthy Richard Stanier, 'gent' (of Wellington, Shropshire), in 1711 had nine rooms containing twelve beds, including those for servants; one chamber alone contained 'One ffeather Bed, Bolster, Bedsteads, Curtains & vallens belonging to the same' which was valued, along with the other furniture in the room, at £14. Elsewhere in the house there were:[70]

	£	s	d
Two dozen & ffour pair of hempen & flaxen Sheets	25	4	0
Two paire of holland Sheets	5	0	0
Two dozen and two paire of hurden Sheetes	7	16	0

Bed hangings made beds warmer, and feather mattresses were more comfortable, while the quality and design of the hangings and covers could make a difference to the appearance of the room. Unfortunately, most of the beds that survive were those of the gentry and aristocracy and therefore do not give a fair picture of their appearance in other households; nor should we assume that the magnificent beds provided models for more modest ones.[71] Beds and bedding, while not the main subject of this book, are a substantial subject in their own right and warrant a study in themselves.[72]

Children

For some men and women the most important and meaningful tasks performed in the household were associated with raising and socializing children, which involved immense physical and emotional activity. As a result of recent research, we now know much more about the relations between children and their families than formerly, but it is still hard to say exactly what people did with them.[73] Many of the activities already described were performed on behalf of children, but there were numerous other things done specifically for children, from suckling them in infancy, encouraging them to walk, nursing them if sick, worrying about them, educating them, and setting them up in life. All this – and much more – was extremely important to the well-being of the household, and the emotions involved are not easily captured in the available written sources. Child-rearing needed few utensils, was not done in any fixed place or at any fixed time, and was taken for granted, but, since roughly three-quarters of all households contained children still at home and since there were about three children in any household that had any children at all, they must have made a large impact on the atmosphere of households.[74] Some of the children were grown up, but when many were small and dependent the life of the household was altered, for children were uncontrolled by adult standards. All the evidence from contemporary writing shows that people cared for them as fully as their resources allowed; the implications for the day-to-day life of the household lay in the provision of some facilities for children, according to their age and needs.

Children were often educated at home and taught practical skills as well, although some went to school and were apprenticed when they were in their early teens. Latham records that books were bought specifically for the children to learn from, and they also received some schooling. James Fretwell was taught to read by his mother at home 'until I could read in my Bible' (as were his brothers and sisters), and he was sent away to school to learn languages, arithmetic, writing, and accounting; he was then taken into his father's business. Teaching children at home added to the activities to be done, and Fretwell's mother, 'tho' she had a large family to oversee and provide for ... would find me proper time every day'.[75] Care of this kind could last into adulthood; John Thomlinson, groomed for life by his uncle, records a number of occasions when he received help; 'Preached at Whickham, was pretty well heard – called it a noble beginning. Uncle Robert took a great deal of pains to teach me how to read well – and as it were musically – by notes.'[76] Care and training could even last into marriage, as Stout records of his brother:

> his wife, who was very young and knew little of housekeeping. But mother having a good maid servant of long experience, let him have her, who, with my mother's advice and assistance, put them into the method of housekeeping according to their abilety.[77]

Play was normal and, although toys have not survived in any numbers, children are quite capable of making games and playing without equipment. People were aware of the need for play; Adam Martindale's comment on how he remembered learning to read suggests that play was expected of small children; he recalls that Anne Simpkin gave him an ABC when he was about six, 'a gift in itselfe exceeding small. ... For till that time I was all for childish play, and never thought of learning.'[78] A surprising number of paintings have children in them, often learning something. Next to the washerwoman in Collett's print, *High Life Below Stairs*, there is a girl copying the behaviour of the adults, partly included as a reflection of adult behaviour, rather than a direct document of children's upbringings, but such images show that play was expected and that children were expected to copy the behaviour of grown-ups, for good or ill. The children in Allan's domestic scenes are playing and doing household tasks. Both artists present an image of children taking a full part in the life of the household.

Leisure

Leisure too was not directly associated with particular goods, but the material culture of a household was influenced by the amount of time that people had to appreciate decorative objects, to read, or to buy their possessions. The possibilities varied according to household composition, the occupations of the individual members, their educational levels, the kinds of friends they had, their interests, and the other things that had to be done. But leisure was essential, and households which did not provide the time and occasion for some leisure, even if it was no more than talking to friends, were deprived. 'Man naturaly desireth Knowledge.... Now recreation ... is of several natures (which are in them selves Innocent, and harmlesse)'.[79] This was recognized by those who were literate and introspective enough to write diaries or memoirs, in spite of the pressures that there could be on their time. Richard Kay claimed to be hard at work in April 1747 – 'I am sent for, I am call'd upon in Haste, I must go; We seldom have a leisure Hour' – but he 'set out upon a Journey for Pleasure towards Buxton-Bath' for a few days in July 1747.[80] Many diarists were, by keeping a diary at all, expressing intellectual and emotional needs beyond the daily round of physical life, and some state explicitly that they had such needs, or could see them in others: 'A man starving of hunger would be deem'd a madman to refuse victuals when offered to him, but how must we term that man who refuses to eat of the bread of life.'[81] A good instance that points to general views occurs in the commentary in William Stukeley's commonplace book about his needs for conversation and company 'to answer the purpose of one of my turn & taste'. He was atypical of the general run of people, for he was an antiquarian of some note, who had also studied medicine and divinity, and valued 'literary conversation' when he lived in London. He left to live in Grantham, but found 'the insufficiency of Country Life' because of 'want of proper relief & variety, in good company & ingenious conversation, the facultys of the mind sink & flag, & at best such an one can be but said to live a dead life there.'[82] He appears to be expressing general views in a more coherent way than the less literate diarists. That the yeomen and tradesmen were less articulate does not mean that they were unaware of the need for rest and relaxation, although they may have done different things. Richard Latham's family went annually to the fair, although they rarely spent more than a few pence there.[83]

At the same time people were ambivalent about leisure, and there are direct and indirect comments about the need for hard work and the dangers of wasting time. Such commentary was often made about other people's lives, sometimes in derogatory terms. Thomlinson's report gives the flavour of this kind of observation: 'Cousin Robinson warned me against Mr Brown's wife's sister coming to be his housekeeper – she is a confident, tatling woman, and she will wast and destroy things by entertaining sparks, etc.'[84] This sounds more like a rather uneasy comment about a sociable woman who was not willing to work all the time. The woman who was always busy met with approval – suggesting some kind of double standard in what was expected of women and men's leisure. Defoe, in addressing the potentially successful shopkeeper or warehouseman, says that 'pleasure is a *thief* to business' and for this reason a tradesman should 'allow himself as few excursions as possible'. By pleasure here he really means the kinds of expensive and time-consuming leisure activities of the gentry, such as riding, hunting, sports, and so on, rather than the more modest recreations, 'intervals from hurry and fatigue'.[85]

The most frequently documented way in which people spent non-working time was in talking and visiting, sometimes for meals and drinks. Virtually every diary, series of letters, or autobiography, no matter what the age and occupation of the writer, records innumerable visits to friends and relatives, apparently for sociable purposes, although sometimes there was a mixture of business with a visit. Marchant, to quote one instance among many, records that he visited or was visited eight times in the first ten days of October 1714; he usually ate meals or had drinks on these occasions, sometimes in immoderate amounts.[86] Misson's observations are of interest, for he comments that 'the ordinary Sort of People' did not visit each other in a formal way in the evening but went 'to see one another with their Work in their Hands and Cheerfulness in their Countenance, without Rule or Constraint'.[87] Many of the visits reported in diaries were not exactly with 'work in their hands', but the occasion for them was often associated with numerous land, trade, or professional transactions between the men concerned. Salusbury dined with Lovett and received rent due twice a year, and he settled accounts with people over dinner.[88] It does not even seem that younger and unmarried people visited more readily than others, although married people often went out together or were visited.

That there was so much visiting, and especially that the visits were basically informal, is of particular importance because visits were frequent enough for people to have time to observe possessions, learn about new possibilities, or be confirmed in existing ones. There is not a great deal of overt commentary on this before the mid-eighteenth century; Thomlinson, who ate out and visited frequently, makes a few comments about possessions that suggest that he cast a shrewd eye over the contents of the houses he went to: 'several old things ... far overvalued ... an old chest of drawers valued 18s – and old fashioned when he may buy a new and fashionable pair for a guinea or a little more.'[89] Observation of this kind is not often the subject matter of diaries and is largely unrecorded, but this does not mean that it did not happen.

This whole chapter has argued that there was more to the inner lives of households than the satisfaction of physical needs. Movable goods had expressive roles and could be used to draw lines in social relationships. What these lines were was unclear to the people concerned, just as our own household furnishings present subconscious images that are hard to define in words. Behaviour and the physical environment communicated in a non-verbal way, and non-verbal communication, often powerful and important to the people concerned, is hard to observe and interpret from written (by definition, verbal) testimony. But it is worth noting that more attractive and varied goods were associated with the expressive 'frontstage' activities, whereas those used 'backstage' with the exception of some beds and bedding, were less liable to change, infrequently decorated, and not overtly expressive. Does this mean that people with different behaviour owned different goods? One way of examining this is to discuss the influence of occupation and social status on the ownership of the goods in inventories, and this is the subject of the next chapter.

8

OWNERSHIP OF GOODS, SOCIAL STATUS, AND OCCUPATION

In the house
one table board one old Joyned Press one old screene
bentches and stooles praised at   0 13 4
(Husbandman, 1681)[1]

In the Hall
Two French Tables & Clothes Eight Stooles Seaven
Chaires Two long Settles a range and froggs a bible
& some little bookes   2   0 0
(Alderman, 1674)[2]

If domestic behaviour and social mores were different among different groups of people, how far was this reflected in ownership of domestic durables? Were some social or occupational groups more inclined to be consumers than others? This chapter examines the patterns of ownership of selected goods in the inventory sample, cross-tabulated according to occupation and status. There are also some comparisons with Scotland using a few testaments, together with the qualitative evidence from descriptions and memoirs.[3] There are pitfalls in doing this, not least the uncertainty in comparing English and Scottish social structures, the different landholding practices, and the concentration in Scottish writing on the domestic behaviour of the upper parts of society. Yet there were many similarities between England and Scotland, for household size, structure, and function were not vastly different in Scotland, although houses were smaller.

The middle ranks

There were many social and economic distinctions between different members of the middle ranks. Contemporary perceptions of the social order, and the ways in which historians have used these, are not without problems, and in particular they tend to conflate occupation and status.[4] Any listing that has a mixture of trades, farmers, professions, and gentry does not necessarily place these in a hierarchical order. In inventories there are both occupations (such as the name of a trade) and status designations (such as yeoman or widow), although these are not usually in the same document. There is therefore a danger of confusing status and occupation, with the undesirable result that interpretation of distinctions between different groups of people in social or economic terms becomes meaningless. Most brief accounts of the social structure of the pre-industrial era are based on contemporary estimates made by Gregory King in the late seventeenth century. Here both status terms and occupations are used, giving no indication of the shape of a hierarchy based on social status within the middle ranks. It is also virtually impossible, without using a lot of guesswork, to 'match' the terms used in the inventories with those used by King. His crucial categories of farmer, freeholder, and craftsman do not match the tradesmen, yeomen, and farmers in the inventories. These remarkable calculations also underestimate the commercial sector and overestimate the agricultural sector, although some recalculations have been done using other sources of information.[5] They are not, however, as useful as they might seem, and different approaches have been used here to group occupations in inventories. First, contemporary perceptions of the status of many common occupations make it possible to position some trade and professional occupations in the recognized hierarchy of gentry, yeomen, husbandmen, and labourers.[6] This gives a listing that concentrates on social status. The information in inventories is also grouped to emphasize general and economic characteristics.

There are no listings of occupations and social position in Scotland comparable with King's estimates and terminology for England. However, scholars have turned their attention in this direction in recent years, and socio-economic designations used in poll-tax returns and elsewhere have formed a basis for making outline distinctions similar to those that are possible for England.[7]

In table 8.1 the inventories are grouped to emphasize social

Table 8.1 A social-status hierarchy: frequencies of ownership of goods in a sample of inventories in England, 1675–1725

Social status	No. of inventories	Total inventory £ (Mean value)	Household goods £	Tables %	Cooking pots %	Sauce-pans %	Pewter %	Pewter dishes %	Pewter plates %	Earthenware %	Books %	Clocks %	Pictures %	Looking glasses %	Table linen %	Window curtains %	Knives and forks %	China %	Utensils for hot drinks %	Silver %
Gentry	122	320	55	93	84	13	93	55	43	39	39	51	33	62	60	26	11	6	7	61
Trades of high status; clergy; professions	152	193	39	97	75	11	95	54	40	53	45	34	35	62	63	21	7	11	7	51
Trades of intermediate status	344	157	32	93	77	25	94	62	50	49	24	25	29	56	58	29	11	9	10	38
Yeomen; large farmers	952	165	23	91	69	5	95	41	20	33	18	19	4	21	35	5	1	1	1	13
Trades of low status	435	92	19	92	74	12	96	56	31	42	17	18	15	37	50	12	3	3	4	23
Husbandmen; small farmers	332	32	8	83	57	2	89	33	9	28	4	4	0	9	16	2	0	0	1	2
Labourers	28	16	5	79	79	11	89	57	14	43	4	0	4	4	18	4	0	4	0	0
Widows and spinsters	217	82	18	77	66	12	89	47	22	33	18	13	12	36	46	17	4	4	2	37
Tradesmen; trade unknown	56	115	31	98	82	27	88	55	32	50	32	29	32	57	61	38	9	11	13	46
Occupation or status unknown	264	62	17	83	70	16	88	48	31	27	17	14	18	36	40	16	5	5	6	23
Total	2,902	128	23	89	70	11	93	48	27	37	19	19	13	33	42	13	4	4	4	23

Note
The criteria are based on work by Dr Vivien Brodsky Elliott; see appendix 2 for full details.

status, and the proportions of each group in which the selected goods were recorded are shown. Social boundaries to the ownership of goods are indicated by the proportions of inventories in different groups. These social-status groupings can be looked at in two parts – first, the well-known hierarchy of gentry–yeomen–husbandmen, and then the other occupations that are so much more difficult to place.

The gentry

The gentry, those of highest status examined in this study, were far from being a homogeneous group, for there were men and women, rural and urban, rich and poor among the inventory sample. The wealthier gentry are not fully represented here because their wills were proven in the superior courts of York and in the Prerogative Court of Canterbury. But the sample is representative of the lesser gentry, with 5 per cent of inventories, as compared with 3 per cent of the middle part of society as a whole.[8] The variety among them can be illustrated by the values assigned to the total inventory, which were extremely spread out, ranging from £5 to £2,677, with no very clear bunching together to form a peak. This gives the quite correct impression that people of gentry status did not always have the most valuable movable goods. The value of movable estate is, of course, a very crude measure of social position, for in contemporary perceptions gentlemen stood apart and the dividing line between gentry and the rest was seen as one of the most fundamental in society. Yet the gentry were not a legally defined group, and there was considerable differentiation among those considered in this study. This is not unexpected, in that gentility was based on local or regional recognition of influence and authority, as well as wealth and lifestyle. The term 'gentry' itself therefore implies considerable variety, as well as a certain similarity, of social position and interests. From the point of view of social standing, however, their influence and authority was considerable.

Yet, in spite of the gentry's superior wealth and social standing, many expressive, decorative goods such as pictures, looking glasses, and china, and even pewter, earthenware, and saucepans, were less frequently recorded in their inventories than in those of the lesser-ranking tradesmen, as table 8.1 illustrates. We tend to think of the gentry as having more decorative household goods

and superior taste, so this is an unexpected pattern. It would be
less unexpected, however, if account is taken of the complexity of
the role and rank of 'gent', for some people were given this status
by virtue of family connections and position in the community,
rather than their economic standing at the time of their death.
John Funston of Newmarket, for instance, had only a bed and a
chest, apart from clothing, a few silver things, a watch, and some
bonds due to him, which added up to £38; he was a bachelor, and
his status derived from his membership of a prosperous family in
the town and his active part in the community; he lived in a room
in his sister's house.[9]

Measurement of frequency also obscures some of the differences in quality and quantity. Take, for instance, goods in the
parlours of two men dying in Burslem, Staffordshire, in about
1720. Samuel Edge was a master potter and had goods in the
parlour valued at £2. 15s.[10]

	£	s	d
In the Parlour			
One Looking Glass and Table	1	0	0
Eleven Chairs & Cupboard	1	10	0
nine pictures & Some small things	0	5	0

Richard Wedgwood, a member of a leading family in the town (on
the boundary between 'gent' and yeomen), had similar goods, but
more of them, and their values were greater.[11]

	£	s	d
In the old parlour 13 Chaires 1 Ovall Table 1 little Square Tale 1 Chest of Drawers 8 pictures Looking glass	5	18	0
In the Hallplace 2 Long Tables 1 forme 4 Turned Chaires 3 Joyned Chaires 1 Skreen	3	8	0

These are subtle differences. By contrast, the parlour of a 'gent'
in Telford in 1711 was valued at four times that of Wedgwood,
contained more expensive furniture, a clock, and pictures, but
included no looking glasses, nor were there any elsewhere in the
house:[12]

	£	s	d
In the parlour			

One large Couch; Ten Tapestry Chaires & two more
of ye same that are in the little Chamber that's over ye
parlour Clossett. Eight Leather Chaires; Two Elbowe

Segg Chaires; one Inlaid Table under the mapp;
one oake ovall Tale; one Clock and weather Glass
one Mapp & other pictures.   22 10 0

Among the upper gentry, who are not of course the subject of this
study, were to be found much more expensive household furnishings, and the example of Sir Thomas Wentworth shows how
much more this could be. His gilt parlour, for instance, had beds,
tables, carpets, curtains, and a looking glass, all valued at £48;
furniture in a chamber, including nothing unusual, was valued at
£120.[13] In Scotland the better-off landowners and lairds
were among the most obvious consumers by the mid-eighteenth
century and were responsible for some very beautiful country
houses, just as their counterparts were in England. We should not
be distracted by the wealth of a few of the richer gentry into
thinking that all the gentry were leaders, for there were more of
the higher-status tradesmen who owned the new and decorative
goods; this is important, and has several implications, to which I
will return later in this and the next chapter.

Yeomen

Yeomen were distinct from the gentry (apart from some overlap at
the upper end). In the inventory sample they were a coherent
group, with the distribution of the values of their estates clearly
concentrated at a clear peak between £65 and £85, although the
range was from £3 to £2,596. The idea of 'yeoman' status was well
recognized at the time, but whether an individual was considered
to be of this rank depended on many factors. However, since
there was no precise norm, the wealth and landholding of the
yeomen varied considerably. It is not unusual to find a wealthy
yeoman referred to as 'gent' on occasions, or referring to himself
as such in his will. Some of the poorer yeomen, especially in the
north-west, were also akin to the lesser farmers and husbandmen.
Individuals could refer to themselves as husbandman or yeoman
at different times in their lives or in different circumstances.
Richard Latham, for instance, was described as 'husbandman' in
1725 when probate on his sister's will was granted, whereas he
called himself 'yeoman' in his own will dated 1764, and his way of
life and expenditure were on the boundary between the two.[14]
The occupations of yeomen also varied, and there are many

instances of people of yeoman status running a business or a trade. The Lancaster shopkeeper, William Stout, certainly came of yeoman family, and many of the master ironworkers in the Midlands and elsewhere were both yeomen and tradesmen, as were craftsmen elsewhere.[15] For the purposes of this analysis, all the yeoman tradesmen have been classified under their trade, so that the yeomen shown in the tables either were farmers or were called 'yeoman' in their probate papers without any indication of their occupation. The tables also group with yeomen the farmers whose estates were valued at over £60 and whose occupations and/or status were not otherwise given; these include some women.[16] Yeomen were also numerous in England as a whole and made up a large part of the sampled inventories.[17]

The Scottish 'tenants' were akin to yeomen in status; they tended to be farmers but, like yeomen, they could also be tradesmen, especially millers and smiths. Like yeomen, they were numerous and their prosperity varied markedly, but there were already some large farmers among them before the end of the seventeenth century, especially among the Lothian 'gudemen'. Tenants were extremely various in their economic position. In many areas where farming was still divorced from the market, farms were still much subdivided between joint tenants, and each tenant might be no better off than a cottar elsewhere.

Ownership of household goods by yeomen was different from ownership by the gentry. This can be seen both in the frequencies with which goods were recorded and in the kinds of furniture that they had. Table 8.1 shows that they less often owned the newer and decorative things; china, knives and forks, utensils for hot drinks, and pictures were almost unknown in these households, whilst looking glasses, silver, curtains, and even earthenware occurred less frequently than in gentry inventories. They also owned these items less often than the low-status tradesmen. At the same time they were well equipped with traditional goods, like pewter and tables. Yeomen, at least those with agricultural occupations, were not inclined to be innovative in their household goods, although their surroundings were comfortable. It is common to find a great deal of pewter, brass, and cooking equipment, with chairs, tables, shelves, and cupboards in large numbers, as well as numerous feather beds and bedding, but small, new, and decorative things were largely absent. Take, for instance, John Steventon of Lilleshall, yeoman (1701), who was among the better-off yeomen, with an inventory valued at £274 and a house of at least nine rooms. In the two main chambers, parlour, and hall alone, goods and furniture were valued at £73; these included:[18]

	£	s	d
Linen of all Sorts vall'd at	22	0	0
In the Parlour Itm One pair of bedsteds wth feather beds bolsters Blanketts Curtains vallons & all things thereto belonging, One Chest one table and form, one Hanging press, one Chair books of all sorts 2 pieces of stuff valled at	12	0	0
In the Hall Itm Twenty eight pewter dishes besides plates porringers flaggons candlesticks & other small things of pewter valu'd at	5	0	0

Thus yeomen are of some interest, for, although few of them owned the newer goods, some of them were well equipped with staple ones.

Memoirs and descriptions, looking back to the mid-eighteenth century after many decades of change, give the impression that the Scottish tenants lived in smaller houses and had more sparse possessions than English yeomen.[19] Robertson's account of the living conditions of farmers in the Lothians in about 1765 suggests that there was little space in the two living rooms for many household goods, and these were mainly basic things like benches, tables, cooking utensils, wooden plates, a few implements, and box beds, although he does mention a clock and looking glasses kept in the parlour. He also stresses that feather beds were unknown and few farmers drank tea at a time when English yeomen certainly had feather beds and were used to tea. The house had also to accommodate several farm servants, who slept in a loft over the kitchen, which served as the main living room. These households were relatively well off, well provided with food grown on the farm, and warmly clothed with home-produced cloth and shoes. Robertson's very vivid picture was probably a simplification of old memories, for he relied on what people told him of the time before he could remember, as he readily admits. Somerville, rather nearer to the events, gives a similar picture of the better-off farmers' families, where 'Household furniture was simple and inexpensive – wooden platters, for instance, being more or less in use in almost every house, and exclusively in those of the farmers, and of many of the clergy.'[20] By contrast, he says that gentry families used pewter and possibly china as well. There was in all this an urge to recall a general picture of the past after considerable change, but it was a common image and is also depicted in David Allan's domestic scenes at the end of the eighteenth century.

The occasional inventory suggests that better-off farmers had larger houses than the two-roomed 'but and ben' of Robertson's description. George Sinclare of Longniddie, for instance, died in 1709 with the high inventory valuation of £8,745.6s. (Scots £ sterling). There were two main rooms, one furnished much as an old-style parlour would be in England, the other the kitchen, which was obviously a general living room, but (unlike kitchens in England) had beds as well. But there were also seven other rooms with household goods and beds in them, as well as several out-houses. There were three looking glasses, some pewter, books, and a Bible, but otherwise there were no new or unusual goods.[21] On the other hand, the Scottish farms were less commercialized than those of English yeomen, and, while locally produced goods could readily be obtained, purchase of many things was restricted by limited cash incomes. In this respect, the retrospective memoirs are reasonably accurate in giving the image of a rural society in which new and decorative goods were as yet rare, even as late as 1765.

Husbandmen and labourers

Husbandmen and small farmers were a clearer group in the inventory sample, with the values of the inventories mostly between £10 and £40, with a range of £2 to £309. Yet the term 'husbandman' is difficult to interpret because it was used in two quite different ways. Sometimes, and especially in the south, it meant simply 'farmer' and could even be used for some very substantial estates; in these cases I have included their estates with those of the large farmers. In the north it generally meant 'smallholder', whose farm and activities fell somewhere between those of yeomen and labourers, usually nearer the latter. Farmers with total valuations under £60 are also included in this group in the tables.[22] In addition, it is not clear how numerous they were, for they are not clearly identified in King's tables.

In Scotland, cottars and sub-tenants were below the tenants; they were very numerous in some areas, as were smallholders and husbandmen in a few parts of England. Their social and economic position varied, but they normally had small plots of land and could also work for wages; some were craftsmen too. Some sub-tenants had larger holdings, and for some this was a stage in their life-cycles and they could become tenant farmers in due course. Thus there were many similarities between sub-tenants and husbandmen, although the cottars were more akin to English labourers or craftsmen/wage-earners in their economic and social position.

The husbandmen are important in this study because they are at the bottom of the society reliably portrayed by inventories, although many smallholders probably escaped probate. It is therefore significant that far smaller proportions of them owned all the goods considered here. Table 6.1 shows that they less often owned staple goods like tables and pewter than the rest of the middle-ranking households, and they rarely owned new or decorative things, although a few recorded earthenware (not necessarily decorative) and looking glasses. Their household goods were often very sparse, the house no more than three rooms, and signs of decoration rare. William Andrews of Dawley (1737) clearly owned enough furniture and equipment for his survival, but there was not much of it and it had a low value; the whole inventory was valued at £16.6s.9d.[23]

	s	d
Item in the Dwelling house		
ffore puter dishes fore chears one little Table	11	0
brass and Iorn	4	0
Item In the Parlar		
One bed one Table one Chest one Chire	18	6
Item In the Chambar over the parlar		
one cofor, two pare of bedstids two Chaff beds	15	0

Descriptions suggest that sub-tenants in Scotland, like husbandmen, would be unlikely to own anything but the most sparse furnishings: 'their plenishings was neither very ample nor very nice'. A box bed was the most substantial item. They had few other things – chests, tubs, wooden utensils, and a cooking pot of iron – but they did own books (or so Robertson reports). Their subsistence was derived from wages paid to them in staple foods, especially oatmeal and milk, their holdings yielded vegetables and other food for subsistence, so (unlike some smallholders in parts of England growing cash crops) they had virtually no cash income to spend on consumer durables or clothing.[24]

The position of smaller farmers has implications for the nature of the social hierarchy, for the influence of the domestic economy on the ownership of goods, and for the depth of the market for manufactured goods, which is discussed in the next chapter.

The labourers' inventories are included as a separate group for interest and comparison. They are too small a proportion of the sample (about 1 per cent) to be representative of *all* labourers in the population, and they were not typical, because labourers did not normally leave probate papers.[25] This is worth emphasizing in order to reduce the possibility of misusing results from inventories. From the values of their estates, they appear as a more clearly defined group than the others, with a range of values between £1 and £38, and the low values of the inventories is in keeping with their low status.

The term 'labourer' is difficult to interpret in this context, for people could earn wages on occasions and not necessarily be of labourer status. For some, wage-earning was a phase in their lives and their ultimate position in the community may have been higher, so it is not clear who is represented by these inventories; but they were not well off, and lower proportions of them owned all kinds of goods. As with husbandmen, it was very unusual for them to own any of the new and decorative goods, and their houses were similarly, and sparsely, furnished. For instance, George Cleaton (labourer of Wellington, 1724) had three rooms with household goods valued at £3.5s.7d.[26]

Tradesmen and craftsmen

The social hierarchy of gentry–yeoman–husbandmen–labourers is reasonably well documented in contemporary perceptions, even if it may not always be clear where particular individuals would be placed in it. The numerous trades and professions pose more serious problems, for there is not a great deal of comprehensive evidence about the status of different occupations. This makes the work of Dr Elliott (upon which the groups in the table are based) especially valuable, for she was able to suggest some ordering of occupations and trades based on contemporary behaviour and perspectives. In addition, and of great significance, the same terms were applied to people of very different status. Building craftsmen, for instance, could be wage-labourers or substantial tradesmen. Blacksmiths could be out-workers in the iron trades or they could be substantial businessmen and tradesmen; there are many other examples.[27] In these and other cases, the name of the trade alone does not give enough information to reveal where any one individual might be placed in the social order. These qualifications do not mean that trades and crafts cannot be placed in order, but they suggest that categories are not absolutely clear, and, as we shall see on occasions, interpretation has to take account of this.

Labourers and husbandmen were certainly at the bottom of the social hierarchy, as the lower mean values of their estates confirms. Some trades were certainly above them in status, but below yeomen, and these included most of the village crafts, like shoemakers, as well as a few 'industrial' ones, like nailers. These lesser tradesmen accounted for about 20 per cent of the inventory sample, and made up about 38 per cent of the households of middle rank in the revisions to King's estimates.[28] Some craftsmen were outside the scope of normal probate because they were too poor; there are, for instance, very few inventories of textile workers (ninety-nine in all), even where they might be expected, as in south Lancashire. The weavers' inventories (forty-five of them) are not among the poorest in the sample, so the poorer weavers whose resources were akin to those of husbandmen and labourers are not documented in probate records. The same is true of ironworkers and many miscellaneous trades, although the village trades (shoemakers, for instance) were more fully represented. Thus, very significantly, the inventory sample represents the better-off craftsmen. The valuations of inventories suggest that there was a reasonable coherence amongst those covered, taken as a group, with frequencies peaking between £15 to £20, although the maximum value was £1,185. In rural Scotland a high proportion of tradesmen were cottars and thus of a lower status than the craft tradesmen represented in inventories.

The lesser tradesmen tended to have more varied domestic possessions than did the husbandmen or even the yeomen. Many more had pictures and window curtains than did yeomen, although ownership of staple goods (pewter and tables) as well as clocks and books was indistinguishable. Individual craftsmen therefore had houses with a slightly different range of domestic goods, for it was likely that there would be the odd new item among a range of possessions otherwise similar to those of the yeomen and husbandmen. Richard Jackson, tailor of Wellington, had the usual furniture, tables, iron pots, and so on, but he also had glass bottles and a 'Glass cage with Tickney ware belonging to it . . . 2s 6d'.[29] (Tickney was a black eathenware.) In Scotland it is impossible to say whether rural tradesmen owned things more often, for it was not a point that struck writers later in the century.

Other trades were distinctly higher in status, and these are given reasonable coverage by the probate sample. King's estimates suggest that about 25 per cent of the middling ranks came into these categories, while about 22 per cent of the inventories are drawn from them. These are divided into two groups in the table so that finer distinctions can be made. Trades of intermediate status include the prosperous manufacturing trades such as clothiers or founders, or those in the commercial sector, such as shopkeepers or innholders. From this it is apparent that dealers generally had greater prestige than either craftsmen or yeomen. The valuations of their inventories also show that they had far greater resources, and a few were even richer than the wealthiest gentry. The median value of their household goods was substantially greater than that of the yeomen, although the valuations for farmers and tradesmen were actually measuring different things, for the former included the value of farm stock, which was a different kind of asset from the trade goods of the tradesmen.

The dealing trades in Scotland tended to be concentrated in towns, some of them very small but fulfilling some of the marketing and other functions of urban areas, and certainly having rights to hold markets and fairs.[30] In this sense, it is difficult to separate urban dealers from rural ones. In Scotland the use of the term 'merchant' included wealthy burgesses who made fortunes from overseas trades, as well as shopkeepers, grocers, chapmen, and other dealers, so their resources varied considerably. In most Scottish towns there were probably shopkeepers and dealers on a modest scale, with only local influence. In Edinburgh and Glasgow there were, on the other hand, merchants whose influence and lifestyles rivalled those of the richer gentry and nobles, although there were enormous variations.[31] These, the élite among the dealers, were not included in the English probate sample, so they are not strictly comparable with the group of dealers from this; they were more akin to some of the freemen of London represented by the Orphans' Court sample.

A large number of consumers were to be found within these

intermediate-status trades, for higher proportions of them owned the selected household goods and especially the new and decorative ones. The Far Eastern imports (china and the utensils for hot drinks) were recorded in about one in ten of their inventories, but only in one in twenty-five of the whole sample. New methods of cookery, as indicated by the ownership of saucepans, were recorded in a quarter of their inventories but in only a tenth overall. Their houses were less sparsely furnished, with upholstered furniture, tables with interesting shapes, hangings, curtains, and even carpets. Take as an extreme case the furnishings of a wealthy Doncaster shopkeeper and alderman in 1674. He had about thirteen rooms, some with fairly ordinary contents, such as the chamber over the hall which had 'A Fether bedd with bedstead & Furniture a Chest & Two Chaires', valued at £2.[32] There were twenty-two pewter plates, nineteen dishes, and all the usual kinds of brass and iron cooking utensils. The parlour was used in the traditional way:

	£	s	d
In the Parlor			
A Fether bedd bedstead and Furniture a Truckle			
bedd with Furniture A Chest Three Trunckes one			
Table a Cubbord Foure Chaires a hanging Shelfe an			
old viol & a little range	4	0	0

But there were also the following well-furnished rooms:

	£	s	d
In the dineing Roome And the Clossett			
Six doozen of Trenchers Three Baskitts Three			
voyders Two seeing glasses Certaine Glasses a Seller			
of Glasses a possitt pott white plates A long Table			
and ovell Table a Forme Nyne Chaires Five Stooles			
a Livery Cubbord Six Qushons a Range a pair of			
Landyrons a peece of matting Twelve pictures Three			
Carpitts & a Cubbord Cloth	7	12	0
In the Hall			
Two French Tables & Cloths Eight Stooles Seaven			
Chaires Two Long Settles a range and froggs a bible			
& some Little bookes	2	0	0

This is an early example when it was very unusual to have a dining room, but this kind of furnishing was to be found on a more modest scale in the houses of many shopkeepers and tradesmen. As in England, the dealers and merchants in Scotland had wider commercial contacts with other places than did farmers or rural tradesmen; they also had more ready cash available than farmers, so we might expect them to acquire more varied household possessions. Yet not every testament lists new or decorative household goods; that of Robert Drysdale, merchant burgess and draper of Edinburgh (1716), listed goods much like the less well-off tradesmen in an English inland town, such as Wellington in Shropshire.[33]

	£ Scots	s	d
In the North roume			
1 stouped bed with hangings	14		
6 Kain chairs & 2 armed ones	16		
1 locking glass	12		
1 wanscot folding table	3		
2 piece of hanging in the roume	8		
1 chamber box & 2 standes	1–	4	

There were five rooms containing cooking pots, linen, pewter, and furniture, but the only unusual goods were an old clock (£1 Scots), three table knives with three forks (14s. Scots), and the looking glass. In London or Newcastle such a draper would have had some at least of the new goods.

The high-status trades include the most prestigious dealing trades, like mercers and drapers, as well as the professions including the clergy.[34] The links between the higher-ranking trades, the professions, and the gentry are not apparent in this way of observing social divisions, but careers in the professions and some trades were often taken up by people of gentle birth, so the upper ranks of the trades and professions maintained strong family links with the gentry. That their ranking was partly a matter of people's perception of prestige and influence, rather than accumulated wealth, can be suggested by the fact that the median values for the whole inventory and for household goods were slightly less than those for the intermediate trades, and the highest value was also rather lower, at £1,284.

These people were also consumers and owned new and decorative goods more often than the gentry. The greatest differences were in book and clock ownership, which reflected the higher literacy and organizational requirements of professional people and clergy. Some of them had very extensive collections of

possessions; Richard Harrison of Lichfield, 'clerk' (1676), owned
£160 worth of furnishings out of an inventory valued at £400.[35]
There was a study with books valued at £50. The parlour and hall
were well furnished, as was the dining room:

	£	s	d
In the parlour			
2 tables, 12 leather chaires, 2 carpets and a couch			
chaire, 6 Turkey worke cushins and 2 other chaires	3	2	4
A grate, fireshovill and tongues		6	8
Pictures, 2 curtaine rodds and a wax candlestik etc.		16	0
In the hall			
A Bible and stand and Booke of Martyrs		14	0
A table, form, 2 leather chairs and other wooden ware		12	0
A grate		4	0
Mapps and pictures		2	6
In the dining roome over the parlour			
3 French tables and 3 carpetts	1	5	0
12 Turkey worke chaires	2	10	0
A folding bedd and furniture	2	10	0
Grate and other materials of iron		5	0
Pictures and curtains		15	0

Only a few of the fifteen rooms in the house were without some
decorative item, such as the 'white ware in a closet'. This was an
unusually well-furnished house, as befitted the Chancellor of
Lichfield Cathedral, and it would be misleading to suppose that
all clergy lived in such comfort. William Cartwright, of Muxton in
Shropshire, a mathematician, lived more modestly, with the total
value of the inventory at £17.4s.4d., although the house had eight
rooms. He had plain pewter, cooking equipment, tables and
chairs in modest numbers; there were feather beds, but also chaff
ones; but he had a new parlour, as well as specialist mathematical
instruments:[36]

	£	s	d
In ye New Parlor			
One Long table one form 3 join stools four Join			
chairs and four Turkey quishions	1	0	0
In the closett			
One hundred books, three leg staffe one plaine table			

one wood Quadrant one small brass Quadrant one brass seal one Brass sights one pair of Brass Compasses One pensell one slate one spectacle Glass	1 12 0
One pair of Globes and box	10 0

The same was probably true in Scotland. Here the better-off clergy, doctors, and lawyers were likely to live in Edinburgh, Glasgow, or Aberdeen, but it is hard to get an accurate impression of their household goods. Edinburgh was a large but crowded city, and even the richest professionals did not have large houses there until later, when the 'New Town' was built. Again, the wealthiest of them are not strictly comparable with the professionals covered by the English evidence from ineventories, but these people had sometimes had a broadly ranging education, not confined to Scotland, and had the reputation for living cultivated lives. Yet even here Scottish households were probably furnished with fewer new and decorative goods. Take, for instance, the impression given by the inventory of goods auctioned after the death of Andro Hog, Writer to the Signet, in 1691. He had basic furniture crowded into four rooms (chamber, little chamber, kitchen, and, probably, a living room). There were five beds and bedding (one folding bed and two couches convertible to beds) for a household consisting of Hog (his wife had died earlier in the year), his two small children, their nurse, and three servants, a total of seven people – a household more overcrowded than those of lesser rank in Norwich.[37] Apart from staple goods like pots, tables, chairs, and pewter, there were only two looking glasses and a Bible.[38] Such a person in London, or a large provincial centre, would have had more decorative items and probably some fashionable furniture as well. In the Orphans' Court sample in 1695, seven out of ten recorded pictures; one in five, cutlery; one in three, china; and over a half, clocks. Hog may have been quite young, for he had been out of his apprenticeship for only a few years. On the other hand, Hog lived in more comfortably furnished surroundings than the farmers.

There are three other groups whose exact status cannot be determined, and these amount to about 18 per cent of the whole sample. Widows and spinsters not included elsewhere could have been the relicts of any kind of household, and their inventoried estates reflect this, with a wide range from £1 to £2,238. They are therefore a residual group, although not without interest as indicators of households headed by women without obvious occupations.[39] The group whose inventories give no indication of occupation or status contains a wide range of different types of estate, from those who had a few household goods left at retirement to those with large investments and households. These may include some wage-earners, but this cannot be assumed even of low-value estates. Some inventories contained evidence of a trade, as 'all the tools of his trade', or 'trade debts'. It was impossible to say what the trade was, so these could not be placed in the hierarchy. On the other hand, their occupations were not totally unknown and so they are listed separately.

Social boundaries

What social boundaries are indicated by this discussion? Ownership of the selected goods, as well as the quantities and qualities of furnishings, did reflect social status, but the pattern has inconsistencies and inversions. The gentry did not predominate, and the goods were more often recorded in the inventories of tradesmen and professional people. Lower down the hierarchy there were similar inversions, with yeomen less inclined to own many of the newer goods than the lower-status craft trades. This has implications for the interpretation of emulation as a mechanism for change and will be discussed next in the chapter. The lower boundary for those tending to own a variety of household goods was between the craftsmen and the husbandmen, since husbandmen's inventories were unlikely to record new and decorative items; even staple goods were less frequent here, and the few labourers' inventories were similar.

These observations enable us to draw two conclusions about the possible nature of consumption patterns in Scotland. One is that, if we had appropriate evidence, we would expect to find that the same kinds of distinctions between people of different rank could be made for Scotland as for England, with some allowance for the slightly different social contexts in Scotland. Tradesmen and professional people were more likely to own new and decorative things than even the better-off farmers, with greater inequalities between town and country. Secondly, it seems that even Lowland Scotland and even Edinburgh would not, at least before 1725, emerge as an area in which consumption of domestic durables was most important. Yet it would not be like the south of England, where the large farmers had very comfortably furnished

Table 8.2 *A consumption hierarchy: frequencies of ownership of goods in a sample of inventories in England, 1675–1725*

Occupation or status	No. of inventories	Mean value Total inventory £	House-hold goods £	Tables %	Cooking pots %	Sauce-pans %	Pewter %	Pewter dishes %	Pewter plates %	Earthen-ware %	Books %	Clocks %	Pictures %	Looking glasses %	Table linen %	Window curtains %	Knives and forks %	China %	Utensils for hot drinks %	Silver %
Dealing trades	452	162	33	95	77	23	95	62	49	49	27	27	33	60	62	28	11	10	10	43
Gentry	122	320	55	93	84	13	93	53	41	39	39	51	33	62	60	26	11	6	7	61
Craft trades	459	96	19	91	72	12	95	55	30	43	17	17	15	36	49	13	2	4	4	22
Yeoman[1]	952	165	23	91	69	5	95	41	20	33	18	19	4	20	35	5	1	1	1	13
Husbandmen[2]	332	32	8	83	57	2	89	33	9	28	4	4	0	9	16	2	0	0	1	2

Notes
1 Includes farmers with total estates valued at over £60.
2 Includes farmers with total estates valued at under £60.
See appendix 1 for details of the goods and appendix 2 for details about the occupational/status groups.

houses. Consumption was not well developed in Lowland Scotland.

This has implications for understanding the social depth of the market for dometic goods in the eighteenth century, and I shall return to it later. Before doing so, it is instructive to examine occupation and status in other ways, in order to emphasize differences between trades, gentry, and farmers in a consumption hierarchy.

A consumption hierarchy

Table 8.2 distinguishes craft trades, dealing trades, husbandmen, yeomen, and gentry in a hierarchy based on consumption.[40] The criterion for this is the tendency towards ownership of goods, the occupations higher up the 'consumption hierarchy' having a higher propensity to ownership than those lower down. The craft trades, as already explained, were not a homogeneous group, and some of the industrial and other crafts represented here were more wealthy than others, although the traditional and village crafts predominated. Some of the inventories are among those of lowest value in the survey, and most of them had values between £10 and £20, although the highest was £1,603. The mean values (£96 and £19) were lower than those for the yeomen. The dealing trades likewise include a wide variety, from small shopkeepers to merchants, and they were the most urban group. The values of the inventories were more spread out, with a rather flat peak from £10 to £50 and a long tail to the highest value in the whole sample, of £4,132.

The consumption hierarchy was not the same as the social hierarchy, although it is not completely different. Husbandmen come out at the bottom in both cases, but above them in the consumption hierarchy are not the lesser trades, but the relatively high-status yeomen, who were less likely to own most of the goods here than the craftsmen. The commercial and dealing trades were at the top, with the gentry and professional people below them, although their social status was much higher. This pattern was especially marked for the new goods, books and clocks being the only clear exceptions. The idea of such a hierarchy suggests ways of looking at the social order and of the influence of social position on the ownership of goods, but there is no need to pursue the idea further at this stage, for there are other aspects of occupation, consumption, and behaviour yet to consider.

Table 8.3 Frequencies of ownership of selected goods in a sample of inventories in England, 1675–1725, subdivided by economic sector of occupations

Economic sector	No. of inventories	Mean value Total inventory £	Mean value Household goods £	Tables %	Cooking pots %	Sauce-pans %	Pewter %	Pewter dishes %	Pewter plates %	Earthen-ware %	Books %	Clocks %	Pictures %	Looking glasses %	Table linen %	Window curtains %	Knives and forks %	China %	Utensils for hot drinks %	Silver %
Primary sector: agriculture; fishery	1,303	130	19	89	66	4	94	39	17	32	14	15	3	18	31	4	1	1	1	11
Primary sector: mining	12*	193	32	92	75	8	100	67	33	42	33	8	17	33	75	0	0	0	0	33
Building sector	71	84	18	93	77	4	94	55	25	32	13	17	7	24	49	13	0	1	0	21
Manufacturing sector	411	101	20	91	72	14	95	56	33	44	17	21	16	39	50	15	3	4	4	23
Transport sector	25*	155	29	96	72	24	88	64	44	48	20	24	32	48	60	16	16	8	16	40
Dealing sector	368	166	34	96	77	23	95	61	50	51	28	27	35	63	60	29	11	11	11	45
Public and professional	44	216	50	100	84	11	100	48	39	52	80	52	20	52	64	18	14	7	7	55
Others	668	116	25	84	73	14	89	50	29	33	22	20	19	41	45	19	6	5	5	35

Notes
* Sample size too small to be meaningful: see appendix 1.
See appendix 2 for details of the economic sectors.

Economic sector and ownership

The economic role of occupations can be discovered by grouping them according to the sector in the economy into which they fall. Table 8.3 reinforces distinctions already made between primary and secondary sectors.[41] At first sight the table seems to show no particular pattern in the ownership of goods, but it does show whether people working in some sectors of the economy were more likely to own the selected goods than others. The differences between the primary, secondary, and dealing sectors are much as might be expected from the differences already observed between yeomen, craft trades, and dealing trades, with the inventories from the primary sector being less likely to record the goods. The inventories from the dealing sector tended, on the other hand, more often to record all kinds of goods, and notably those that were newly available, with the transport sector akin to the dealing one in this respect. The table also lists the professions separately and shows that here too higher proportions of inventories recorded the goods than those in the primary and the craft sectors, but often lower proportions than in the dealing occupations.

These distinctions can be further emphasized by examining the individual trades for which there are reasonable numbers of inventories in the sample, as in table 8.4.[42] The commercial occupations (merchants, shopkeepers, and innkeepers) were much more likely to own the newer and more decorative items than were the tailors, butchers, and blacksmiths. Ownership of books and clocks was much higher among the shopkeepers and merchants than among the others.

Material culture and status

Ownership patterns also show that the main differences between those of different occupation and status were in ownership of goods that expressed something about the household; ownership of goods used in the course of 'backstage' activities varied less between social groups. For instance, china and the utensils for hot drinks were not very common in the inventory sample as a whole, and ownership was concentrated in a few groups, so that by 1725 they were recorded in over half the tradesmen's inventories in London and in virtually all the London freemen's inventories from the Orphans' Court sample, but in very few yeomen's

Table 8.4 Frequencies of ownership of selected goods in a sample of inventories in England, 1675–1725: selected occupations

Occupation	No. of inventories	Mean value Total inventory £	Household goods £	Tables %	Cooking pots %	Sauce-pans %	Pewter %	Pewter dishes %	Pewter plates %	Earthen-ware %	Books %	Clocks %	Pictures %	Looking glasses %	Table linen %	Window curtains %	Knives and forks %	China %	Utensils for hot drinks %	Silver %
Shoemakers	45	63	17	91	64	8	93	58	33	51	16	8	8	38	47	2	2	4	2	16
Tailors	32	56	16	91	78	16	100	69	41	44	22	16	16	34	44	6	0	0	13	17
Carpenters	32	70	18	90	81	6	97	56	22	38	9	16	3	22	56	13	0	0	0	19
Weavers	48	85	13	88	67	8	96	48	19	44	15	17	2	27	29	4	0	0	2	8
Blacksmiths	49	56	15	82	63	14	90	41	18	35	10	22	8	33	39	12	0	4	0	8
Butchers	37	129	24	97	76	8	97	59	41	32	16	19	19	46	59	11	0	3	3	43
Shopkeepers	87	124	29	98	86	25	95	64	53	48	37	25	34	67	68	40	15	13	11	45
Innkeepers and victuallers	101	151	43	99	81	37	98	72	67	57	19	30	39	70	65	40	21	9	17	46
Mariners	40	85	30	98	70	8	98	68	45	60	18	25	48	70	73	20	3	23	25	60
Merchants	16*	223	46	100	75	6	81	44	38	56	50	38	44	75	56	38	19	25	19	75
Drapers and mercers	21*	303	34	95	81	19	95	43	38	48	43	24	43	67	43	24	5	5	10	43

Notes
* Sample too small to be meaningful.
See appendix 1 for details about the goods.

inventories. Goods such as these had social functions as well as associations with new forms of domestic behaviour, and their uneven distribution points towards social differentiation. In this case, the concentration was also due to easier supply in the London area. Looking glasses, suggestive of a certain self-awareness and a desire to set the atmosphere of rooms, were three times as common in the dealers' inventories as in those of the yeomen, suggesting a greater aesthetic awareness on the part of those in the non-agricultural sector. The expectations and lives of people in the commercial sector led them to be more interested in innovation and in varied domestic goods. These were the fore-runners of the middle classes, noted in later periods for their materialism and their elaborate domestic interiors.

Other kinds of goods, such as those indicative of a household's contacts with a wider commercial or intellectual world, also show considerable variation in ownership, some of it arising from the requirements of particular occupations and activities. Books were recorded in virtually all inventories of professional people, who were literate, and their high ownership of clocks reflects their need to co-ordinate their time with other people in the community. The gentry also tended towards higher book and clock ownership because they had an identity of interest with gentry elsewhere, with whom they exchanged information, some of it through books and publications of various kinds. Yet it is also notable that professional people and gentry did not have the highest pro-portions of the new and decorative goods, although we might expect them to have wanted to express their social standing in this way. What this means is that these people were especially likely to look to a wider world beyond their immediate household and locality, and it shows that the social expectations of these groups were not the same as those of the traders.

9

CONCLUSIONS AND IMPLICATIONS

The consumption patterns examined in this book contain specific implications about people's lifestyles and values in the early modern period and about the forces acting upon them. From a social perspective we can see various social boundaries to consumption. From an economic perspective consumption can be seen to influence, and be influenced by, trade and economic growth. But the meanings of consumption patterns are multi-layered and, transcending these specific implications, there are more general implications which are not always explicitly visible.

Social boundaries

The relationships between ownership of goods, social status, and occupation show clear-cut distinctions, as well as some paradoxes. Ownership patterns show that those in agricultural occupations were less likely to own new kinds of domestic goods than those in trades or commercial and professional occupations. A clear boundary can be seen between the main body of consumers and the less well-off farmers, with their sparse domestic possessions. Patterns also reveal how complex was the use of domestic goods for enhancing status or displaying social rank. The lesser gentry, in spite of higher social standing, were less likely to own most kinds of goods than the commercial and professional people.

There were certainly limits to consumption, because small farmers and husbandmen were unlikely to have had the items upon which the early growth of manufacturing was based. This is extremely important, for the evidence from inventories does not even pretend to extend to those in the lowest ranks; it refers only to those with sufficient goods and property to have left probate papers. The position of labourers is difficult to establish from this small sample, which cannot be taken as representing all such people, since they were atypical by the very fact of having left probate records. The domestic economies of labourers and wage-earners were different from those of small farmers, for they relied more heavily on cash wages, and many of them lived in towns. In their ownership of goods, the twenty-eight found in the sample of inventories were not notably different from the husbandmen, although they were a little more likely to own staple goods, and there is the odd new item. The main limit to the market for many household goods was, however, between the husbandmen and craftsmen. In saying this it must not be forgotten that the crafts-men represented here are the small masters, rather than the journeymen or wage-earners in the same crafts, and this evidence should not automatically be extended to include anyone working in craft trades.

This lower limit to the market for household goods sheds light on the questions that have been raised by historians of early industrial and economic development about who actually bought imported new goods and the products of industries in the countryside. In two notable contributions to our understanding of the later seventeenth century, one examining the development of the consumer-oriented trades and the other the trade of the petty chapman, it is argued that a wide range of goods suited the needs of a large proportion of the population and thus implied that a 'mass' market was already in existence by the early eighteenth century.[1] In both studies there is a tendency to conflate evidence from the middle ranks of society (notably inventories, but also some contemporary comment) with conclusions that the 'extra cash' available among 'wage labourers, cottagers and small-holders' resulted in greater purchasing power for the kinds of consumer goods produced in the expanding rural industrial areas. Thus 'the labouring classes found cash to spare for consumer goods in 1700 that had no place in their budgets in 1550'.[2] While it may be true that these people were able to buy things that had not been available in the sixteenth century, it does not follow that they made up a significant part of the market in the late seventeenth century. The difficulty in defining the lower bounds of the 'poor' or 'humble' can also be seen in examining the chain of itinerant distributors of miscellaneous personal goods to urban and rural households of the seventeenth century. To the question of who bought chapmen's goods, the answer is stated as being 'the wage labourers and the poor husbandmen ... from at least the 1680s'. Yet the evidence offered about the appearances of the goods, their uses, and who owned them is not drawn from data relating directly to wage-labourers, and only a few 'poor' husbandmen are quoted; most of the evidence is again from general commentary and probate inventories.[3]

These difficulties are widespread and have been elaborated here by reference to two good books in order to show that scholars have found it very difficult to admit that many people about whose lives we would like to know are hidden from sight. The observations about the relationships between the ownership of goods and social position suggest that we should be very cautious about accepting that the market extended as far down the social hierarchy as these writers have suggested. It is certainly clear that the consumption and ownership of the goods selected here, which were chosen because they were representative of many others, were not confined to the social and economic élites, and so the market for such goods had considerable social depth, as well as geographical extension. This supports Eversley's view that the important markets for consumer goods were to be found between the upper gentry and the labourers, that is to say in the middle ranks. It does not confirm the view that there was a 'mass' market for these kinds of goods, or a 'humble consumer society', in the late seventeenth or early eighteenth century. There were limits, and those limits were reached at some point between the craftsmen and the small farmers. This is why it is important to stress that the craftsmen represented by these inventories were probably those with greater resources than people who were called by the name of the craft but were either working for wages or were not fully established in the trade. To conclude from this evidence that, for example, 19 per cent of *all* textile workers had clocks would be a misuse of probate inventories, which only give evidence about the craftsmen with sufficient resources to have left probate papers.

The exaggerated claims for consumption among the lower orders are based on two serious problems in how other evidence about consumer behaviour has been used. One problem is that much commentary actually refers to textiles, and especially to clothing, the need for which was different from the need for domestic utensils. King's calculations that there were enough stockings produced for everyone to have a pair every year does reveal something about the economy and people's needs, but it is not necessarily applicable to other commodities.[4] Clothing, as shown in chapter 6, was second only to food in household expenditure. Secondly, there is a lack of reliable evidence about the possessions of those who did not leave inventories or accounts; we simply do not know what they owned and how they spent their incomes. The impression can be given that we *do* know something about them from the inventories with low valuations, but we have no way of knowing how typical the inventories were. Likewise, arguments based on increases in real wages already imply that wage-earners spent their surplus on household goods and clothing, although it is difficult to see how they could have done so. Even an income of £20 a year, suggesting a high wage and regular work, would leave little spare for significant quantities of household goods.

Emulation

One of the most persuasive and powerful theories, implicit if not explicit, in most accounts of increasing consumption of goods at any time seeks to explain it by saying that the main motivation was a desire to emulate those of higher social rank, in order to keep up appearances, and (in slightly dated slang) 'keep up with the Joneses'. The notion of social emulation has been used to explain changes in the goods available during industrialization and economic change in the second half of the eighteenth century, although it is often applied to earlier periods. Perkin argued, for instance, that the key to industrial growth was 'the infinitely elastic home demand for mass consumer goods and ... the key to that demand was social emulation ... the compulsive urge for imitating the spending habits of one's betters'.[5]

Emulation of this kind, it is argued, led to penetration down the social scale in the ownership of various goods, with the proviso that this was made possible by price reduction or by increased availability of cheaper (but similar) versions of the same kinds of goods. The evidence quoted for this kind of process is usually based on contemporary observation of the habits of other (often lower) social ranks in copying specific fashions or clothing or adopting some specific new behaviour, such as drinking tea. Sometimes there is a tone of horror at the 'luxury' of the poor in using some item which they had not previously used; thus 'in a few years we shall probably have no common people at all.'[6] Most often quoted of manufacturers' comments are those of Josiah Wedgwood to his partner Thomas Bentley in the 1770s. His letters discuss many aspects of production and marketing in great detail, and in 1772, writing about increasing his production of ornamental vases, he observed:

> The Great People had these Vases in their Palaces long enough for them to be seen and admired by the *Middling Class* of People ... their character is established, and the middling People would probably buy quantities of them at a reduced price.[7]

Yet if we want to generalize about this kind of mechanism, and say that the *main* motive for people's acquiring more, or new, goods was to emulate others of higher rank, then we need to ask whether such comment was reasonably representative; did this apply to the other parts of the pottery trade producing less unusual items? Josiah Wedgwood's remarks arose from a particular situation, namely the need to produce more ornamental vases to make production economical and profitable. Can we tell whether the same mechanisms were at work in the expanding trades, such as pewter and clocks, stoneware and cabinet making? Most, but not all, writers take their evidence from the second half of the eighteenth century, but their conclusions are often applied to the late seventeenth century onwards, so that some theories originating in attempts to explain industrialization in the later eighteenth century are applied more generally to the 'pre-industrial' period and have become part of historians' 'stock responses' to questions of changing living standards in general.

The frequency tables in the previous chapter, showing ownership of goods by those of different social rank and occupation, provide some specific observations against which ideas of this kind can be tested. Although there was a social dimension to the ownership of goods, those higher up the social hierarchy did not necessarily own the goods most often. This alone suggests that the theory of emulation, while applicable in some cases, can easily be overstated with little regard for the practical and social situations of people's lives or the exact nature of the social hierarchy.

The limitations of taking emulation as the most powerful motivation can best be demonstrated by considering the likely role of the gentry as leaders. If social emulation were at work as a dynamic force behind people's motivation in owning goods, then we would expect higher proportions of the most highly regarded group to own many of the items examined here, and we would also expect them to be the first to own the new things. Yet, as already observed, this was not the case, for a higher proportion of tradesmen and professional people owned the goods associated with 'frontstage' areas of the house, with the exception of clocks. Likewise, while the gentry were among the earliest to record china and hot drinks, they were not in advance of the dealers and the crafts.

Do these observations arise out of limitations in the evidence? There are two limitations to the evidence about the gentry. One is that the sample is rather small and patchy; however, it is not out of keeping with the proportion of gentry in the population at the time, and the gentry were, in spite of a certain coherence of interest, a very varied group, so the numbers in the sample are large enough to give coherent results. The other limiting factor is that the gentry represented by the sample of inventories are confined to those of lesser rank; those of greater wealth and standing are not included. Yet, although this limitation should not be forgotten, these lesser gentry were still highly regarded in local communities, they were of observably higher social rank than all but the richest tradesmen, and they normally had greater means at their disposal.

Emulation could not have worked in such a simple way as historians imply, and the processes by which people learned about consumer goods were much more complex. It is not even established that people of middle rank approved of copying people of higher rank. The first entry of sayings in the account and memorandum book of Lee Warley, a well-to-do Kentish yeoman, states: 'In our Expenses we should neither ape those that are placed in a more exalted sphere, nor ... sink beneath our proper station'.[8] Of greater importance, however, is that the emulation model looks at the problem of expanding consumption in a very limited way because it only admits ownership of goods to have one social function. But goods had many functions, and there were many ways of learning about them. Furthermore, there were other relationships influencing ownership, notably the economy and trade in the particular areas of the country in which particular individuals lived.

Supply and trade

The first part of this book concentrated on consumption at a national level, for the economy as a whole was responsive to the requirements of the many individual consumers. Trade with the Far East brought attractive consumer goods on to the market at modest cost. The range of these, and the large quantities available in the early eighteenth century, had a profound influence on domestic decoration, eventually stimulating new products and production methods in industries as diverse as furniture, textiles, and ceramics.

Domestic goods were also made in Britain. Many established items, such as pewter, continued to be made in craft workshops; production of others, such as clocks, knives, forks, or ironwares, was organized in a variety of complex ways, and there were many producers on a relatively small scale orientated towards extensive home (as well as overseas) markets. Some trades, such as pottery, came to be organized on an increasingly large scale, so that consumption both was influenced by the goods available and itself influenced the changing location and methods of production.

Increasing supply, whether of imported or of home-produced goods, required retail outlets as well as increasingly well-organized internal trade networks. The importance of the inland trades was stressed in the discussion of both urban and regional consumption patterns; ownership of some goods was more likely in regions with well-established trading contacts with London. It is a valuable conclusion of this study that such relationships between consumption patterns and inland trade can be established.

Economic growth

The late seventeenth and early eighteenth centuries are often presented as a time of restricted economic and social development, even of stagnation. Yet this is a misrepresentation, as many recent detailed studies have shown. The conclusions derived from the sample of inventories also indicate that these were decades of considerable change. Not only did more people own more ordinary things, but they also chose more decorative and expressive household goods, many of them imported from the Far East. Thus there was already, at a very early stage in industrialization, an extensive potential market for a wide range of goods among the middle ranks.

There are also specific implications for the way in which we might look at the impact of decreases in the prices of basic foodstuffs in the 1730s and the impact of the agricultural depression of that time on the market for many household items, as well as clothing. It has been argued, notably by T.S. Ashton and A.H. John, and subsequently by others, that low food prices in 1717–24 and between 1730 and 1740 (owing to a succession of favourable harvests) allowed large sections of the working population to feed well, yet retain a margin between income and expenditure which was spent on consumer goods. Workers, it is argued, spent part of their earnings on manufactured commodities, resulting in increases in production or imports. This provided buoyancy in the home market for the development of industrial production of many kinds and enabled many wage-earners to afford new kinds of goods. Others have taken an alternative view – that bad harvests might be more beneficial to consumption because the incomes of farmers and landlords were higher in years of short harvests, and this would be of greater consequence than the cheapness of food.[9] One of the major weaknesses in this kind of argument is that a considerable number of speculations are made on the basis of very little evidence. To begin with, Flinn has questioned whether prices were low enough in the 1730s to produce the kinds of effects that have been suggested, since prices were erratic and only moderately low for a relatively short time; they were no lower in the 1730s and 1740s than they had been in the late 1680s and the mid-1720s, with the secular trend from the 1660s to the late 1720s being only slightly downwards. Yet these ideas have remained in the imaginations of historians, although we do not even know whether income formerly spent on grain was actually spent on other food, on drink, or on manufactured goods.

Two suggestions can be made which draw attention to the need for more evidence about some crucial issues, if growth in the early eighteenth century is to be understood. First, the agricultural sector, even the yeomen and gentry, did not contain those who were most likely to acquire a variety of goods, and they did not constitute the main consumers of the domestic items upon which economic growth was based. This can most clearly be seen in the differences between the yeomen and all kinds of tradesmen, shown in table 8.2, where both new and established goods are more frequently recorded in tradesmen's inventories, with the exception of the established things like pewter. This means that the market for domestic utensils and other possessions would not necessarily be affected by reductions in farm incomes, and a depression of incomes in the agricultural sector would be less important to the long-term development of imports and industries producing goods for household use than it may seem. Agricultural depression in grain-growing areas was not incompatible with expanding consumer demand in the nation as a whole, although it could have influenced some areas more than others, as chapter 3 shows.

The argument that a consumer boom in this period was caused by lower food prices – which gave wage-earners a margin between 'subsistence' and income that they could spend on manufactured goods – is questionable in a number of ways (quite apart from the problem of knowing what is meant by 'subsistence'). The evidence does show that new goods were not available to the upper classes alone, but, as has been demonstrated, wage-earners and the less well-off farmers were not acquiring the goods examined here. In the vocabulary of writers about consumption of goods in the late seventeenth and eighteenth centuries, there is in fact considerable doubt as to who *exactly* they are writing about. Eversley, in his very perceptive and wide-ranging account of the home market, argues (perfectly correctly) that the market for manufactured goods after 1690 lay in the middle-income groups, but he often presents arguments of a qualitative kind as if he were referring to a 'mass' market including wage-earners. He conflates the small-scale ironworkers of the Sedgley area in south Staffordshire, for instance, with 'ordinary industrial workers', and draws on their inventories for evidence about the lower ranks in society. But they were not 'ordinary' workers. Similarly, his conclusion that there was a broadly based and expanding home market for industrial products during the eighteenth century is a perfectly valid one, but it contains the implication that this was based on consumption by wage-earners ('Had food shortages, labour displacement by mechanisation, or the subsistence theory of wages won the day, there would have been no industry') – which contrasts with his earlier (and more accurate) definitions of the markets as lying within the middle ranks.[10] So there was a limit to consumption in the eighteenth century, just as there was in the seventeenth century, for there is no evidence in the inventories that wage-earners were able and willing to spend their incomes on many domestic goods, and it is more likely that they spent additional income (if there was any) on a wider variety of food, drink, and clothing.

By the late seventeenth century there is every sign that the commercial and trading classes in England were active consumers of household goods. There is little sign amongst the middle ranks that surplus resources were used for a few conspicuous occasions or on a few valuable possessions. Households, even in rural areas, were rarely self-sufficient and there was already a predisposition to value material life and to acquire a wide range of domestic goods.

There were many reasons why people wanted to own material goods, some practical, some financial, some psychological. This makes it necessary to explore social, as well as economic factors. It also makes once-and-for-all conclusions both impossible and intellectually dishonest. There is no single answer. The emphasis of the approaches in this book has been on the expressive, social functions of consumer goods in the daily lives of the middle classes. Through trying to understand material goods in these ways, with their many non-verbal cues, we come closer to understanding the humanity of the past.

Appendix 1

WAYS OF USING PROBATE INVENTORIES

Inventories present the researcher with many technical problems both in collecting and analysing them. Some of these are referred to in the text, but the purpose of this appendix is to give more detail about how the sample was taken and about some of the decisions made in selecting the goods, in order to clarify the methods used in the research for this book. Appendix 2 deals with the specific problems associated with occupation and status. Published collections of inventories are listed in the second section of the Bibliography.

The sample

Probate inventories are very numerous and can be sampled and used in a bewildering variety of ways.[1] How it is done in any particular case depends on the questions to be answered, the detail to be examined, and the kinds of practical limitations anticipated in data collection. It is essential to pay attention to the way in which the sample is taken, for the kind of sample limits, controls, and defines the conclusions that can be drawn. In general, relatively small, carefully contrived samples are to be preferred, for these give the most flexible results. There are, unfortunately, substantial practical problems in taking a random probability sample of English probate inventories. This is due to the complexity of the mechanisms by which inventories were made and subsequently kept. There was a hierarchy of local and church courts with responsibility for probate, so that there are considerable practical difficulties in obtaining all the inventories for a particular place, even if the indexes are reasonably easy to use, which many are not. If a sample is taken from one of the local diocesan courts alone, it does not cover all the inventoried population, for estates could have been subject to probate in consistory, archdeaconry, or peculiar courts, or the Prerogative Courts of Canterbury or York. Inventories have mainly found their way into the keeping of county record offices, with the result that the records for some dioceses are split between different county archives. In other cases, several counties are to be found in one place, as at Lichfield, where Staffordshire, Derbyshire, and parts of Shropshire are held. Each archive has its own method of storage, search facilities, and indexes of various kinds. Extracting inventories for selected people or places can be a lengthy if not impossible undertaking. A truly random sample is therefore complex and time-consuming to take, even when the kinds of variation in the data are known, which they were not when this study began.

As a result of these practical limitations, and because I was not sure of the kinds of problems I would encounter, I opted for a simplified and unsophisticated quasi-probability sample. There is no obvious bias due to the sample technique in the data, but the extent of the error due to the sample cannot validly be calculated. I have taken samples of the same size (65) from each diocese, regardless of its geographical size or population, from the middle year of each decade from 1675 to 1725. I have selected which dioceses or counties to examine to give a broad geographical coverage, and I did not choose the areas to be examined at random. Details about each diocese are in table 3.2 in the text.[2] In the archive itself I have taken the inventories unseen from the boxes in which they were kept, rejecting those which seemed incomplete or which did not give details of the contents of individual rooms. Scottish inventories are less numerous and less detailed, so I have not been able to include them in the sample.

Another possibility would have been to take a random probability sample from a large diocese with good inventories, perhaps Lichfield, which covers much of the Midlands. This would have given good results for some questions but it would not have satisfied the requirement that the survey should give expression to change at a national level. The most important limitation of the sample is that it does not pretend to be representative of everyone in England, or even of those who might have left an inventory. On the other hand, the aim of this study was not to produce national aggregations but to explore the mechanisms behind patterns of behaviour, so, while a limitation, it does not render the results meaningless.

The selection of 'key' goods

Inventories contain a great deal of detail about individual items, although sometimes they are annoyingly sparse in their listings. It is tempting to try to examine everything, but the amount of information thus generated is overwhelming, so I have not even tried to collect comprehensive data on all furniture and utensils. Instead I have concentrated on a few goods which seem to have been reasonably fully appraised and which were also representative of patterns of behaviour in a more general way, as explained in chapter 1. It is, however, worth pointing to a few problems in making the selection of 'key' goods, and it is especially necessary to comment on the extent to which I feel household goods were deliberately, or accidentally, left out of the inventories.

The question of how often goods were present in a household and were subsequently left out of an inventory is obviously a crucial one in interpreting the results of much of the investigation reported in this book. There is no one answer to this problem, simply because we do not have any evidence at all about what was not there, but only what was actually listed. The possibility that unexpected patterns may be due to different levels of recording has to be remembered. But the important point is that most of the patterns discussed in the text were not due to variations in recording.

It is evident from the wording of some inventories that minimal detail is being given on some items; 'all the linen', for instance, may or may not have included table linen; 'all the pewter' did not distinguish dishes or plates; 'pewter, brass, iron and treen' does not name vessels such as pots which could well have been present. This would not matter for comparative purposes, if the inventories lacking detail were evenly spread throughout time and space, but this was not so, and in some dioceses they were less detailed than in others. In particular, detail was more sparse in the Carlisle, Lancashire, and Staffordshire inventories than elsewhere. This problem only influences a few of the goods (notably table linen, saucepans, pots, pewter dishes, and plates), although some items were so poorly listed that they were not included in the first place.

The other major reason why things were left out is that some goods may have been too small, or of too little value, to be appraised in detail. Many personal items, such as hair combs, were rarely listed. There may have been some doubt about whether personal effects, including even clothing, should be listed at all, for over 10 per cent in inventories do not record clothes, although everyone must have had some items of clothing. More important is the fact that many household utensils were, then as now, part of the clutter of the living area and were sometimes grouped together, so that things of low value could be hidden away and overlooked as 'lumber' or just discounted; this was probably the case with the low-value but extremely common and useful wooden trenchers and plates, which had to be left out of this study entirely because they were erratically listed. The only other such utensil included here is earthenware, which could have a very low value and was probably overlooked on occasions. On the other hand, the patterns of change in ownership of earthen-ware are entirely in keeping with what is known about the growth of production of the industry, so that, even if it were sometimes overlooked, it was included often enough and consistently enough to give meaningful results. Some of the small items, like china or pictures, were relatively new and unusual and probably caught the eye of the people making the inventory; they were therefore less likely to be excluded.

Some things included here were quite large or had a certain value in themselves, so that they were not so likely to be left out by accident. Silver, for instance, was usually quite valuable, and care was taken in listing it; clocks were sometimes the most valuable single item, valued at more than £1. 10s. each. The objective of the main text is to get round the problem of omissions by being aware of the likelihood of problems in coverage and avoiding naïve conclusions. In the last resort there is no way of our knowing for certain if something has been left out, for we are only told about what was put in.

Goods selected

Valuations of these goods are listed in chapter 5, table 5.3.

FURNITURE

This research concentrates on utensils and household goods, so furniture was not noted, except for tables. Beds would make a very meaningful study in themselves.

Tables These were consistently listed and all kinds were noted. Sometimes details are given about sizes, shapes, and the woods used, but this was not frequent enough for the data to be cross-tabulated, so no attempt is made here to trace new types.

COOKING EQUIPMENT

Inventories often list this in great detail, including all the fire tools, jacks, pots, pans, and roasting tools. A few items were selected here to represent different kinds of cookery. Many of the smaller things were not consistently listed in detail. I also noted frying pans, but these were so like pots that I have not included them in the study.

Cooking pots There is internal evidence in three dioceses (Carlisle, Lancashire, and Lichfield) that these were not consistently listed, for they could have been included in entries like 'all the brass' that were common in these areas. They were sometimes singled out, as in 'brass pot and all the other brass and ironware'. I included all kinds of materials, although iron pots were not common; they were usually made of brass. I have included kettles here as well, for these were round vessels like pots at this time, rather than vessels with spouts. Some were very large and of high value.

Saucepans These were rare in the dioceses where metal vessels were not listed separately; elsewhere they seem consistently listed. They were vessels with handles, much as we use now, for small amounts of food, such as sauces. They were least useful over the traditional open fire, and more suited to the enclosed ranges.

EATING EQUIPMENT

Many of the most interesting goods in households were associated with meals and drinking. I would have liked to have had more information on wooden utensils, especially trenchers and bowls, for these were cheap and practical for everyday use. They were often mentioned in accounts and inventories, but are not consistently listed and are not therefore included in the tables.

Pewter This is consistently listed, usually in some detail. This alone shows that it was valued.

Pewter dishes and plates These were selected for comparison, because the plates were associated with new ways of eating and new table layouts. They are not consistently listed, especially in the three dioceses already mentioned. I have left them in the tables for interest and to show the differences between them.

Earthenware This is consistently listed, although it was the kind of low-value item that was easy to overlook or include with other things. Here it includes stoneware (becoming more available from the 1680s), white ware, and delftware. It had many different household and dairy functions, but it is normally listed as just 'earthenware' with little detail; some inventories refer to specific vessels like plates or cups; some list it in the buttery or dairy, separately from earthenware in the house itself. But this kind of detail is not given often enough for any of the distinctions to be used in the tables.

Knives and forks It surprises many people to learn that these were not used as we now use them until the mid-eighteenth century or later (see chapter 7). They seem to have been consistently listed, and listed separately from knives and 'flesh forks' used in cookery. I have included any entries that seemed to be for table use and excluded kitchen equipment.

China Chinaware was imported in large quantities and was made in England until the 1740s. It was lighter in shape and usually white with blue or coloured decoration. It seems to be well recorded because it was new and decorative. Often the vessels are specified in some detail.

Utensils for hot drinks These too seem to have been consistently listed, for they were new and obvious. I have included any references to utensils that could have been used for these drinks, such as teapots, tea kettles, coffee pots, teacups and teaspoons.

DOMESTIC TEXTILES

These are the most difficult kind of item to select because there were many different kinds and they were all poorly listed. Some just list 'all the linen', and this could have included table and bed linen, as well as hangings and curtains. Cushions and upholstered furniture would have been interesting as indicators of comfort, but neither item is well listed; cushions are hardly mentioned after

1690, although they had become more common before then. No solution is satisfactory.

Window curtains These seem to have been consistently listed, possibly because they were appraised *in situ* rather than among other things. I did not include references that might have been to bed curtains.

Table linen This is the least satisfactory of all the selected goods. It includes any references to napkins or tablecloths or towels. Some inventories give immense detail, others obviously include table linen with all the linen together, but in these cases I have not included it, for I do not wish to include this kind of assumption in the data.

OTHER HOUSEHOLD GOODS

The other goods were included because they were representative of behaviour and because they were consistently listed. Other things of considerable interest were also too infrequently owned for it to be useful to tabulate their ownership, notably musical instruments and ornaments (images).

Looking glasses All kinds from small to large are included. They were well listed.

Pictures All pictures and prints are included. They seem well listed. Detail is rare, but where a title is given they are normally landscapes or portraits.

Books These too seem consistent. I have not included Bibles in the cross-tabulations, although these were only recorded in a small proportion of inventories (5 per cent). The titles are almost never given, and in some places they are listed with clothing.

Clocks These seem fully appraised; they were harder to overlook than many things because of their high value. Details are rarely given.

Silver I have included all silver utensils and oddments, as well as a few references to gold and jewellery. There is a very wide variation, from a few silver spoons to substantial holdings of vessels.

Appendix 2

OCCUPATIONS AND STATUS IN INVENTORIES

Inventories and other probate papers often give good information about occupations, because these are either directly stated or can be deduced from the contents of the inventory or will. They form the basis for much of the discussion in the text of the influence of social rank on behaviour and possessions. Individual occupations and other designations that occurred in the inventory sample are listed in table A2.1, including occupations that were unstated and could not be deduced. The listing also has some outline information about the inventories found. The rest of this appendix outlines three ways in which the occupations have been grouped, to emphasize different social and economic functions.

Three ways of grouping occupations

Identification of social and occupational groups is essential in order to be able to discuss relationships between social and consumer behaviour. The well-known distinctions based on such contemporary opinion as Gregory King can be misleading in many ways, not least because they give a dangerously explicit way of defining the social order. They are also based on a mixture of occupations and status designations, rather than one set of criteria. It is necessary to look at the middle ranks in more than one way, in order to take specific account of different economic sectors and parts of the social hierarchy. The occupations given in the inventories provide a basis for this, and it is possible to group them in three ways, which are discussed here and used in the text, especially in chapter 8. The first takes account of the social hierarchy; the second classifies according to the definitions that

Table A2.1   *Occupations and status in the sample of inventories*

1	2	3	Occupation or status	No. in sample	No. of women	No. in rural areas	Mean value Whole inventory £	Household goods £
4b	4	5	anchor smith	1	0	0	23	19
7a	5	2	apothecary	4	0	1	93	52
6a	5	3	badger	1	0	1	66	17
4g	5	5	baker	10	0	3	147	29
6c	5	3	barber	11	1	2	121	32
7a	1	2	barber-surgeon; surgeon; bone-setter	6	0	3	322	37
4h	4	5	basketmaker; corve maker	2	0	1	53	24
4b	4	5	blacksmith	49	1	37	56	15
4b	4	5	brazier, kettleman; mettleman	3	0	1	69	8
4g	4	3	brewer, distiller	6	1	3	92	25
3	4	5	bricklayer	9	0	4	40	16
2	4	5	brickmaker	3	0	1	223	37
6a	5	5	butcher	37	0	22	129	24
3	4	5	carpenter	32	1	28	70	18
5	5	5	carrier	4	0	2	206	36
5	5	5	carter	3	1	3	232	51
4d	4	5	chair-maker; cabinet-maker	1	0	0	432	9
4h	5	3	chandler	8	3	2	95	19
6a	5	3	chapman	7	0	7	295	30
7a	5	2	chemist	1	0	1	165	43
7b	1	2	clergyman	14	0	11	182	60
7b	1	2	clerk	10	0	9	266	40
4e	4	3	cloth finisher	3	0	1	289	58
6a	5	3	clothier	16	0	11	404	34
4e	4	3	clothworker; clothmaker	20	0	17	120	23
4a	4	5	coller-maker	2	0	2	62	17
2	4	5	collier	6	0	6	106	19
4d	4	5	cooper	9	0	5	89	18
4a	4	5	cutler	1	0	0	69	32
6c	5	3	dealer in rags	1	0	0	7	6
7a	1	2	doctor of physic	4	0	3	84	42
6a	5	2	draper	12	1	2	274	34
4e	4	3	dyer	2	0	1	75	15
1	2	4	farmer: inv. valued over £60	392	45	373	169	23
1	3	6	farmer: inv. valued under £60	256	43	245	31	8
4c	5	3	fellmonger	4	0	2	146	54
4e	4	5	feltmaker	3	0	2	104	21
1	4	5	fisherman	11	0	8	129	28
4e	4	5	flax dresser	1	0	1	76	7
4e	5	3	flaxman	3	0	2	210	22
4b	4	3	founder	1	0	0	1,603	36
1	5	5	gardener	7	0	3	37	15

1 2 3					Mean value	
	Occupation or status	No. in sample	No. of women	No. in rural areas	Whole inventory £	Household goods £
8 1 1	gent	92	2	56	361	56
4h 4 5	girdler	1	0	0	18	13
3 4 5	glazier	3	0	1	279	37
4f 4 5	glover	7	0	3	32	10
7b 1 2	goaler	1	0	1	104	73
6 4 2	goldsmith	1	0	0	825	76
1 2 4	grazier	1	0	1	771	104
6a 5 2	grocer	13	2	7	111	19
4a 4 5	gunner	1	0	0	135	32
4f 4 5	hatter	4	3	1	85	17
5 5 5	hoyman	2	0	0	625	82
1 3 6	husbandman stated	76	0	75	34	9
6b 5 3	innkeeper; innholder	24	1	13	138	44
6a 5 2	ironmonger; iron dealer	8	1	2	382	61
4b 4 5	ironworker	3	0	3	111	21
3 4 3	joiner	4	0	1	48	20
8 6 7	labourer; servant	26	0	22	15	5
8 6 7	laundress	1	1	0	7	7
6a 5 3	leather dealer; leather seller	3	0	2	229	27
3 4 5	locksmith	2	0	0	428	28
4g 5 3	maltster	16	1	11	189	24
6d 5 2	mariner	40	2	7	85	30
3 4 3	mason	13	0	10	60	14
7b 1 2	master of attendance at dockyard	1	0	0	1,043	162
6a 5 2	mercer	9	0	7	341	35
6d 5 2	merchant	16	0	0	223	46
7a 5 5	midwife	1	1	0	104	63
4g 4 5	miller	15	0	12	138	22
4a 4 3	millwright	1	0	1	82	35
8 1 1	Mr; Mrs; esq.	30	7	18	194	53
4b 4 5	nailer	2	0	2	47	19
8 8 10	occupation unknown: value of inv. under £15	104	15	57	8	6
8 8 10	occupation unknown: value of inv. £16 to £80	111	24	57	46	14
8 8 10	occupation unknown: value of inv. over £81	49	10	20	210	49
4h 4 9	occupation unknown: craft	14	0	7	116	28
6a 5 9	occupation unknown: dealer	3	2	1	290	53
8 8 9	occupation unknown: trade	38	6	21	102	31
4b 4 3	pewterer	3	0	0	54	10
4h 4 3	potter	2	0	1	19	13
4h 4 3	printer	1	1	0	356	98
4e 4 5	ropemaker	6	1	1	149	13
4a 4 5	saddler; whittaver	4	0	0	192	45

Table A2.1   *Continued*

1 2 3						Mean value	
		Occupation or status	No. in sample	No. of women	No. in rural areas	Whole inventory £	Household goods £
2 4 2		salt-maker	3	0	0	339	53
7b 1 2		schoolmaster	1	0	0	34	9
7b 1 2		scrivener	1	0	1	206	27
5 5 5		seaman; waterman; trowman	13	0	8	77	13
4b 4 5		shearman	2	0	1	46	17
1 6 7		shepherd	1	0	1	29	11
5 5 2		ship's master	2	0	0	29	28
4a 4 3		shipwright; boatwright	12	0	1	109	31
4f 4 5		shoemaker; cordwainer	45	0	24	63	17
6c 5 3		shopkeeper: general	67	20	27	133	32
6c 5 3		shopkeeper: specialized	20	3	1	92	21
4e 4 5		silk thowster	2	1	0	116	48
4e 4 5		silk weaver	3	0	0	36	18
4c 5 2		skinner; currier	3	0	2	33	13
3 4 5		slater	3	0	1	30	16
8 7 8		spinster: no occupation	30	30	26	56	8
6 5 2		stationer; bookseller	1	0	0	82	36
4f 4 5		stocking maker	1	0	0	38	18
4f 4 5		tailor	32	0	20	56	16
4h 5 3		tallow chandler	1	0	0	133	60
4c 4 3		tanner	12	0	6	146	21
3 4 5		thatcher	3	0	3	51	5
5 5 5		tidesman	1	0	0	41	38
3 4 5		tilemaker	2	0	2	219	34
4d 5 3		timber dealer; woodmonger	2	0	0	668	26
4b 4 5		tin-plate worker	1	0	0	81	56
4h 4 9		toynt-maker	1	0	1	68	17
4h 4 3		upholsterer	1	0	0	218	40
6b 5 3		victualler	77	8	12	155	43
6b 5 2		vintner	1	0	0	39	20
4h 4 3		watchmaker; clockmaker	2	0	1	194	18
4e 4 5		weaver	45	0	30	88	12
4e 4 5		webster	11	0	11	52	15
4a 4 5		wheelwright	9	0	8	86	20
4b 4 5		whitesmith	1	0	0	36	22
8 7 8		widow: no occupation	187	187	102	86	20
4d 4 5		woodworker; carver; turner	16	0	8	98	22
1 2 4		Yeoman, stated: no trade	559	3	530	162	23
		Totals	2,902	430	2,075	128	24

Notes
1 Column 1 is the economic sector into which each occupation was put; see table A2.4 for the details and codes.
2 Column 2 represents the general groups into which each occupation was put; see table A2.3 for the details and codes.
3 Column 3 is the social status into which each was put; see table A2.2 for the details and codes.

Table A2.2   *Some characteristics of inventories in ten social-status groups*

Social status	No. of inventories			Total value of inventory		Value of household goods	
	All	Women	Rural	Mean £	Median £	Mean £	Median £
1 Gentry	122	9	74	320	154	55	38
2 Trades of high status; clergy; professionals	152	7	57	193	79	39	27
3 Trades of intermediate status	344	39	137	157	85	32	33
4 Yeomen; large farmers	952	48	904	165	104	23	17
5 Trades of low status	435	9	268	92	45	19	14
6 Husbandmen; small farmers	332	43	320	32	30	8	7
7 Labourers	28	1	23	16	13	5	5
8 Widows; spinsters	217	217	128	82	30	18	13
9 Tradesman: trades unknown	56	8	30	115	60	31	21
10 Occupation or status unknown	264	49	134	62	20	17	9

Notes and sources
See text and chapter 8 for discussion. The criteria are based on the work of V. Brodsky Elliott, 'Mobility and marriage in pre-industrial England', Cambridge University PhD thesis (1978), pp. 1–149.
The trades and occupations in each group are shown in table A2.1.

are often used by historians, based on contemporary perceptions; the third groups occupations according to economic sector.

SOCIAL STATUS

The groups listed in table A2.2, and analysed in the text, are based on the results of research done by Dr Vivien Brodsky Elliott, in which she ordered about fifty occupations and status designations according to the observed trade to which sons were apprenticed and according to the occupations and status of marriage partners. I have used her results, as well as other commentary about status, to place the occupations of the inventoried population into groupings which give an indication of status. The table shows seven groups, ranging from those of gentry status to labourers, together with three others which could not be positioned in the hierarchy because there was too little information about them. In effect this places the trades alongside

Table A2.3   *Some characteristics of inventories in eight general occupational groups*

| Occupation or status | No. of inventories | | | Total value of inventory | | Value of household goods | |
	All	Women	Rural	Mean £	Median £	Mean £	Median £
1 Gentry; pro-fessional; clergy	160	9	102	300	148	54	37
2 Yeomen; large farmers	952	48	904	165	104	23	17
3 Husbandmen; small farmers	332	43	320	32	30	8	7
4 Tradesmen: crafts	459	9	278	96	45	19	14
5 Tradesmen: dealers	452	48	165	162	80	33	24
6 Labourers	28	1	23	16	13	5	5
7 Widows; spinsters	217	217	128	82	30	18	13
8 Unknown	302	55	155	67	23	19	10

Notes and sources
See text and chapter 8 for discussion. The criteria are those commonly used by historians. See D. Cressy, 'Describing the social order of Elizabethan and Stuart England', *Literature and History*, 3 (1976), 29–44; K. Wrightson, *English Society*, (London, 1982), pp. 17–38; P. Corfield, *The Impact of English Towns* (Oxford, 1982), pp. 124–45. The trades and occupations in each group are shown in table A2.1.

the well-known groups of gentry, yeomen, husbandmen, and labourers. The groups are not inflexible, and Dr Elliott's research points towards a great deal of diversity, as we would expect in a complex society. The advantage of this method of grouping is that it allows us to examine the impact of social status *per se* on behaviour.

GENERAL CRITERIA

The most obvious and easiest way of classifying the occupations recorded in inventories is to use the distinctions made in King's tables, in combination with the terminology of the inventories themselves. This produces a listing, as in table A2.3, basically similar to that used by historians in analysing various aspects of social and economic life in this period, and it relies on the distinctions between gentry, yeomen, and husbandmen. It is, however, unsatisfactory for many purposes, since it refers to neither occupation nor status. It is retained because it is a common way of presenting the social order of pre-industrial England. The table shows eight groups, some of which are the same as in the first table. The difference lies in the treatment of the trades and professions: the small number of professional and

Table A2.4 *Some characteristics of inventories in different economic sectors*

Economic sector	No. of inventories			Total value of inventory		Value of household goods	
	All	*Women*	*Rural*	*Mean £*	*Median £*	*Mean £*	*Median £*
1 Primary sector: agriculture; fishery	1,303	91	1,236	130	78	131	13
2 Primary sector: mining	12	0	7	193	94	32	25
3 Building sector	71	1	50	84	38	18	13
4 Manufacturing sector	411	12	236	101	51	20	15
5 Transport sector	25	1	13	155	58	29	19
6 Dealing sector	368	41	124	166	78	34	25
7 Public and pro-fessional	44	2	30	216	104	50	36
8 Others	668	282	379	116	32	25	14

Notes and sources
See text and chapter 8 for discussion. The criteria are based on W.A. Armstrong, 'The use of information about occupation', in E.A. Wrigley (ed.), *Nineteenth-Century Society* (Cambridge, 1972), pp. 191–310, especially part 2, pp. 226–310, which deals with an industrial classification; see also A.J. and R.H. Tawney, 'An occupational census of the seventeenth century', *Economic History Revue*, 5 (1934), 25–64. The trades and occupations in each group are shown in table A2.1

clergy inventories are included with the gentry; the trades are roughly divided in two, distinguishing those who made things and those who dealt.

ECONOMIC SECTOR

The occupations can also be grouped according to the economic sector into which they fell, as in table A2.4. This too poses problems, especially if attempts are made to use the divisions suggested by the Tawneys, for their divisions again mix economic and social criteria. I therefore used the headings given in Armstrong's account of Booth's classification based on the occupations stated in censuses. Although these were devised for nineteenth-century conditions, many of the distinctions (and even many of the trades) can be seen in the late seventeenth century, and I felt it was instructive to apply them to the inventory data. The main practical problem here is that some sectors contain very few inventories, while nearly a half of them fall into the primary sector. The section of 'Others' is also rather large and contains a very disparate grouping. But this approach is not without its use in showing the influence of occupation on the ownership of goods.

NOTES

Note: Where full details are not given, short titles refer to works listed in the Bibliography.

1 Introduction

1 Josiah Wedgwood to Thomas Bentley, 23 August 1772 in *The Selected Letters of Josiah Wedgwood*, ed. Ann Finer and G. Savage (London, 1965), p. 131.
2 The most accessible text on consumer behaviour, which acknowledges economic, social, and psychological approaches, is G.R. Foxall, *Consumer Behaviour: A Practical Guide* (London, 1980); a comprehensive text is J.F. Engel, D.T. Kollat, and R.D. Blackwell, *Consumer Behaviour* (London, 1968).
3 Probate inventories have been used by historians in many ways, and there are several editions of collections from different parts of the country; those used in this study are listed in the 'Bibliography of contemporary sources'. For a full bibliography, see M. Overton, *A Bibliography of British Probate Inventories* (Geography Department, University of Newcastle upon Tyne, 1983). The law covering probate in Scotland means that full listings of goods are rare, although a few have survived.
4 City of London Record Office. The inventories of the Court of Orphans of the City of London were similar to inventories made for probate. The court assessed the estate and determined how it was to be administered on behalf of the child or children. This small sample represents a wealthy group of consumers not covered by the main sample.
5 See studies reported in 'Probate inventories: a new source for the historical study of wealth, material culture and agricultural development, papers presented at the Leeuwenborch Conference, 1980' in *A.A. Bijdragen*, 23 (1980). Students of colonial North America have made fuller use of them, partly because they were kept there in greater detail. See, for example, Gloria Main, *Tobacco Colony: Life in Early Maryland, 1650–1720* (Princeton,

NJ, 1982). The most helpful introductions to printed editions are in Trinder and Cox, *Telford*, and Vaisey, *Lichfield Inventories*. Other editions are listed in the Bibliography.

6 The sample is not formally statistically representative of the whole of England, since the areas sampled were chosen for practical convenience, not at random. See appendix 1 for full details of the sample.

7 Diaries have been utilized by many historians, especially of family life; see note 2 to chapter 5. I have tried to be as comprehensive as possible in choosing those written by people below the gentry in rank. Those used, and household manual and accounts, are listed in the Bibliography.

8 Van Aken was one of several Flemish artists who visited, or lived in, Britain. He came to England before 1720 and painted draperies for portrait painters and a few scenes of interiors. There are several little-known artists who are not well documented; I have become aware of their work through the Witt Collection of photographs in the Courtauld Institute of the University of London. There is an outline of his career in R. Edwards, 'The conversation pictures of Joseph Van Aken', *Apollo*, 132 (February 1936), 79–85. D. MacMillan, 'Scottish painting 1500–1700', documents Jacob de Witte and Sir John Medina, who both settled in Scotland. See also R.H. Wilenski, *Flemish Painters, 1430–1830* (London, 1960), which gives an account of the careers of Flemish painters who visited London. There are reasons for not using the Dutch and Flemish interiors for detailed analysis, although they are a useful way of seeing into households in these countries. Many of the conventions about furniture, the shapes of the fireplaces, and other details are known to have been different here, so it does not seem appropriate to use them on any scale. See W. Bernt, *The Netherlandish Painters of the Seventeenth Century*, 3 vols (London, 1970); P.C. Sutton (organizer), *Masters of Seventeenth-Century Dutch Genre Painting: Exhibition Catalogue* (Royal Academy of Arts and Philadelphia Museum of Art, 1984).

9 This kind of approach to material goods is particularly well expressed in a study of modern consumer behaviour, Mary Douglas and B. Isherwood, *The World of Goods: Towards an Anthropology of Consumption* (Harmondsworth, 1980).

10 Full references are in chapter 5 notes 3 and 4.

11 There is an overwhelming literature on individual buildings; see R. de Zouche Hall (ed.), *A Bibliography on Vernacular Architecture* (Newton Abbot, 1972). Only those that I have found most helpful are noted here: E. Mercer, *English Vernacular Houses: A Study of Traditional Farmhouses and Cottages*, Royal Commission on Historical Monuments in England (London, 1975); J.T. Smith, 'The evolution of the English peasant house to the late seventeenth century: the evidence of buildings', *Journal of the British Arch. Assoc.*, 3rd series, 33 (1970), 122–47; Linda J. Hall, *The Rural Houses of North Avon and South Gloucestershire, 1400–1720*, City of Bristol Museum and Art Gallery (Bristol, 1983), a useful and well-documented account; A. Dyer, 'Urban housing: a documentary study of four Midland towns, 1530–1700', *Post-Medieval Arch.*, 15 (1981), 207–18; D.H. Richards, 'The chimney', *Journal of the British Arch. Assoc.*, 3rd series, 24

(1961), 67–79; A. Fenton, *The Hearth in Scotland*, National Museum of Antiquities (Edinburgh, 1981). There are many references to individual houses in the annual listings of sites in *Post-Medieval Arch.*, and several longer accounts, such as R. Taylor, 'Town houses in Taunton, 1500–1700', *Post-Medieval Arch.*, 8 (1974), 63–79; A.F. Kelsall, 'The London house plan in the later seventeenth century', *Post-Medieval Arch.*, 8 (1974), 80–91; P. Crummy and R.H. Moyes, 'Portreeves House, Colchester, and a method of modernizing Essex houses in the sixteenth and seventeenth centuries', *Post-Medieval Arch.*, 10 (1976), 89–103. The small size of houses in East London is examined in M.J. Power, 'East London housing in the seventeenth century', in P. Clark and P. Slack (eds), *Crisis and Order in English Towns, 1500–1700* (London, 1972), pp. 237–62. Open-air museums give evocations of the buildings and are highly recommended, especially the one in West Sussex; see F.G. Aldsworth and R. Harris, 'A medieval and seventeenth-century house at Walderton, West Sussex, dismantled and re-erected at the Weald and Downland Open-Air Musuem', *Sussex Arch. Coll.*, 120 (1982) 45–92.

12 Evidence for this is drawn from inventories. There are many published series, and those used in this book are listed in the Bibliography. Details of room use and house size were not collected in the main sample of inventories because such detail was not given often enough to be used in a comprehensive way. Only 57 per cent of the inventories from Telford give information on rooms; see Trinder and Cox, *Telford*. A good impression of urban houses is outlined in Vaisey, *Lichfield Inventories*. For a very useful summary of room use in an advanced urban area, see Ursula Priestley and Penelope Corfield, 'Rooms and room use in Norwich housing, 1580–1730', *Post-Medieval Arch.*, 16 (1982), 93–123.

13 Linda J. Hall, op. cit.

14 These generalizations are based on the published collections of inventories, as well as on the main sample. Instances of 'one up and one down' houses are not numerous, but see Trinder and Cox, *Telford*, p. 396.

15 M. Daunton, *House and Home in the Victorian City: Working-Class Housing, 1850–1914* (London, 1983). For ideas of this kind, see A. Rapoport, *The Meaning of the Built Environment: A Nonverbal Communication Approach* (London and Beverly Hills, California, 1982) and *The Mutual Interaction of People and their Built Environment* (The Hague, 1976); see also E. Leach, *Social Anthropology* (London, 1982), and N.W. Jerome, R.F. Kandel, and Gretel H. Pelto (eds), *Nutritional Anthropology: Contemporary Diet and Culture* (New York, 1980).

16 I have used the ideas and vocabulary in E. Goffman, *The Presentation of Self in Everyday Life* (Harmondsworth, 1969; first published in the USA in 1959); Alice W. Portnoy, 'A micro-archaeological view of human settlement space and functions', in R.A. Gould and M.B. Schiffer (eds), *Modern Material Culture: The Archaeology of Us* (London and New York, 1981), which also contains other articles on this problem.

17 The vocabulary of 'front' and 'back' is rather uncomfortable, but it does convey the impression of self-presentation. The terms 'private' and 'public' do not convey the same kinds of behaviour.

18 The generalizations about room use are based on the sample of inventories and the published collections listed in the Bibliography. See also Priestley and Corfield, op. cit.

19 Trinder and Cox, *Telford*, p. 409. The total value of the inventory was £64. 13s. 4d., £44 of which was money on bond, and the rest was household goods.

20 Robertson, *Rural Recollections*, pp. 72–3; see also the discussion of Scotland in chapter 8 below.

21 Robertson, *Rural Recollections*, pp. 74–5.

22 John Webster of Doncaster, 14 January 1674/5, in Brears, *Yorkshire Inventories*, p. 141.

23 Edward Sackley of Rochester, Kent, 'saylesman', 1 September 1717, in Margaret Spufford, *The Great Reclothing of Rural England: Petty Chapmen and their Wares in the Seventeenth Century* (London, 1984), p. 222.

24 James Spender of Lilleshall, Shropshire, yeoman, 21 July 1748, in Trinder and Cox, *Telford*, pp. 246–7.

25 See notes 5 and 6 to chapter 8. Full details of assumptions about social position used in this book are outlined in appendix 2.

26 Daniel Defoe, *Robinson Crusoe* (1719).

27 These concepts are most fully discussed in D.E.C. Eversley, *Social Theories of Fertility and the Malthusian Debate* (Oxford, 1959); Joyce Appleby, 'Ideology and theory: the tension between political and economic liberalism in seventeenth-century England', *American Historical Review*, 81 (1976), 499–515; Douglas and Isherwood, op. cit.

28 Eversley, op. cit., p. 23.

29 Adam Ferguson, *An Essay on the History of Civil Society* (1767), 4th edn (London, 1773), pt vi, sect. 2, p. 375; quoted in Eversley, op. cit., p. 24.

30 Douglas and Isherwood, op. cit., pp. 112 and 118; F. Braudel, *Capitalism and Material Life, 1400–1800* (London, 1974).

31 Porter conveys this with great verve, but also a sensitivity to the contrasts between 'haves' and 'have-nots', in R. Porter, *English Society in the Eighteenth Century*, Pelican Social History of Britain (Harmondsworth, 1982), pp. 232–68; this is also the main theme in N. McKendrick, J. Brewer, and J.H. Plumb, *Birth of a Consumer Society: The Commercialization of Eighteenth-Century England* (London, 1982); on the other hand, the role of wage-earners and out-workers is examined in Mazine Berg, *The Age of Manufactures, 1700–1820* (London, 1985), pp. 169–75.

32 Studies of the industrial revolution, or of the economy in the eighteenth century, have some comment on the home market, but see, in particular, M.W. Flinn, *The Origins of the Industrial Revolution* (London, 1966); A. Thomson, *The Dynamics on the Industrial Revolution* (London, 1973); T.S. Ashton, *An Economic History of England in the Eighteenth Century* (Oxford, 1955); Phyllis Deane and W.A. Cole, *British Economic Growth, 1688–1959* (Cambridge, 1969). For the home market in particular, see D.E.C. Eversley, 'The home demand and economic growth in England, 1750–80', in E.L. Jones and G.E. Mingay (eds), *Land, Labour and Population in the Industrial Revolution* (London, 1967), pp. 206–59; Elizabeth Gilboy, 'Demand as a factor in the industrial revolution' reprinted in

R.M. Hartwell (ed.), *The Causes of the Industrial Revolution* (London, 1967), pp. 121–38; N. McKendrick, 'Home demand and economic growth: a new view of the role of women and children in the industrial revolution', in N. McKendrick (ed.), *Historical Perspectives: Studies in English Thought and Society in Honour of J.H. Plumb* (London, 1974), pp. 152–210. There is a recent summary in W.A. Cole, 'Factors in demand, 1700–1780', in R. Floud and D. McCloskey (eds), *The Economic History of Britain since 1700* (Cambridge, 1981), pp. 36–65; C.G.A. Clay, *Economic Expansion and Social Change: England 1500–1700*, vol. 2 (Cambridge, 1984), pp. 22–43; Berg, op. cit. For the role of overseas trade, see R. Davis, *The Industrial Revolution and British Overseas Trade* (Leicester, 1979), especially ch. 5.

33 B.A. Holderness, *Pre-Industrial England: Economy and Society from 1500–1750* (London, 1976); L.A. Clarkson, *The Pre-Industrial Economy of England, 1500–1750* (London, 1971); D.C. Coleman, *The Economy of England, 1450–1750* (Oxford, 1977); Joan Thirsk, *Economic Policy and Projects: The Development of a Consumer Society in Early Modern England* (Oxford, 1978); P. Earle, 'The economics of stability: the views of Daniel Defoe', in D.C. Coleman and A.H. John (eds), *Trade, Government and Economy in Pre-Industrial England: Essays Presented to F.J. Fisher* (London, 1976).

34 Gilboy, op. cit., pp. 121–2.

35 Cole, op. cit., p. 45.

36 McKendrick, op. cit.; J. Mokyr, 'Demand versus supply in the industrial revolution', *Journal of Economic History*, 37 (1977), 981–1008.

37 There are studies of many major firms and industries. See note 3 to chapter 2.

38 D.C. Coleman, *Courtaulds: An Economic and Social History*, vol. 1, (Oxford, 1969), pp. 10–23. There is half a page on consumer behaviour and the market.

39 Joan Thirsk, op. cit.; Margaret Spufford, op. cit.

40 Deane and Cole, op. cit., p. 78. Cole's more recent estimates have not modified the narrow range of series used; see W.A. Cole, 'Eighteenth-century economic growth revisited', *Explorations in Economic History*, 2nd series, 10 (1973), 327–48.

41 There are studies of many major industries. See note 3 to chapter 2.

42 P. Mathias, *The Brewing Industry in England, 1700–1830* (Cambridge, 1959); P. Clark, *The English Alehouse: A Social History, 1200–1830* (London, 1983).

43 A.H. John, 'Agricultural productivity and economic growth in England, 1700–1760', *Journal of Economic History*, 25 (1965), 19–34; M.W. Flinn, 'Agricultural productivity and economic growth in England, 1700–1760: a comment', *Journal of Economic History*, 26 (1966), 93–8; J.D. Gould, 'Agricultural fluctuation and the English economy in the eighteenth century', *Journal of Economic History*, 22 (1962), 313–33; Eversley, 'The home demand and economic growth in England, 1750–80'.

44 H. Phelps Brown and Sheila V. Hopkins, 'Seven centuries of the price of consumables, compared with builders' wage-rates', in H. Phelps Brown

and Sheila V. Hopkins (eds), *A Perspective on Wages and Prices* (London, 1981), pp. 13–59 (first published in *Economica* in 1956). This is a *tour de force* stressing the long-term continuities in expenditure patterns for wage-earners. It displays a due sensitivity to the limited evidence about actual expenditure patterns, but, in weighting the price of bread, meat, clothing, and so forth, it is making assumptions, sometimes 'in the half light of general knowledge' (as the authors put it), about the behaviour of some consumers (i.e. wage-earners) over long periods.

45 D. Woodward, 'Wage-rates and living standards in pre-industrial England', *Past and Present*, 91 (1981), 28–45.

46 N.B. Harte, 'State control of dress and social change in pre-industrial England', in Coleman and John (eds), op. cit.

47 J.J. Hecht, *The Domestic Servant in Eighteenth-Century England* (1956; London, 1980), pp. 200–28; Braudel, op. cit.; McKendrick, Brewer, and Plumb, *op. cit.;* H.J. Perkin, 'The social causes of the British industrial revololution', *Trans. of the Royal Historical Society*, 18 (1968), 123–43; J. de Vries, 'Peasant demand patterns and economic development in Friesland, 1550–1750', in W.N. Parker and E.L. Jones (eds), *European Peasants and their Markets* (Princeton, NJ, 1975), pp. 205–68; W.E. Minchinton, 'Convention, fashion and consumption: aspects of British experience since 1750', in H. Baudet and M. Bogucka (eds), *Types of Consumption, Traditional and Modern*, Eighth International Economic History Congress publication (Budapest, 1982). It finds its way into other kinds of problems, even the influence of towns on consumer life; see P. Borsay, 'The English urban renaissance: the development of provincial urban culture, 1680–1760', *Social History*, 5 (1977), 581–603.

48 See, for instance, encyclopedias and guides for collectors, such as G.A. Godden, *An Illustrated Encyclopedia of British Pottery and Porcelain* (London, 1965); R. Edwards, *The Shorter Dictionary of English Furniture* (London, 1964).

49 Such as *Post-Medieval Archaeology* and *English Ceramic Circle Transactions*.

50 Such as *Furniture History* and *Textile History*.

51 One way in which this can be done is by meetings at which scholars from different disciplines participate, such as that organized by the Pasold Research Fund in September 1985 on the social and economic history of dress in the early modern period. Here the curators of museum collections, designers, and historians met and discussed the history of textiles and clothing. Sometimes an individual study bridges the gap; see Patricia Kirkham, 'Furniture making in London, *c.* 1700–1870', PhD thesis (London, 1982).

52 P. Thornton, *Seventeenth-Century Interior Decoration in England, France and Holland* (London, 1978); J. Fowler and J. Cornforth, *English Decoration in the Eighteenth Century* (London, 1974); B. Denvir (ed.), *The Eighteenth Century: Art, Design and Society, 1689–1789* (London, 1983). Doll's house interiors are oddly evocative; see Constance King, *The Collector's History of Doll's Houses* (London, 1983).

53 Spufford, op. cit.

54 Lorna Weatherill, *The Growth of the Pottery Industry in England, 1660–1815* (New York, 1986).

2 Growth

1 Daniel Defoe, *A Tour Through the Whole Island of Great Britain*, Everyman edn (London, 1962), p. 1.
2 Phyllis Deane and W.A. Cole, *British Economic Growth, 1688–1959* (Cambridge, 1969), p. 78. Recent discussion derived from their work recognizes this as a problem and seeks to examine a wider range of industries; see NFR Crafts, 'British economic growth, 1700–1831: a review of the evidence', *Economic History Review*, 36 (1983), 179–81. The focus of these works is the course of economic growth in the eighteenth century and the industrial revolution; they are less concerned with the early eighteenth century in its own right and with the mechanisms of demand.
3 The generalizations in this chapter are based on specific series, as well as general surveys: B. Mitchell and Phyllis Deane, *Abstract of British Historical Statistics* (Oxford, 1962); Elizabeth B. Schumpeter, *English Overseas Trade Statistics* (Oxford, 1960); K.N. Chaudhuri, *The Trading World of Asia and the East India Company, 1660–1760* (Cambridge, 1978), pp. 519–20; T.S. Ashton, *Economic Fluctuations in England, 1700–1800* (Oxford, 1959); Phyllis Deane and W.A. Cole, *British Economic Growth, 1688–1959* (Cambridge, 1969); W.R. Scott, *The Constitution and Finance of English, Scottish and Irish Joint Stock Companies to 1720* (Cambridge, 1912); D.W. Jones, 'The "hallage" receipts of the London cloth markets, 1562–1720', *Economic History Review*, 25 (1972), 567–87; Lorna Weatherill, 'The growth of the pottery industry in England, 1660–1815', *Post-Med. Arch.*, 17 (1983), 38–9; J. Hatcher and T.C. Barker, *A History of British Pewter*, (London, 1974), pp. 272, 279, 294; R. Burt, 'Lead production in England and Wales, 1700–1770' *Economic History Review*, 22 (1969), 257; S.R.H. Jones, 'The development of needle manufacturing in the West Midlands before 1750', *Economic History Review*, 31 (1978), 354–68; M. Overton, 'Estimating crop yields from probate inventories: an example from East Anglia, 1585–1735', *Journal of Economic History*, 39 (1979), 363–78.
4 For the higher-quality interiors, see P. Thornton, *Seventeenth-Century Interior Decoration in England, France and Holland* (London 1978); J. Fowler and J. Cornforth, *English Decoration in the Eighteenth Century* (London 1974); S.V. Smith (ed.), *Polite Society by Arthur Devis, 1712–1787: Catalogue of the Exhibition*, Harris Museum and Art Gallery (Preston, 1983); Constance King, *The Collector's History of Doll's Houses* (London 1983). None of these really conveys the atmosphere of middle-ranking homes. Spufford had shown how difficult it is to find surviving clothing from these social ranks for the seventeenth century and found very few examples in the costume collections in English and Scottish museums; see Margaret

Spufford, *The Great Reclothing of Rural England: Petty Chapmen and their Wares in the Seventeenth Century* (London, 1984), pp. 130–41.

5 Patricia Kirkham, 'Furniture making in London, *c.* 1700–1870', PhD thesis (London, 1982), especially pp. 19–37.

6 Trinder and Cox, *Telford*, p. 203, Thomas Newell of Lilleshall, 3 January 1676/7. The value of the estate was £91. 2s.

7 Lichfield JRO, Joshua Astbury of Shelton, potter 1721/2. The value of the estate was £435.6s.

8 Lichfield JRO, Thomas Heath of Shelton, potter, 1742. The value of the estate was £102. 13s.

9 Mr Mortimer, *The Universal Director* (London, 1763), lists several pages of them.

3 Contrasting localities

1 J. Langton, 'The industrial revolution and the regional geography of England', *Trans. Inst. Brit. Georgr.*, n.s., 9(1984), 145–67; the quotation is from p.165.

2 For this reason it was not possible to take one area as being representative of likely developments in the country as a whole, although in-depth studies of single communities can be immensely valuable for some purposes.

3 A. Everitt, 'Country, county and town: patterns of regional evolution in England', *Trans. of the Roy. Hist. Soc.*, 5th series, 29 (1978), 78–108; D. Grigg, 'Regions, models and classes', in R.J. Chorley and P. Haggett (eds), *Integrated Models in Geography* (London, 1967), pp. 461–510; J.F. Hart, 'The highest form of the geographers' art', *Annals of the Assoc. of American Geographers*, 72 (1982), 1–29; Langton, op. cit.

4 For geographical and agricultural background to all the localities discussed in this chapter, see J.B. Mitchell (ed.), *Great Britain: Geographical Essays* (Cambridge, 1962); L. Dudley Stamp and S.H. Beaver, *The British Isles: A Geographical and Economic Survey*, 5th edn (London, 1963); E. Kerridge, *The Agricultural Revolution* (London, 1967). Joan Thirsk (ed.), *The Agrarian History of England and Wales*, vol. 5, pt 1: *Regional Farming Systems* (Oxford, 1984).

5 The generalizations are based on a number of works: see F.J. Fisher, 'The development of London as a centre of conspicuous consumption in the sixteenth and seventeenth centuries', *Trans. of the Roy. Hist. Soc.*, 4th series, 30 (1948), 37–50; D.V. Glass, 'Socio-economic status and occupations in the City of London at the end of the seventeenth century', in A.E.J. Hollaender and W. Kellaway (eds), *Studies in London History* (London, 1969), pp. 373–92; G. Rudé, *Hanoverian London, 1714–1808* (London, 1971); J. Stevenson, 'London, 1660–1780', unit 13 of English Urban History, 1500–1780, Open University; E.A. Wrigley, 'A simple model of London's importance in changing English society and economy, 1650–1750', *Past and Present*, 37 (1967), 44–70.

6 P.W. Brassley, 'The agricultural economy of Northumberland and Durham

in the period 1640–1750', B. Litt. thesis (Oxford, 1974); Joyce Ellis, 'A dynamic society: social relations in Newcastle-upon-Tyne, 1660–1760', in P. Clark (ed.), *The Transformation of English Provincial Towns, 1600–1800* (London, 1984); P. Brassley, 'Northumberland and Durham', in Thirsk (ed.), op. cit., vol. 5, pp. 30–58.

7 The sample is biased here away from yeomen and farmers because these inventories tended to list all agricultural goods in detail but group all household goods with too little detail to be useful. This may suggest the priorities of yeomen and farmers, but it has meant that many farming inventories had to be excluded.

8 M.G. Jarret and S. Wrathmell, 'Sixteenth and seventeenth-century farmsteads: West Welpington, Northumberland', *Agricultural History Revue*, 25 (1977), 108–19.

9 Richard Pocock, letter to his sister of 8 October 1760, in 'Letters from Pocock on a northern journey, 1760', in 'North country diaries', ed. J.C. Hodgson, *Surtees Society*, 124 (1914), 244; I am very grateful to Keith Wrightson for this reference.

10 B.M. Short, 'The south-east: Kent, Surrey and Sussex', in Thirsk (ed.), op. cit., vol. 5, pp. 270–316; J.H. Andrews, 'The Thanet seaports, 1650–1750', in Margaret Roake and J. Whyman (eds), *Essays in Kentish History* (London, 1973), pp. 118–26; C.W. Chalklin, *Seventeenth-Century Kent* (London, 1965).

11 Chalklin, op. cit., pp. 172–82; Andrews, op. cit.

12 H.C. Darby, *The Changing Fenland* (Cambridge, 1983); B.A. Holderness, 'East Anglia and the Fens', in Thirsk (ed.), op cit., vol. 5, pp. 197–238, especially the map on p. 196.

13 D. Hey, 'Yorkshire and Lancashire', in Thirsk (ed.), op. cit., vol. 5, pp. 59–88; A.P. Wadsworth and Julia de Lacy Mann, *The Cotton Trade and Industrial Lancashire, 1600–1780* (Manchester, 1931).

14 J.R. Wordie, 'The south', in Thirsk (ed.), op. cit., vol. 5, pp. 317–57 (the map on p. 318 is useful); A. Temple Patterson, *A History of Southampton, 1700–1914* (Southampton, 1966).

15 F.W. Holling, 'A preliminary note on the Pottery industry of the Hampshire-Surrey borders', *Surrey Arch. Coll.*, 68 (1971), 57–88.

16 D. Hey, 'The north-west Midlands', in Thirsk (ed.), op. cit., vol. 5, pp. 128–58.

17 Marie Rowlands, *Masters and Men in the West Midland Metal Working Trades* (Manchester, 1975); B.S. Trinder, *The Industrial Revolution in Shropshire* (Chichester, 1973); Lorna Weatherill, *The Pottery Trade and North Staffordshire, 1660–1760* (Manchester, 1971).

18 It is also more fully researched than many other areas as a region: A.B. Appleby, *Famine in Tudor and Stuart England* (Liverpool, 1978); E.J. Evans and J.V. Beckett, 'Cumberland, Westmorland and Furness', in Thirsk (ed.), op. cit., vol. 5, pp. 3–29; J.V. Beckett, 'Landownership in Cumbria, 1680–1750', PhD thesis (Lancaster, 1975); J.V. Beckett, *Coal and Tobacco: The Lowthers and the Economic Development of West Cumberland, 1660–1760* (Cambridge, 1981). J.D. Marshall, 'Agrarian wealth and social structure in pre-industrial Cumbria', *Economic History*

Revue, 33 (1980), 503–21, concentrates on a different part of the area than that covered by the other studies quoted and by the sample of inventories.

19 Appleby, op. cit., pp. 158–68.

20 This is because the law relating to probate was different in Scotland; usually enough assets were listed to cover a person's debts, and detailed listing of household and other goods is rare, although there are a very few scattered through the records. It was not possible in the time available for writing this book to study these in depth, but it would be worthwhile to collect all those that have details in them.

21 J.H.Farrent, 'The seaborne trade of Sussex, 1720–1845', *Sussex Arch. Coll.*, 114 (1976), 97–120.

22 PRO, Excise and Treasury Letterbooks, CUST/48/13, p. 206, dated 17 February 1737/8. I am indebted to John Chartres for these figures.

23 This was a very complex trade, for some of the parts were made in Lancashire and were assembled and put into cases in London.

24 J. Hatcher and T.C. Barker, *A History of British Pewter* (London, 1974); Patricia Kirkham, 'Furniture making in London, *c.* 1700–1870', PhD thesis (London, 1982).

25 J. de Vries, 'Peasant demand patterns and economic development in Friesland, 1550–1750', in W.N. Parker and E.L. Jones (eds), *European Peasants and their Markets* (Princeton, NJ, 1975), pp. 205–68.

26 Warley, 'Accounts', p. 5, at the back. See also the quotation at the head of chapter 6.

27 Misson, *Travels*, under 'Christenings, feasts and weddings'.

28 Burrell, 'Journal'.

29 Marchant, 'Diary'.

30 May, *Newmarket Inventories*, pp. 18–19; the total value of the inventory was £306. 19s. 2d.

31 Ramsey, *Scotland and Scotsmen*, vol. 2, p 82.

32 Mure, 'Observations', p. 64.

33 Somerville, *Own Life and Times*, p. 327.

34 Robertson, *Rural Recollections*, pp. 232–3.

35 Ramsey, *Scotland and Scotsmen*, vol. 2, pp. 73–4.

36 Ramsey, *Scotland and Scotsmen*, vol. 2, p. 67.

37 Somerville, *Own Life and Times*, p. 344.

4   The influence of towns

1 F. Braudel, *Capitalism and Material Life, 1400–1800* (London, 1974), p. 373.

2 M. Daunton, 'Towns and economic growth in eighteenth-century England', in P. Abrams and E.A. Wrigley (eds), *Towns in Societies: Essays in Economic History and Historical Sociology* (Cambridge, 1978), p. 253.

3 The best introductions to urban history are P. Clark and P. Slack, *English Towns in Transition, 1500–1700* (Oxford, 1976), and P.J. Corfield, *The*

Impact of English Towns, 1700–1800 (Oxford, 1982). See also P. Clark *et al*. (eds), 'English urban history, 1500–1780: a course in urban history' (Open University, 1977), for excellent summaries of the many problems in studying early modern towns. For stress on the importance of towns, see Braudel, op. cit., pp. 373–440.

4 F.J. Fisher, 'The development of London as a centre of conspicuous consumption in the sixteenth and seventeenth centuries', *Trans. of the Roy. Hist. Soc.*, 4th series, 30 (1948), 37–50; E.A. Wrigley, 'A simple model of London's importance in changing English society and economy, 1650–1750', *Past and Present*, 37 (1967), 44–70; P. Borsay, 'The English urban renaissance: the development of provincial urban culture, *c*. 1680–1760', *Social History*, 5 (1977), 581–603.

5 Daunton, op. cit., pp. 245–77.

6 Gloria L. Main, *Tobacco Colony: Life in Early Maryland, 1650–1720* (Princeton, NJ, 1982), pp. 42–3; C.V. Earle, 'The evolution of a tidewater settlement system: All Hallow's Parish, Maryland, 1650–1783' (University of Chicago, Department of Geography research paper no. 170, 1975), pp. 78–82.

7 Daniel Defoe, *A Tour Through the Whole Island of Great Britain*, Everyman edn (London, 1962); Fiennes, *Journeys*.

8 For instance in William Wycherley, *The Country Wife*, first performed in 1675.

9 C.W. Chalklin, *The Provincial Towns of Georgian England: A Study of the Building Process, 1740–1820* (London, 1974).

10 This is particularly well and forcefully stated in the work of P.J. Corfield; see Corfield, *The Impact of English Towns*, pp. 5–16, and 'Economic growth and change in seventeenth-century English towns', unit 10 of English Urban History, (Open University, 1977), pp. 37–45, where a population of 5,000 is used as a limit for towns.

11 Corfield, *The Impact of English Towns*, p. 3.

12 Chalklin, op. cit., pp. 16–18.

13 P. Borsay, 'The English urban renaissance: the development of provincial urban culture, *c*. 1680–1760', *Social History*, 5(1977), 581–603; 'All the town's a stage: urban ritual and ceremony, 1660–1800', in P. Clark (ed.), *The Transformation of English Provincial Towns, 1600–1800* (London, 1984), 228–58. His views find wide acceptance, much as the ideas of emulation have done. There is something appealing in discussions of personal display, luxury, and leisure – perhaps vicarious living by historians.

14 Braudel, op. cit.; P. Borsay, 'All the town's a stage'.

15 There is a large literature on urban housing, but less on the way in which houses were used, and nothing on perceptions of overcrowding. Mobility of people over short distances within towns has made it hard to trace individuals, even where the evidence exists for us to do so, but see N.J. Alldridge, 'House and household in Restoration Chester', *Urban History Yearbook* (Leicester, 1983), pp. 39–52; also several essays in P. Clark (ed.), *The Transformation of English Provincial Towns, 1600–1800* (London, 1984).

16 Lichfield JRO, Aaron Shaw of Burslem, potter, 23 April 1714; the value of the inventory was £19.5*s*.6*d*.

17 William Cookson of Wellington, weaver: Trinder and Cox, *Telford*, p. 338; the value of the inventory was £18.12s7d.
18 William Watkis, blacksmith of Dawley: Trinder and Cox, *Telford*, p. 178; the value of the inventory was £16.7s.6d.
19 The late eighteenth century is better documented, and some impression of retailing can be seen in D. Alexander, *Retailing in England during the Industrial Revolution* (London, 1979); see also S.I. Mitchell, 'The development of urban retailing, 1700–1815', in P. Clark (ed.), *The Transformation of English Provincial Towns*, pp. 259–83.
20 Mitchell, op. cit., pp. 260–70; Corfield, *The Impact of English Towns*, pp. 19–21; Sheena Smith, 'Norwich china dealers of the mid-eighteenth century', *English Ceramic Circle Trans.*, 9 (1974), 193–211.
21 Some of the problems in studying the inland trades can be seen in Margaret Spufford, *The Great Reclothing of Rural England* (London, 1984); Lorna Weatherill, 'The business of middleman in the English pottery trade before 1780', *Business History*, 28 (1986), 51–76.
22 This is based on Lorna Weatherill, *The Growth of the Pottery Industry in England, 1660–1815* (New York, 1986), chs 4 and 7; Weatherill, 'The business of middleman'.
23 D.G. Vaisey and F. Celoria, 'Inventory of George Ecton, potter of Abingdon, Berks. 1696', *Journal of Ceramic History*, 7 (1974), 13–42; it contained six coffee 'chainy cupps' at 6d. (and these may even have been the cheaper, white delftware), the only reference out of a stock valued at £39.14s.5d. Lincoln RO, inventory of Richard Hargrave, March 1720/21, Wills O., 2019; it contained seven white teapots at 2s.4d. and two sugar dishes at 1s. 6d. out of a stock of £6.7s.4d.
24 Weatherill, *The Growth of the Pottery Industry*, p. 126, for details.
25 Blundell, 'Diurnal', vol. 1, p. 262, and vol. 2, p. 260.
26 Weatherill, *The Growth of the Pottery Industry*, pp. 192–3: the counts are based on all references in three producers' ledgers, Bailey's Directory and miscellaneous references in advertisements, inventories, and insurance records.
27 Daunton, op. cit., pp. 253–5.

5   Financing the household: income, wealth, and prices

1 Oliver Goldsmith, 'The deserted village', in A. Friedman, *Collected Works of Oliver Goldsmith* (Oxford, 1966), pp. 282–304.
2 The best general introduction is in K. Wrightson, *English Society, 1580–1680* (London, 1982). There are important insights in Linda Pollock, *Forgotten Children* (Cambridge, 1983). Other studies are not sensitive to domestic life, such as R. Houlbrooke, *The English Family, 1450–1700* (London, 1984); J.L. Flandrin, *Families in Former Times: Kinship, Household and Sexuality* (first published in French in 1976), English translation (Cambridge, 1979), stresses the image of the European, often Catholic, French tradition.

3 Mean household size in the English listings was 4.8: P. Laslett, 'Size and structure of the household in England over three centuries', *Population Studies*, 23 (1969), 199–223. In Scotland, detailed listings have not been analysed in the same way as English ones, but the hearth-tax records suggest a mean size of around 5: see D. Adamson, 'The hearth tax', *Trans. of the Dunfermline and Galloway Natural Historians and Antiquaries Society*, 47 (1970), 147–58; M. Flinn *et al.*, *Scottish Population History* (Cambridge, 1977), pp. 194–8.

4 Laslett, op. cit.; N. Goose, 'Household size and structure in early Stuart Cambridge', *Social History*, 5 (1980), 347–85; Adamson, op. cit., pp. 150–4.

5 This is obviously because the records about large establishments are more accessible, and most of the manuscript accounts in local archives and in the British Museum are from the larger gentry and aristocratic households. It is especially true of accounts of Scottish domestic life in the eighteenth century; see M. Lochhead, *The Scots Household in the Eighteenth Century* (Edinburgh, 1948), and Baillie, 'Household book'.

6 Josselin, *Diary*; A. MacFarlane, *The Family Life of Ralph Josselin: a Seventeenth Century Clergyman: an Essay in Historical Anthropology* (Cambridge, 1970), pp. 47, 93, and 147.

7 Latham, 'Account book'.

8 Stout, 'Autobiography'; Fretwell, 'Family history'.

9 Three household accounts have been studied in detail for the study, together with one household budget; the full references are in the Bibliography. See Latham, 'Account book'; Pengelly, 'Accounts'; Fell, *Account Book*. Also King, 'Budget', and Baillie, 'Household book'.

10 Even wage-earners could have many sources of income, see D. Woodward, 'Wage-rates and living standards in pre-industrial England', *Past and Present*, 91 (1981), 28–45. The complexity of middling incomes is evident from diaries and memoirs such as those listed in the Bibliography. For a summary, see Dorothy Marshall, *English People in the Eighteenth Century* (London, 1956), pp. 118–59.

11 P.H. Lindert and J.G. Williamson, 'Revising England's social tables, 1688–1812', *Explorationsin Economic History*, 19 (1982), 385–408. See also note 5 to chapter 8 for further discussion of King.

12 Mildred Campbell, *The English Yeoman under Elizabeth and the Early Stuarts* (London, 1960 edn), pp. 217–19.

13 Josselin, *Diary*, p. 44.

14 Martindale, 'Life', pp. 168–9 and 239.

15 Rosemary O'Day, *The English Clergy: The Emergence and Consolidation of a Profession, 1558–1642* (Leicester, 1979), pp. 172–89, p. 175; in 1649/50 a survey of stipends in Derbyshire showed that only a third of the clergy in the county reached this level.

16 Stout, 'Autobiography', pp. 206 and 239.

17 Stout, 'Autobiography'.

18 Lorna Weatherill, *The Pottery Trade and North Staffordshire, 1660–1760* (Manchester, 1971), pp. 96–108.

19 Lorna Weatherill, *The Growth of the Pottery Industry in England, 1660–1815* (New York, 1986).
20 Campbell, op. cit., pp. 217–19; she also estimates the 'better sort' of yeomen at over £100.
21 MacFarlane, op. cit., p. 36.
22 Moore, 'Journal', pp. 66–7, 89, 91, and 103.
23 Stukeley, 'Memoirs'.
24 Yonge, *Journal*, pp. 162, 206–8, and 227.
25 Martindale, 'Life', pp. 172–5.
26 Stout, 'Autobiography'; there is an estimate at the end of every year.
27 Pengelly, 'Accounts'; see also chapter 6.
28 King, 'Budget', LCC Burns journal, p. 250.
29 Burrell, 'Journal', pp. 117–72 (he summarizes his expenditure at the end of each year); Fell, *Account Book*; see also chapter 6.
30 Latham, 'Account book'; Martindale, 'Life'.
31 MacFarlane, op. cit., pp. 34–9. This book is based on the diary and on his own summaries, as well as on MacFarlane's calculations. It is rare to find so much detail.
32 Rogers, 'Diary', pp. 37 and 60.
33 Stout, 'Autobiography'.
34 Latham, 'Account book'.
35 Martindale, 'Life', 1668, p. 190.
36 See, for instance, Sue Wright, '"Churmaids, Huswyfes and Hucksters": the employment of women in Tudor and Stuart Salisbury', in L. Charles and Lorna Duffin (eds), *Women and Work in Pre-Industrial England* (London, 1985), pp. 100–21.
37 Alice Hanson Jones, working on colonial North America, has been able to trace the full wealth of those in her sample, but the records are fuller, and she was working with a smaller sample for only one year. *The Wealth of a Nation To Be* (New York, 1980). Likewise, Peter Earle has been able to trace other evidence than probate records about London freemen. Spufford has shown, in tracing the assets of chapmen, that an inventory total can give a misleading impresion of 'wealth' because debts owed are not recorded, and these could exceed the value of the inventory: Margaret Spufford, *The Great Reclothing of Rural England: Petty Chapmen and their Wares in the Seventeenth Century* (London, 1984).
38 The estates with low valuations should not be taken as representing labourers or poor groups in society, for there were many reasons why someone of higher status could leave few movable goods, especially at the end of their lives. There were probably labourers among these but they are not representative of all such people. See chapter 8 and appendix 2.
39 Weatherill, *The Growth of the Pottery Industry*, pp. 95–9, where data from various places are drawn together.
40 *Journals of the House of Commons*, 11 (17 February 1696/7), 709, 'Upon the petition of Jonathon Chilwell'; for an account of this in context, see Rhoda Edwards, 'London potters', *Journal of Ceramic History*, 6 (1974), 45.

6 Financing the household: expenditure and priorities

1 Warley, 'Accounts', p. 5.

2 Household accounts are not easy to find, and it is possible that they were not as frequently kept by relatively small households as the larger ones. They have, however, been much neglected and overlooked, for they are often unimpressive volumes and sometimes seem to have survived merely by good fortune. They obviously contain a great deal of detailed information. Farm and household may not have been perceived as distinct as far as accounting was concerned, and household expenses may be found in farm accounts. I have looked at the holdings of many county archives for such accounts, but they are often not well indexed, and it is necessary to be very persistent. But a larger body of accounts would be useful in showing many things about the organization of life at this time. The accounts used here are: Lancashire RO, Latham, 'Account book'; British Museum, Dept of MSS, Pengelly, 'Accounts'; Fell, *Account Book*. There are several Scottish accounts, but these refer to households of much higher status than those that are the subject of this study, for they are those of the landowners, the equivalent of the county gentry in England. These are used in Lochhead, *The Scots Household in the Eighteenth Century*.

3 King, 'Budget'; Baillie, 'Household book'.

4 The mixture of house and farm says something about perceptions of expenditure; there are few separate household accounts, and production and domestic consumption were not seen as distinct.

5 The manuscript accounts have unnumbered pages, but the year is always clear from the manuscript, although the precise date is not often given.

6 Work on colonial North America shows a different context, where the food produced on many farms was intended primarily for home consumption, especially in New England. Yet, even here, farms were not independent of others for food, so not only were tools purchased but there was a good deal of local, small-scale trading in food between farms. See Bettye Hobbs Pruitt, 'Self-sufficiency and the agricultural economy of eighteenth-century Massachusetts', *William and Mary Quartery*, 41 (1984); Sara F. Mahon, 'A comfortable subsistence: the changing composition of diet in rural New England, 1620–1840', *William and Mary Quarterly*, 42 (1985), 26–51.

7 This was even true of households other than those used here; see Anne Buck, 'Buying clothes in Bedfordshire: tradesmen, customers and fashion, 1700–1800', paper given at the Pasold Research Fund Conference on the Economic and Social History of Dress in 1985.

8 Omissions could have occurred if Sarah were not responsible for cash payments for some items, like groceries; likewise, individual groceries would not show up if they were paid in a lump sum, and a false impression of self-sufficiency would be gained.

9 The differences in date probably only matter to the Fells, whose accounts occur before hot drinks and imported china became available.

7   The domestic environment

1 T. Tusser, *Five Hundred Points of Good Husbandry* (London, 1580).
2 Markham, *Housewife*, p. 49.
3 This was not an unreasonable assumption, given the mores of the time and the needs engendered by domestic tasks. Attempts by historians of women's life to stress their economic roles are perfectly proper, but we should not forget that their role in housekeeping was essential and was expected for them. See Alice Clark, *The Working Life of Women in the Seventeenth Century* (London, 1919). See also, on attitudes to work, M. Roberts, '"Words they are women and deeds they are men": images of work and gender in early modern England', in L. Charles and Lorna Duffin (eds), *Women and Work in Pre-Industrial England* (London, 1985), pp. 122–80; R.E. Pahl, *Divisions of Labour* (Oxford, 1984), esp. pp. 15–63.
4 Stout, 'Autobiography'; Fretwell, 'Family history'.
5 The range of advice available is summarized, with much other commentary, in Kathleen M. Davies, 'Continutiy and change in literary advice on marriage', in R.B. Outhwaite (ed.), *Marriage and Society* (London, 1981), pp. 58–80; Alice C. Carter, 'Marriage counselling in the early seventeenth century: England and the Netherlands compared', in J. Van Dorsen (ed.), *Ten Studies in Anglo-Dutch Relations* (London, 1974), pp. 94–127.
6 Markham, *Housewife*, frontispiece; the most interesting and well-illustrated book on housework is Caroline Davidson, *A Woman's Work is Never Done: A History of Housework in the British Isles, 1650–1950* (London, 1982).
7 Fretwell, 'Family history', pp. 182 and 216.
8 Stout, 'Autobiography', p. 68.
9 Defoe, *Everybody's Business*, p. 6.
10 Pepys, *Diary*, vol. 1, p. 29, 25 January 1660.
11 The literature on servants tends to concentrate on those in gentry and even aristocratic households, rather than on those in more modest households: J.J. Hecht, *The Domestic Servant in Eighteenth-Century England* (London, 1956); Sara C. Maza, *Servants and Masters in Eighteenth-Century France* (Princeton, NJ, 1983).
12 Stout, 'Autobiography', p. 105. Ellin also worked in the shop.
13 Newcome, 'Autobiography', vol. 2, July 1652, p. 296. See also commentary about Josselin in A. MacFarlane, *The Family Life of Ralph Josselin*, pp. 147–8.
14 Latham, 'Account book'.
15 Brereton, 'Travels', p. 106.
16 Kay, 'Diary', 1737–8 and p. 25.
17 His mother ran the household; he was deeply religious and was unsure whether to join his father in the medical practice or whether to become a minister. In the event he continued to help his father and eventually went to Guy's Hospital in London in 1743 for a year for formal training. He

then shared the practice with his father until his death in October 1751; he remained unmarried and continued to live with his parents.

18 This is a very sparsely documented subject, but see J. Rule, *The Experience of Labour in Eighteenth Century England* (London, 1981).

19 This is true of the inventories used in the main sample here and in the published collections.

20 Stout, 'Autobiography', pp. 90 and 96. For general accounts of the kinds of work involved in shopkeeping, see T.S. Willan, *The Inland Trade* (Manchester, 1976); D. Alexander, *Retailing in England during the Industrial Revolution* (London, 1970).

21 Kay, 'Diary', pp. 7–13; Martindale, 'Life', 1668, p. 190.

22 Rogers, 'Diary', pp. 2–3, 14 November 1727. He was married with several children living at home, and he also farmed. Salusbury, 'Diary', pp. 49–77.

23 Stapley, 'Diary', pp. 102–28, 2 June to 4 August 1694.

24 Latham, 'Account book'.

25 Lowe, *Diary*, 16 February 1668/9, p. 121.

26 Markham, *Housewife*, p. 49.

27 Fiennes, *Journeys*, pp. 217 and 223.

28 Misson, *Travels*, no page numbers; this is under the entry 'Table'. He visited in 1685.

29 Newcome, 'Diary' 21 December 1663, p 146.

30 Cookery, as done in households of middle rank in the late seventeenth century, is not well documented because collections of 'traditional' recipes tend to have a nineteenth-century origin, although they can give useful insights. The best are: F. Marion McNeill, *The Scots Kitchen* (London, 1929); Dorothy Hartley, *Food in England* (London, 1954). More concern with change and social context can be found in C. Anne Wilson, *Food and Drink in Britain* (Harmondsworth, 1976). There is an out-of-date, but useful, listing of contemporary cookery books, which were mostly aimed at the aristocracy and upper gentry, A. Whittaker, *English Cookery Books to the Year 1850* (Oxford, 1913). I have used two printed collections of recipes kept by women running gentry households: 'Diana Astry's Recipe Book c. 1700', ed. Bette Stitt, *Pubs. of the Beds. Hist. Soc.*, 37 (1957); *The Compleat Cook or the Secrets of a Seventeenth Century Housewife by Rebecca Price*, ed. M. Masson (London, 1974). The most useful contemporary cookery book referring to the middling ranks is Mrs Hannah Glasse, *The Art of Cookery made Plain and Easy*, 1st edn (London, 1747). See also Davidson, op. cit., for a review of housework and cookery.

31 Misson, *Travels*, under the topic of 'Table'.

32 The extent to which people expected to eat meat is not easily demonstrated. Gregory King, in calculating the per capita consumption of meat, commented that about half the population never, or rarely, ate meat, including unweaned children. Of the rest, some families (440,000) did not 'by reason of their poverty ... eat not flesh above 2 days in 7' and a further 440,000 'receive alms and consequently eat not flesh above once a week': King, 'Budget', pp. 54–5.

33 Glasse, *Art of Cookery*.

34 Glasse, *Art of Cookery*. This seems rather quick in comparison with times in an electric oven.

35 They are often recorded in the Orphans' Court inventories by this time. See appendix 1 for a description of these inventories.

36 For an interesting account of self-sufficiency in a different context, but one that is of relevance here, see Bettye Hobbs Pruitt, 'Self-sufficiency and the agricultural economy of Massachusetts', *William and Mary Quarterly*, 41 (1984); Sarah F. McMahon, 'A comfortable subsistence: the changing composition of diet in rural New England, 1620–1840', *William and Mary Quarterly*, 42 (1985), 26–51.

37 Price, *Compleat Cook*, especially pp. 1–19.

38 Pepys, *Diary*. Especially in the early years.

39 Stout, 'Autobiography'.

40 Glasse, *Art of Cookery*, p. 1. She was addressing the gentry at this point.

41 Ursula Priestley and Penelope Corfield, 'Rooms and room use in Norwich housing, 1580–1730', *Post-Medieval Arch.*, 16 (1982), 93–123.

42 Trinder and Cox, *Telford*. The other generalizations are based on the published collections of inventories and the inventory sample.

43 Anon., 'A woman's work is never done', quoted in Davidson, op. cit.

44 Fiennes, *Journeys*, p. 237; see also note 15 above.

45 Mary Douglas, *Implicit Meanings: Essays in Anthropology* (London, 1975); this emphasizes that meals have many symbolic elements in them.

46 Fiennes, *Journeys*, p. 235.

47 Glasse, *Art of Cookery*, p. 2.

48 Fiennes, *Journeys*, under 'Food'; Misson, *Travels*, under 'Table'; Baillie, 'Household book', pp. 281–304. There are menus of large formal dinners that give the impression of this way of eating, although they refer to a large household; Colville (ed.) 'Ochtertyre House Book of Accompts' gives an excellent impression of the food eaten in a large household for dinner and supper, but there is no indication of how it was served. It also distinguishes the servants' food from the rest. Pepys, *Diary*, vol. 9, 23 January 1669/70, p. 423; the diary contains some evocative descriptions of large dinners with family and friends, as well as the amount of work that went into preparing a special meal.

49 Ramsey, *Scotland and Scotsmen*, p. 180.

50 See note 53 to chapter 1.

51 Misson, *Travels*, under 'Table'.

52 Most diaries before 1740 record dinner in the middle of the day. Later commentary suggests that some people took to having dinner later in the day from the mid-eighteenth century, and this then served to distinguish working people from those of higher status, but this seems to have happened only at the very end of the period covered by this study. A much later description is J.P. Malcolm, *Manners and Customs of London* (London, 1810), quoted briefly in A.F. Scott, *Every One a Witness* (London, 1970), pp. 28–30.

53 There are extracts from these, aimed largely at the gentry, in N. Elias, *The Civilizing Process*, English trans. (Oxford, 1978; first published in

German in 1939). There are good descriptions of the conventions, again aimed at those of the upper ranks, in Woolley, *Guide.*

54 Trinder and Cox, *Telford.*
55 Priestley and Corfield, op. cit.
56 Pepys, *Diary*, vol. 9, 22 January 1669/70, p. 423.
57 J. Hatcher and T.C. Barker, *A History of British Pewter* (London, 1974), pp. 139–41.
58 Robertson, *Rural Recollections* (of the1760s, but written in the 1820s), p. 276. The Scottish commentary tends to be later and more retrospective; it is also more aware of change than the English a century earlier, because the commentary was self-conscious and intended to document rapid change.
59 Misson, *Travels*, under 'Visits'; Claver Morris, *Diary*; Fiennes, *Journeys*, Tunbridge, p. 153, Lichfield, p. 194, Bath, p. 41, Epsom, pp. 379 and 391.
60 This section is based on P. Clark, *The English Alehouse: A Social History, 1200–1830* (London, 1983), pp. 195–242. Inns had always catered for wealthier clients; inventories show that they were often well furnished.
61 Moore, 'Journal', 4 February 1668/9, p. 105 (in Latin).
62 Marchant, 'Diary', 1 November 1727, p. 194. See also Rogers, 'Diary', 30 January 1729/30, p. 4.
63 The exact chronology of tea making is not well documented. For imports, see K.N. Chaudhuri, *The Trading World of Asia and the East India Company, 1660–1760* (Cambridge, 1978); C. Anne Wilson, *Food and Drink in Britain* (Harmondsworth, 1973), pp. 361–72.
64 Thomlinson, 'Diary', 16 October 1717, p. 85.
65 Priestley and Corfield, op. cit.; Trinder and Cox, *Telford.* See also the other published series of inventories listed in the Bibliography.
66 Scottish testaments are not normally as full in their listings of household goods as the English inventories and have not therefore been used in the main sample. There are, however, individual inventories that show the kinds of goods in Scottish, especially urban, households.
67 Priestley and Corfield, op. cit.
68 Elias, op. cit., pp. 161–3.
69 Trinder and Cox, *Telford*, p. 356; the value of the inventory was £3.5s.7d.
70 Trinder and Cox, *Telford*, pp. 339–42; the value of the inventory was £1,327.15s.9d.
71 P. Thornton, *Seventeenth-Century Interior Decoration in England, France and Holland* (London, 1978). The discussion in this is of the most lavish and expensive beds, and beds that have survived in country houses or in museums tend to be of the highest quality. Even the smaller pieces of beds displayed in the woodwork study room of the Victoria and Albert Museum in London are of higher quality than the ordinary bedsteads listed in the inventories.
72 They are also difficult to pinpoint, although inventories sometimes have considerable detail about beds and bedsteads. Some of the problems in dealing with linen are given in Margaret Spufford, *The Great Reclothing of*

Rural England: Petty Chapmen and their Wares in the Seventeenth Century (London, 1984), pp. 114–16.

73 Linda Pollock, *Forgotten Children* (Cambridge, 1983); K. Wrightson, *English Society, 1580–1680* (London, 1982), pp. 104–18. Virtually all diaries and autobiographies make some reference to one or other aspects of childhood – which suggests in itself how important they were. One of the best is in Thornton, 'Autobiography', with its detailed descriptions of childbirth and moving accounts of maternal love.

74 P. Laslett, 'Size and structure of the household in England over three centuries', *Population Studies*, 23 (1969), pp. 217 and 221.

75 Fretwell, 'Family history', p. 183; Margaret Spufford, 'First steps in literacy: the reading and writing experiences of the humblest seventeenth-century spiritual autobiographies', *Social History*, 4 (1970), 407–35.

76 Thomlinson, 'Diary', 11 August 1717, p. 72; 4 January 1717/18, pp. 72 and 99.

77 Stout, 'Autobiography', p. 119.

78 Martindale, 'Life', p. 5.

79 Holme, 'Academy of Armoury', p. 55.

80 Kay, 'Diary', April and July 1747, p. 119.

81 Dawson, 'Diary', 10 March 1761, p. 255.

82 Stukeley, 'Memoirs', vol. 1, pp. 108–9.

83 Latham, 'Account book'.

84 Thomlinson, 'Diary', 17 August 1717, p. 73.

85 Daniel Defoe, *The Compleat English Tradesman*, 2 vols (London, 1726–7), 1, 61–70.

86 Marchant, 'Diary', 1–11 October 1714, p. 167. He was a substantial yeoman farmer and became agent to the Duke of Somerset after 1727.

87 Misson, *Travels*, under 'Visits'.

88 Salusbury, 'Diary', 5 May 1758, p. 62.

89 Thomlinson, 'Diary', 26 January 1717/18, p. 102.

8   Ownership of goods, social status, and occupation

1 Edward Jones, husbandman of Wellington, 1681, in Trinder and Cox, *Telford*, p. 266; the total value of the estate was £22.18s.10d.

2 John Webster of Doncaster, alderman, 1674, in Brears, *Yorkshire Inventories*, p. 140; the total value of the inventory was £548.18s.0d.

3 This is because the law relating to probate was different in Scotland; usually enough assets were listed to cover a person's debts, and detailed listing of household and other goods is rare, although there are a very few scattered through the records. It was not possible in the time available for writing this book to study these in depth, but it would be worthwhile to collect all those that have details in them.

4 This is fully discussed in appendix 2. The best discussion of social position is in K. Wrightson, *English Society, 1580–1680* (London, 1982), pp. 17–38; for a wider interpretation, see K. Wrightson, 'The social

order of early modern England: three approaches', in L. Bonfield, R. Smith, and K. Wrightson (eds), *The World We Have Earned* (Oxford, 1986), pp. 178–202. This account is confined to England, although there were similar distinctions in Scotland. There is a brief, useful, comparative survey in R. Houston, *Scottish Literacy and the Scottish Identity, 1660–1800* (Cambridge, 1985), pp. 22–37.

5 I have used the recalculations in P.H. Lindert and J.G. Williamson, 'Revising England's social tables, 1688–1812', *Explorations in Economic History*, 19 (1982), 393. These take some account of occupational structure as seen in other sources, such as parish registers, and go some way towards answering criticisms of King's original estimates, especially those in G.S. Holmes, 'Gregory King and the social structure of pre-industrial England', *Trans. of the Roy. Hist. Soc.*, 5th series, 27 (1977), 41–68. The main differences lie in King's apparent over-emphasis on the agricultural sector and his underestimates of commercial and craft occupations. His listing has 63 per cent of the middle ranks in farming, only 12 per cent in crafts and manufacturing, and 8 per cent as shopkeepers. Neither is wholly satisfactory, but the recalculations do give a better expression to the variety of occupations at the time and go some way towards answering criticisms made by Holmes. See also P.H. Lindert, 'English occupations, 1670–1811', *Journal of Economic History*, 40 (1980), 685–712; P. Mathias, 'The social structure in the eighteenth century', in *The Transformation of England* (London 1979), pp. 171–189.

6 Vivien Brodsky Elliott, 'Mobility and marriage in pre-industrial England' (Cambridge University PhD thesis, 1978), pp. 1–149. She ordered about fifty occupations on the basis of observed choice of marriage partners and apprenticeship choices; see appendix 2 for further commentary on this.

7 The account of social structures is based on Houston, op. cit., especially pp. 27–37; I.D. Whyte and K.A. Whyte, 'Some aspects of the structure of rural society in seventeenth-century lowland Scotland', in T.M. Devine and D. Dickenson (eds), *Ireland and Scotland, 1600–1850*, (Edinburgh, 1983), pp. 32–45, and especially the table on p. 36. There are useful insights into rural society in I.D. Whyte, *Agriculture and Society in Seventeenth Century Scotland* (Edinburgh, 1979); R.A. Dodgshon, *Land and Society in Early Scotland* (Oxford, 1981), especially pp. 203–76. There are accounts of urban and rural society in T.C. Smout, *A History of the Scottish people, 1560–1830* (London, 1971).

8 Revisions to King's calculations suggest that about 680,000 families (of about 1,390,000) were of middle rank. Of these, 18,000 were lesser gentry or esquires. See note 5 above.

9 May, *Newmarket Inventories*, pp. 23–4. This is an extreme case and would not have been included in the main sample, because his was not a 'household' in the sense that there is not evidence here for the full range of activities, and cookery is absent. Small households of people called 'gent' are well illustrated in Lichfield; see Vaisey, *Lichfield Inventories*.

10 Lichfield Joint Record Office, Samuel Edge of Burslem, 'Earthpotter,' 9 May 1721; the value of the inventory was £75. 17s.

11 Lichfield JRO, Richard Wedgwood, of Burslem, 23 April 1719; the value of the inventory was £408.8s.2d.

12 Trinder and Cox, *Telford*, p. 340; the value of the inventory was £1,327.15s.

13 I have deliberately chosen an inventory in print for this example, and Wentworth was not among the rich and fashionable; Brears, *Yorkshire Inventories*, pp. 145–53. His silver was valued at £591 and 'three Indian Cabinetts with Jewells' at £800.

14 Latham, 'Account book'.

15 Stout, 'Autobiography'; Lorna Weatherill, *The Pottery Trade and North Staffordshire, 1660–1760* (Manchester, 1971), pp. 139–41; Marie Rowlands, *Masters and Men in the West Midland Metal Working Trades* (Manchester, 1975); D.G. Hey, *The Rural Metalworkers of the Sheffield Region* (Leicester, 1972).

16 The farmers with an inventory valuation over £60 were not very different from the yeomen: the mean values were £162 for yeomen (N = 559) and £169 for farmers (N = 392). These are grouped together to avoid too many subdivisions in the tables. See appendix 2.

17 References to King are fully given in note 5 above.

18 Trinder and Cox, *Telford*, pp. 219–20; the value of the inventory was £274.7s.6d.

19 Robertson, *Rural Recollections*, pp. 71–81 and 91–100. See also Somerville, *Own Life and Times*, pp. 325–85, where he takes a brief retrospect of Scotland in the early part of his life; he wrote in 1814. See also Ramsey, *Scotland and Scotsmen*; Mure, 'Observations'.

20 Somerville, *Own Life and Times*, p. 335.

21 Scottish RO, Edinburgh Commissariat Testaments, Testament Testamentar of George Sinclare, farmer in Longniddrie, died October 1709. I am grateful to Professor Mitchison for this reference.

22 In the sample, 74 per cent of husbandmen and small farmers came from north of the river Trent. In all, there were 76 husbandmen and 256 farmers with estates under £60, although the two are grouped together here for convenience. See also J.D. Marshall, 'The domestic economy of the Lakeland yeoman, 1660–1749', *Transactions of the Cumberland and Westmorland Antiquarian and Archaeological Society*, n.s., 73 (1973), 190–219. The point is less well documented for counties to the east of the Pennines.

23 Trinder and Cox, *Telford*, p. 189.

24 Robertson, *Rural Recollections*, pp. 99–100.

25 See note 5 above for references to King.

26 Trinder and Cox, *Telford*, p. 356; the value of the inventory was £3.5s.7d.

27 D. Woodward, 'Wage-rates and living standards in pre-industrial England', *Past and Present*, 91 (1981), 28–45.

28 See note 5 above for references to King's tables.

29 Trinder and Cox, *Telford*, p. 311; the value of the inventory was £30.6s.0d.

30 I.H. Adams, *The Making of Urban Scotland* (London, 1978); G. Gordon and B. Dicks (eds), *Scottish Urban History* (Aberdeen, 1983).

31 M. Lynch, *Edinburgh and the Reformation* (Edinburgh, 1981), pp. 52–3;

T.C. Smout, 'The Glasgow merchant community in the seventeenth century', *Scottish Historical Review*, 47 (1968), 53–71; T.M. Devine, 'The merchant class of the larger Scottish towns in the later seventeenth and early eighteenth centuries', in Gordon and Dicks (eds), op. cit., pp. 92–111.

32 Brears, *Yorkshire Inventories*, pp. 140–1; the value of the inventory was £548.18s. 2d.

33 Scottish RO, Edinburgh Commissariat, Testament Dative of Robert Drysdale, merchant burgess and draper of Edinburgh, 10 February 1716; the value of the inventory was £1,837.14s. Scots.

34 There has been more interest in the professions of late: see G. Holmes, 'The professions and social change in England, 1680–1730', *Proceedings of the British Academy*, 65 (1979), 314–54; Rosemary O'Day, *The English Clergy: The Emergence and Consolidation of a Profession, 1558–1642* (Leicester, 1979), especially pp. 172–89; C. Ehrlich, *The Music Profession in Britain since the Eighteenth Century* (Oxford, 1985).

35 Vaisey, *Lichfield Inventories*, pp. 252–3; the value of the inventory was £400.13s.4d.

36 Trinder and Cox, *Telford*, p. 240; the value of the inventory was £17.4s. 4d.

37 Ursula Priestley and Penelope Corfield, 'Rooms and room use in Norwich housing, 1580–1730', *Post-Medieval Archaeology*, 16 (1982), 93–123; see also discussions of this in chapter 1.

38 R. Scott-Moncrieff (ed.), 'Household plenishings belonging to the deceist Andro Hog, Writer to the Signet, Publicklie Rouped and Sold upon the 19th, 20th, 21st, 22nd, 23rd and 24th days of Octr., 1691 Yeares', *Proceedings of the Society of Antiquaries of Scotland*, 5th series, 5 (1918–19), 52–63. He had only been admitted to the Society of Writers to the Signet on 28 July 1690, although he was probably a few years out of his apprenticeship when he died, for his master died in 1688.

39 Other women are listed under a trade or occupation. There were 430 women in the whole sample (15 per cent), of whom 217 were widows or spinsters. See Lorna Weatherill, 'A possession of one's own: women and consumer behaviour in England, 1660–1760', *Journal of British Studies*, 25 (1986), 131–56.

40 The idea of a hierarchy based on consumption is discussed in a different context in Mary Douglas and B. Isherwood, *The World of Goods: Towards an Anthropology of Consumption* (Harmondsworth, 1980), ch. 9, based on the idea that those in the higher-consumption classes spend a higher proportion of their incomes on information and are thus more firmly linked to the culture of their time. They apply it to a definition of poverty in modern Britain, but the idea of a consumption hierarchy has meaning for other times and places.

41 A.J. and R.H. Tawney, 'An occupational census of the seventeenth century', *Economic History Revue*, 5 (1934), 25–64; W.A. Armstrong, 'The use of information about occupation', in E.A. Wrigley (ed.), *Nineteenth Century Society* (Cambridge, 1972), pp. 191–310, especially part 2, pp. 226–310, which deals with an industrial classification.

42 See appendix 2 for a full list of occupations.

9   Conclusions and implications

1 Margaret Spufford, *The Great Reclothing of Rural England: Petty Chapmen and their Wares in the Seventeenth Century* (London, 1984); Joan Thirsk, *Economic Policy and Projects: The Development of a Consumer Society in Early Modern England* (Oxford, 1978).
2 Thirsk, op. cit., pp. 174–5.
3 Spufford, op. cit., p. 6.
4 Thirsk, op. cit., p. 176.
5 H.J. Perkin, 'The social causes of the British industrial revolution', *Trans. of the Roy. Hist. Soc.*, 18 (1968), 123–43; see also D.E.C. Eversley, 'The home demand and economic growth in England, 1750–80', in E.L. Jones and G.E. Mingay (eds), *Land, Labour and Population in the Industrial Revolution* (London, 1967); F. Braudel, *Capitalism and Material Life, 1400–1800* (London, 1974).
6 *British Magazine* (1763), quoted in Perkin, op. cit., p. 140.
7 Josiah Wedgwood to Thomas Bentley, 23 August 1772; in Ann Finer and G. Savage (eds), *The Selected Letters of Josiah Wedgwood* (London, 1965).
8 Warley, 'Accounts', p. 1. This has several pages of sayings and sentences of advice of this kind; many are concerned with getting and spending, giving an unusual insight into common perceptions of these matters.
9 A.H. John, 'Agricultural productivity and economic growth in England, 1700–1760', *Journal of Economic History*, 25 (1965), 19–34; M.W. Flinn, 'Agricultural productivity and economic growth in England, 1700–1760: a comment', *Journal of Economic History*, 26 (1966), 93–8; J.D. Gould, 'Agricultural fluctuation and the English economy in the eighteenth century', *Journal of Economic History*, 22 (1962), 313–33. This debate was a creature of the 1960s, and there has been little recent interest in its resolution except in so far as the importance of consumption in Britain is now recognized, but the issues are ones that should interest economic and social historians more than they do. The debate was perhaps a response to a growing awareness that there were long-term origins to growth, and these issues are now being explored in different ways, as in N.F.R. Crafts, 'British economic growth, 1700–1831: a review of the evidence', *Economic History Revue*, 36 (1983), 177–99.
10 Eversley, op. cit., pp. 230 and 237.

Appendix 1

1 There is no text on how to sample inventories, but I found the following most practical and useful: C. Dixon and B. Leach, *Sampling Methods for Geographical Research* (Geo Abstracts, University of East Anglia, 1978); Alice Hanson-Jones, *American Colonial Wealth, Documents and Methods*, 2nd edn (New York, 1977); Alice Hanson-Jones, 'Estimating the wealth of the living from a probate sample', *Journal of Interdisciplinary History*, 13

(1982), 273–300. I do not agree with the views in P.H. Lindert, 'An algorithm for probate sampling', *Journal of Interdisciplinary History*, 11 (1981), 649–68.

2 For general guides to inventories and probate papers, see M. Overton, *A Bibliography of British Probate Inventories* (University of Newcastle upon Tyne, 1983). My sample was taken from the following areas:

(a) *Diocese of Durham*, 1675–1715: Department of Palaeography and Diplomatic, University of Durham. This covers County Durham, Northumberland, and Berwick-on-Tweed. The inventories for the coastal plain are fuller than those from the Pennine areas, so the coverage is biased towards the more economically developed areas, as discussed in chapter 8. There were too few inventories for 1725 to take a sample.

(b) *Diocese of Carlisle*, 1675–1725: Cumbria Record Office, Carlisle. This covers the northern part of Cumbria, Carlisle, and the Eden valley, but it does not include Whitehaven.

(c) *Diocese of London*: 1675 and 1695–1725 from the City division of the consistory court of the diocese, which covered the eastern parishes of the City and some places, notably Whitechapel, outside. These are kept in the Guildhall Library, London. The sample for 1685 was taken from the Middlesex division because records of this date were missing in the Guildhall. These are kept in the Greater London Record Office.

(d) *Diocese of Winchester*, 1675–1705: Hampshire Record Office, Winchester. These cover Hampshire and the Isle of Wight, and the sample is from both archdeaconry and consistory courts. There are too few inventories to sample after 1705.

(e) *Diocese of Chester*, south Lancashire division, 1675–1725: Lancashire Record Office, Preston. The sample covers Lancashire south of the River Ribble.

(f) *Diocese of Canterbury*, 1675–1725: Kent Record Office, Maidstone. These cover the eastern part of Kent only.

(g) *Diocese of Ely*, 1675–1725: Cambridge University Library, archive department. The sample is from the county of Cambridgeshire.

(h) *Diocese of Lichfield*, 1675–1725: Lichfield Joint Record Office, Lichfield Public Library. The diocese covers a very large part of the Midlands, including Derbyshire, Staffordshire, northern Shropshire, and parts of Warwickshire and Nottinghamshire. The sample was confined to Staffordshire and north Shropshire.

BIBLIOGRAPHY OF CONTEMPORARY SOURCES

Diaries, autobiographies, memoirs, and household books

Astry, 'Recipe book': 'Diana Astry's recipe book, *c*. 1700', ed. Bette Stitt, *Bedfordshire Historical Record Society*, 37 (1957), 83–199.

Baillie, 'Household book': 'Lady Griselle Baillie's household book, 1693–1733', ed. R. Scott-Moncrieff, *Scottish History Society*, 2nd series, 1 (1911).

Blundell, 'Diurnal': 'The great diurnal of Nicholas Blundell of Little Crosby, Lancashire', ed. F. Tyrer and J.J. Bagley, *Record Society of Lancashire and Cheshire*, 110 (1968), 112 (1970), 114 (1972). It covers the years 1702–28.

Bradley, *Coffee*: Richard Bradley, *The Virtue and Use of Coffee with Regard to the Plague*, London, 1721. A pamphlet.

Brereton, 'Travels': 'Travels in Holland, the United Provinces, England, Scotland and Ireland by Sir William Brereton, Bart', ed. E. Hawkins, *Chetham Society*, 1 (1844).

Brockbank, 'Diary': 'Diary and letterbook of Rev. Thomas Brockbank', ed. R. Trappes-Lomax, *Chetham Society*, n.s., 89 (1930). It covers the years 1671–1709.

Burrell, 'Journal': 'Journal and account book of Timothy Burrell Esq., 1683–1714', ed. R. Willis Blencowe, *Sussex Arch. Coll.*, 3 (1850), 117–72.

Claver Morris, *Diary*, *The Diary of a West Country Physician, 1709–1726*, ed. E. Hobhouse, London, 1934.

Colville, James (ed.) 'Ochtertyre house book of accompts, 1737–39', *Scottish History Society Publication*, 55 (1907).

Cunningham, 'Diary' 'The diary and general expenditure book of William Cunningham of Craigends, 1673–1680', ed. J. Dodds, *Scottish History Society*, 2 (1887).

Dawson, 'Diary': 'Diary of John Dawson of Brunton', ed. J.C. Hodgson, *Surtees Society*, 124 (1914), 253–94 (*c*.1761).

Defoe, *Everybody's Business*: Daniel Defoe, *Everybody's Business is No-Body's Business*, London, 1725.

Doddridge, 'Correspondence': 'Calendar of the correspondence of Philip Doddridge (1702–1751)', ed. G.F. Nuttall, *Northants. Record Society*, 29 (1979).

Eyre, 'Diurnall': 'The diurnall of Adam Eyre', ed. H.J. Morehouse, *Surtees Society*, 65 (1875).

Fell, *Account Book*: *The Household Account Book of Sarah Fell of Swarthmoor Hall*, ed. N. Penney, Cambridge, 1920.

Fiennes, *Journeys*: *The Journeys of Celia Fiennes*, ed. C. Morris, London, 1983.

Freke, *Diary*: *Mrs Elizabeth Freke, her Diary, 1671–1714*, ed. Mary Carbery, Cork, 1913.

Fretwell, 'Family history': 'A family history begun by James Fretwell', ed. C. Jackson, *Surtees Society*, 65 (1875), 163–244.

Glasse, *Art of Cookery*: Mrs Hannah Glasse, *The Art of Cookery made Plain and Easy*, 1st edn, London, 1747.

Hay, 'Diary': 'The diary of Andrew Hay of Craignathan, 1659–1660', ed. A.G. Reid, *Scottish History Society*, 39 (1901).

Holme, 'Academy of Armoury': Randle Holme, 'The Academy of Armoury and Blazon', *Roxburgh Club*, London, 1905.

Jackson, 'Diary': 'James Jackson's diary, 1650–1685', ed. F. Grainger, *Trans. of Cumberland and Westmorland Antiqu. and Arch. Soc.*, n.s., 21 (1921), 96–129.

Jolly, 'Notebook': 'Notebook of the Rev. Thomas Jolly, 1671–1693', ed. H. Fishwick, *Chetham Society*, n.s., 33 (1894).

Josselin, *Diary*: *The Diary of Ralph Josselin, 1616–1683*, ed. A. MacFarlane, British Academy, London, 1976.

Kay, 'Diary': 'The diary of Richard Kay, 1716–1751: a Lancashire doctor', ed. W. Brockbank and Rev. F. Kenworthy, *Chetham Society*, third series, 16 (1968).

King, 'Budget': *The Earliest Classics: John and Gregory King*, ed. P. Laslett, London, 1973, p. 250.

Latham, 'Account book': 'Account book of Richard Latham of Scarisbrick, Lancashire, 1723–1767', Lancashire Record Office, DP 385.

Lowe, *Diary*: *The Diary of Roger Lowe, 1663–1674*, ed. W.L. Sachese, London, 1938.

Marchant, 'Diary': 'The Marchant diary, 1714–28', ed. E. Turner, *Sussex Arch. Coll.*, 25 (1873), 63–203.

Markham, *Housewife*: Gervaise Markham, *The English Housewife*, London, 1683.

Martindale, 'Life': 'The life of Adam Martindale, written by himself', ed. R. Parkinson, *Chetham Society*, old series, 4 (1845).

Misson, *Travels*: Henri Misson, *Memoirs and Observations in his Travels over England*, trans. Mr Ozell, London, 1719. He visited in 1685.

Moore, 'Journal': 'Extracts from the journal and account book of the Rev. Giles Moore, rector of Horstead Keyes, Sussex, 1655–1679', ed. R. Willis Blencowe, *Sussex Arch. Coll.*, 1 (1847), 65–127.

Mure, 'Observations': 'Some observations of the change of manners in my own time, 1700–1790', ed. J.G. Fyfe, *Scottish Diaries and Memoirs, 1746–1843*, Stirling, 1942, pp. 61–81.

Neville, *Diary*: *The Diary of Sylas Neville, 1767–88*, ed. B. Cozens-Hardy, London, 1950.

Newcome, 'Autobiography': 'The autobiography of Henry Newcome', ed. R. Parkinson, *Chetham Society*, old series, 27 (1852).

242   *BIBLIOGRAPHY*

Newcome, 'Diary': 'The diary of Rev. Henry Newcome, 1661–3', ed. T. Haywood, *Chetham Society*, 18 (1849).

Pengelly, 'Accounts': Rachael Pengelly, 'Household accounts, 1693–1709', British Museum, Add. MS, 32, 456.

Pepys, *Diary: The Diary of Samuel Pepys*, ed. R. Latham and W. Matthews, 9 vols, London, 1970–83.

Price, *Compleat Cook: The Compleat Cook or the Secrets of a Seventeenth Century Housewife by Rebecca Price*, ed. M. Masson, London, 1974.

Ramsey, *Scotland and Scotsmen*: Alexander Allardyce, *Scotland and Scotsmen in the Eighteenth Century: from the MSS. of John Ramsey of Ochtertyre*, 2 vols, London, 1888. There are extracts in J.G. Fyfe (ed.), *Scottish Diaries and Memoirs, 1746–1843*, Stirling, 1942, pp. 164–201.

Robertson, *Rural Recollections: John Robertson, Rural Recollections; or, The Progress of Improvement in Agriculture and Rural Affairs*, Irvine, 1829. There are extracts in J.G. Fyfe (ed.), *Scottish Diaries and Memoirs, 1746–1843*, Stirling, 1942, pp. 257–88.

Rogers, 'Diary': 'The diary of Benjamin Rogers, rector of Carlton, 1720–1771', ed. C.D. Liddell, *Beds. Hist. Record Soc.*, 30 (1949).

Ryder, *Diary: The Diary of Dudley Ryder, 1715/16*, ed. W. Matthews, London, 1939.

Salusbury, 'Diary': 'John Salusbury of Leighton Buzzard, 1757–9', ed. Joyce Godber, *Beds. Hist. Record Soc.*, 40 (1959), 46–77.

Savage, 'Diary': Mrs S. Savage, 'Diary', Bodleian Library, Oxford, MS Erg. Misc., e 331.

Somerville, *Own Life and Times*: Thomas Somerville, *My Own Life and Times, 1714–1814*, ed. W. Lee, Edinburgh, 1861; written *c.* 1815. There are extracts in J.G. Fyfe (ed.), *Scottish Diaries and Memoirs, 1746–1843*, Stirling, 1942, pp. 203–54.

Stapley, 'Diary': 'Extracts from the diary of Richard Stapley of Twineham, Sussex, 1682–1724', ed. E. Turner, *Sussex Arch. Coll.*, 2 (1849), 102–28.

Stout, 'Autobiography': 'The autobiography of William Stout of Lancaster', ed. J.D. Marshall, *Chetham Society*, 3rd series, 14 (1967).

Stukeley, 'Memoirs': 'The family memoirs of the Rev. William Stukeley, MD', ed. W.C. Lukis, *Surtees Society*, 73 (1880).

Symcotts, 'Diary': 'A seventeenth century doctor and his patients: John Symcotts, 1592–1662', ed. F.N.L. Poynter and W.J. Bishop, *Beds. Hist. Record Soc.*, 31 (1950).

Taylor, 'Diary': 'Henry Taylor of Pulloxhill, 1750–1772', ed. Patricia Bell, *Beds. Hist. Record Soc.*, 40 (1959), 38–45.

Thomlinson, 'Diary': 'The diary of the Rev. John Thomlinson', ed. J.C. Hodgson, *Surtees Society*, 118 (1910), 64–167.

Thornton, 'Autobiography': 'The autobiography of Alice Thornton (nee Wandesford), 1627–1707', ed. C. Jackson, *Surtees Society*, 62 (1875).

Turner, *Diary: The Diary of Thomas Turner, 1754–1765*, ed. D. Vaisey, Oxford, 1984.

Warley, 'Accounts': Lee Warley, 'Accounts and memos', Reading University Library, KEN 14.2/1.

Woodforde, *Diary: James Woodforde: The Diary of a Country Parson, 1758–1802*, ed. J. Beresford, 5 vols, Oxford, 1924–31.

Woolley, *Guide*: Hannah Woolley, *The Gentlewoman's Companion or a Guide to the Female Sex*, London, 1675.

Yonge, *Journal*: *The Journal of James Yonge, 1647–1721: Plymouth Surgeon*, ed. F.N.L. Poynter, London, 1963.

Collections of printed probate inventories

For a general bibliography of probate inventories, see M. Overton, *A Bibliography of British Probate Inventories*, University of Newcastle upon Tyne, Department of Geography, 1983.

Brears, *Yorkshire Inventories*: P.C.D. Brears (ed.), 'Yorkshire probate inventories, 1542–1689', *Yorkshire Arch. Soc., Record Series*, 134 (1972).

May, *Newmarket Inventories*: P. May (ed.), *Newmarket Inventories 1662–1715*, Newmarket, 1976.

Moore, *Clifton and Westbury*: J.S. Moore (ed.), *Clifton and Westbury Probate Inventories, 1609–1761*, Bristol, 1981.

Moore, *Frampton Cotterell*: J.S. Moore (ed.), *The Goods and Chattels of our Forefathers: Frampton Cotterell and District Probate Inventories, 1539–1804*, London, 1977.

Roper, *Sedgley*: J.S. Roper (ed.), *Sedgley Probate Inventories, 1614–1787*, Sedgley, 1960.

Steer, *Mid-Essex Inventories*: F.W. Steer, *Farm and Cottage Inventories of Mid-Essex, 1635–1749*, Essex Record Office, 1950.

Trinder and Cox, *Telford*: B. Trinder and J. Cox (eds), *Yeomen and Colliers in Telford*, Chichester, 1980.

Vaisey, *Lichfield Inventories*: D.G. Vaisey (ed.), 'Probate inventories of Lichfield and district, 1568–1680', *Staffordshire Record Society*, 4th series, 5 (1969).

INDEX

Note: italics refer to Tables

Aberdeen 182
Abingdon 86
agriculture *see* farming
Allan, David 5, 11, 68, 151, 162, 174; pictures 12, 68, 154
Andrews, William 175

'backstage' activities *see* 'frontstage/backstage'
Baillie, Lady Griselle *133*, 134
barley 55, 56
Bedfordshire *see* Price, Rogers
beds and bedding 159–61, 181; Kent 56; in living room 10; Scotland 10, 11, 12 (illus.), 160, 175, 182
beer production 41
Berkshire 61
Bibles 174, 182, 207
blacksmiths 84, 101, 177
Blundell, Nicholas 86
books 10, 28, 29, 207; for children's learning 162; in household accounts *116–17*, 120, *124–5, 129–30*, 133; regions *49* (London) 50; (northwest England) 55; (Scotland) 174, 175; and social status 177, 180–1; urban/rural comparisons 77, 79, 83, *88*, 89; *see also* Bibles, Tables of key goods

bread 145, 146, 147, 148–9; prices 40, 41
Brereton, Sir William 142
brewing, home 115, 127, 128, 138, 145; in household accounts *116, 124, 129*
Bristol 86, 87, 101
Bullock, Elizabeth 10
Burrell, Timothy 65, 102
Burslem (Staffordshire) 83, 170
'but and ben' 10–11, 174

Cambridge: size of households 94
Cambridgeshire *53–4*; china 87; crops 104; 'frontstage' goods 43; hot drinks utensils 31, 62; knives and forks 54; looking glasses 30; pictures 54; saucepans 54; silver 29; trades and occupations 104–5
Canterbury (diocese) *see* Kent
Carlisle 58, 59; looking glasses 30; population 74; silver 29; *see also* Cumbria
Carlton (Beds.), rector of 104, 145
carpets 7
Cartwright, William 181
celebrations, feasts and special occasions *64–9*, 68 (illus.), 121
cereals *see* crops
chairs 7, 33; *see also* furniture
chambers (upper rooms) 6, 11, 159–61

change, patterns of 28–32, *88*; chronology 38–41
Chester (diocese) *see* north-west England
Chester (town) 85
children 94–5, 105, 121, 161–2
china 8, 110, 206; cost 159; increasing use 28, 31, 32, 41; London 50, 187; and social status 169, 172, 179, 187–8; in taverns 157; trade and supply 41, 63, 86–7; urban/rural comparisons 79, *88; see also* Tables of key goods
chinamen 86
chocolate 28, 65, 131; *see also* hot drinks utensils
christenings 64
Christmas celebrations 65
City of London 48 *see also* Orphans' Court
cleaning and washing 120, 139, 140 (illus.), 141 (illus.), 142, 151; accounts *117, 124, 129, 133*; expenditure on 126
Cleaton, George 160, 176
clergy 180–1; incomes 98–9, 100, 103–4; *see also* Rogers
clocks 25, 27, 31, 40, 109, 207; Latham's 121; manufacture 55, 63, 197; regions (Kent) 56; (Scotland) 10, 173, 180; and social status 177, 180; urban/rural comparisons 77, 79, 83, *88*, 89; *see also* Tables of key goods
clothing and cloth 145, 173, 193–4; cloth industry 55; in household accounts *116–17*, 119–20, *124–5, 129–30*, 131–2; *see also* spinning
coal mining and trade 51, 52, 58
Cobbett, William 111
coffee 28, 41, 158; dealers 61–2; in Pengelly household 126; *see also* hot drinks utensils
Colius, R., picture by 35
Collett, John 139, 162; picture 140
conduct books 138, 154, 155, 160

consumption hierarchy 21, 185
cookery *see* cooking equipment, food and cookery
cooking equipment 109, 136, 146, 147–8, 205; continuity of style 33; in yeomen households 172; *see also* food and cookery, saucepans, Tables of key goods
Cookson, William (weaver) 83–4
cost of goods 109–11
cottars (Scotland) 175, 177
cotton: spinning at home 118, 119; in household accounts *116*
craft trades *46*, 100–1, *184*, 185, 192, 193; home as workplace 144; *see also* pottery industry, woodworking trades, ironworkers, tradesmen and craftsmen
crockery *see* earthenware
crops: Cambridgeshire 54; grain trade 61–2; north-west England 55; Richard Latham's 118; *see also under* names of crops
Cumberland 52
Cumbria 47, *58–9*; china 59; clocks 43, 59; hot drinks utensils 62; pewter 43, 59; pictures 59; *see also* Carlisle
curtains, bed 161
curtains, window 7–8, 40, 207; regions (Kent) 56; (London) 50; and social status 172, 177; urban/rural comparisons 77, 83; *see also* Tables of key goods
cushions 207
cutlery *see* knives and forks

dairy produce as part of income 103
Dawley (Shropshire) 84, 175
Dawson, John (quoted) 163
dealing trades *46*, 178, *184*, 185, *186*, 189; *see also* shopkeepers
Defoe, Daniel 71, 139, 164; (quoted) 1, 25, 26
delftware 101, 110, 206
Devon 87
diaries 4–5; as leisure activity 163
dioceses 44, 46, 48, 239

doctors 102; *see also* Kay
Doncaster inventories 11, 166, 179
Dorset 61
drinking 157–9; *see also* chocolate,
    coffee, tea
Drysdale, Robert 180
Durham (diocese) 31, 43, 51, 52,
    74; *see also* north-east England
Durham (town) 51

earthenware 28, 32, 40, 41, 206;
    changing styles 34, 111; cost 110;
    regions *49* (Hampshire) 56;
    (Kent) 29, 30, 63; (north-west
    England) 30, 55, 56, 63;
    (Orphans' Court) 30; shop
    inventories 86; and social status
    169, 172, 175; trade and
    manufacture 55, 57, 63, 86–7,
    101; urban/rural comparisons
    77, *88*; *see also* pottery industry,
    Tables of key goods
East India Company and Far East
    trade 25, 37, 41, 86, 197
eating equipment 205; *see also*
    pewter, earthenware, china,
    knives and forks, hot drinks
    utensils
economic sector, ownership by *186*,
    187, *214*
economy and economic factors 16–
    19, 39–40, 57, 60–1, 197–9
Edge, Samuel 170
Edinburgh 59, 178, 180, 182, 183;
    Baillie 134
education 182; in accounts *117*,
    129, *133*; children's 161–2;
    literacy 55, 127, 180, 189;
    schoolmasters' incomes 100,
    102, 104; women's 138, 149
Ely, diocese of *see* Cambridgeshire
emulation as ownership factor 20,
    194–6
expenditure patterns *112–36*;
    accounts used 112–14; Fell
    household 128–32; Latham
    household 114–23; Pengelly

household 123–8; ways of
    interpreting 134–6

Far East trade *see* East India
    Company
farmers: contents and value of
    inventories 33, 106; effect of
    place on ownership 79; *see also*
    husbandmen, yeomen
farming: agricultural depression
    and ownership 198–9; regions
    (Cambridgeshire) 54;
    (Hampshire) 56, 57; (Kent) 54;
    see also livestock
Fell, Margaret 128
Fell, Sarah 102, *128–32*; clothing
    and cloth 131–2; food
    expenditure 131; furniture and
    utensils 132; livestock and
    farming 131; scope of accounts
    128; size of household 128
Fiennes, Celia 71, 146, 151, 152
flax 54, 104, *129*; home spinning
    114, 115, 119, 145
food and cookery *145–51*, 148
    (illus.), 154 (illus.); central role of
    cookery 146; cooking methods
    147–9; proportion of income
    spent on *116*, 119, *124*, *129*, *133*,
    135; rooms used 150; storing and
    preserving 149; wife's
    responsibility 149–50; *see also*
    cooking equipment
forks *see* knives and forks
Fox, George 128, 132
freemen of City of London *see*
    Orphans' Court
Fretwell, James 95, 138, 162
'frontstage/backstage' activities 9,
    11, 145, 165; cleaning and
    washing 151; meals 155, 156;
    and new goods 28
funerals 64, 65, 121
Funston, John 170
furniture 136, 204; expenditure on
    115; home-made 145; in
    household accounts *117*, 120,
    125, 127, *130*, 132; manufacture

33, 63; regions (Kent) 56; (Scotland) 173; and social status 172, 179; upholstered 207; *see also* beds, tables, Tables of key goods

gardening and garden produce 103, 145; accounts *116, 124, 129*
gentry *169–71*, 189, 196; incomes 101–2; inventory values *213, 214*; in status hierarchy *168, 184*, 185
geographical areas sampled *see* regions
Glasgow 182
glass 55, 86
Glasse, Hannah 147, 150, 152
Gloucestershire 6
gold 207; *see also* silver
Goldsmith, Oliver (quoted) 93
grain trade 61–2
growth, patterns of 28–32

hall 10; *see also* living rooms
Hampshire 47, *56–7*; clocks 43; hot drinks utensils 62; pewter 43; silver 66; trade with London 61–2
Harrison, Richard 181
heating and lighting 120, 126, 147; in household accounts *117, 124, 129, 133*
hemp 54
Henley-on-Thames 84
Hog, Andro 182
home produce as part of income 103
hot drinks utensils 28, 32, 41, 110, 159, 206; regions *49*; (Cambridgeshire) 31; (Kent) 31; (London) 31, 50; and social status 172, 179; trade and supply 61–2, 63; urban/rural comparisons *88*, 89; *see also* Tables of key goods
house (name for living room) 10
household: domestic schedules 142–5; men's role 138; size and

composition 6, 94–5, 182; as unit of consumption 6; women's role 137–9; *see also* houses
household accounts 4–5, 112–14; *see also* Fell, Latham, Pengelly
household goods: patterns of change 28–32, 37–41; (in style and quality) 32–5; studies and collections 21–2; *see also* incomes, key goods, regions, social status, trades and occupations, urban/rural comparisons *and under* names of goods
household manuals 4–5
houseplace 10; *see also* living rooms
houses: arrangement and use of rooms 9–13, 137, 150, 155; (bedrooms) 159–61; size 6, 174, 181; used as workplace 144; *see also* household
husbandmen 14, *174–6*, 185, 191–2, 193; incomes 100; inventory values *212, 213*; in status hierarchy *168, 184*, 185

incomes *95–105*; clergy 101–2; complex nature of 95–6; effect of wages on consumption 19–21; lawyer 65; range in middle ranks 98–102; schoolmasters 100, 102, 104; Scotland 175–6; sources 103–5; *see also* wealth
inventories: contents and nature 2–3, 106; methods of interpretation 5–6; regions used in sample 3–4; size of sample 3–4; values *209–14*
ironware 58, 197
ironworkers 101, 105, 172, 177

Jackson, Richard 178
jewellery 207; *see also* silver
Josselin, Ralph 94, 98, 101, 103–4

Kay, Richard 142–3, 145, 163
Kent *52–3*; china 87; clocks 31; earthenware 30, 63; 'frontstage'

goods 43; hot drinks utensils 31, 62; inventory 12; pewter 29, 43; silver 66; *see also* Warley

key goods 3, *203–8*; *see also* under names of goods; *Tables*, economic sector *186*; inventory values *107, 108, 110*; Orphans' Court *27*; regional *44*; social status *168*; trades and occupations *184, 188*; urban/rural comparisons *76, 78, 80*; whole sample *26*

King, Gregory 13, 73, 98, 100, 167, 178; own budget 102, 113, *133*, 134–6, 147

kitchens 10–11, 140 (illus.), 141 (illus.), 150

knives and forks 8, 35, 36 (illus.), 153, 206; Cambridgeshire 54; cost 111; manufacture 197; Scotland 180; in yeomen households 172; *see also* Tables of key goods

labourers and wage-earners 3, 54, 176, 192–4; effect of economy on 19–21, 198–9; size of household 94

Lancashire: clocks 31, 43; earthenware 30, 63, 87; 'frontstage' goods 43; income of lesser gentry 102; *see also* Fell, Latham, north-west England

Lancaster 99, 104, 131

Latham, Richard 95, 103, 105, *114–23*; books 121, 162; children's education 121; cleaning and washing 120; clock 121; cloth 145; food purchases 118–19; furniture and utensils 115, 118, 120; heating and lighting 120; lease 122; leisure activities 163; livestock 115; loan 122; medical and childbirth expenses 121; servants 140, 142; size of household 115; social status 171; special occasions 121; sugar and salt 149; wool and flax 145

lawyer's income 65

leisure 163–5

letters, payments for 132

Lichfield: Cathedral Chancellor's inventory 181

Lichfield (diocese) *see* north-west Midlands

lighting *see* heating and lighting

Lilleshall (Shropshire), inventories from 13, 33, 172

linen *see* table linen, textiles

literacy 55, 127, 180, 189

Liverpool 55, 63, 74, 86

livestock 115, *116, 124, 129*, 131

living rooms 10, 11–13, 33–5, 150

loans 122, 127, 128, 131

London 29, 40, *47–51*, 75; books 43, 50; china 50, 86–7, 187; clocks 31, 63; curtains 50; 'frontstage' goods 43; hot drinks utensils 31, 50, 62; looking glasses 30; pictures 50; population 47, 73; saucepans 50; silver 66; size of household 94; trade and manufacturing 50–1, 61–3, 86–7, 101; *see also* urban/rural comparisons

London, archdeaconry of 48

London, City of 48; *see also* Orphans' Court

Longniddrie 174, 237

looking glasses 10, 28, 30, 41, 207; cost 109, *110*, 111; regions 30; (London) 29, 30, 40; (Scotland) 173, 174; and social status 169, 172, 175, 177, 189; trade and supply 63; urban/rural comparisons 77, 79; *see also* Tables of key goods

Lowe, Roger 145

luxury v. necessity 14–16

Manchester 55

Marchant, Thomas (diarist) 157, 164

marketing *see* supply and trade

Markham, Gervaise 138, 146

Marsh Grange 128

Martindale, Adam 98–9
Massie, James 13, 14, 98, 100
mattresses 160, 161
meals and mealtimes 7 (illus.), 35
(illus.), *151–7*, 158 (illus.);
behaviour 153–5; equipment
152–4, 155–6; presentation 151–
3; rooms used 155; times of
meals 152, 153
meat 146–7
medical expenses *117*, 121, *125*,
127, *129*, *133*
merchants *see* dealing trades
middle ranks: definition used 13–
14
Middlesex, archdeaconry of 48
Midlands (part) *see* north-west
Midlands
midwife, payments for 121
mirrors *see* looking glasses
Misson, Henri 64, 153, 157, 164
Moore, Giles 101–2, 157
Mure's 'Observations' (quoted) 67
musical instruments 207
Muxton (Shropshire) 181

napkins *see* table linen
necessity v. luxury 14–16
'new goods' 3, 31–2, 77, 147–8; *see
also* china, hot drinks utensils,
etc.
New Year celebrations 65
Newcastle (upon Tyne) 51, 74, 86,
131
Newcome, Elizabeth 140
Newcome, Henry 146
Newmarket 66, 170
north-east England 47, *51–2*; books
43; china 52, 87; clocks 52;
'frontstage' goods 43; hot drinks
utensils 62; silver 66; trade with
London 61
north-west England *54–6*
north-west Midlands 47, *57–8*;
clocks 43, 58; hot drinks utensils
62; saucepans 58
Northumberland 51, 52; *see also*
north-east England

Norwich 73, 86, 150, 155, 159–60

oats 55
ornamentation, rarity of 7–8
Orphans' Court inventories 3–4,
27, 38–40, 48, 50; books 38;
china 39, 182, 187; clocks 31, 39,
182; cutlery 182; earthenware
39; knives and forks 38; looking
glasses 29, 30, 39; pictures 31,
38, 39, 182; silver 29, 66;
window curtains 31, 39
Oxfordshire 61

parlour 11–13; *see also* living
rooms
pattern books 33
Pengelly, Rachael 89, *123–8*;
cleaning and washing 126;
clothing 126; food expenditure
126, 135; furniture and utensils
127; heating and lighting 126;
income of household 102;
livestock and dairy produce 126;
size of household 123
Pepys, Samuel (quoted) 139, 149,
156
pewter 41, 109, 136, 205; cost 110,
111; manufacture 28, 63, 197;
regions (Kent) 29, 56; (Scotland)
174; and social status 169, 172,
175, 177; in taverns 157; *see also*
Tables of key goods
pewter dishes and plates 8, 30–1,
153, 156, 206
pictures, prints and drawings 8, 10,
40, 41, 207; production 37, 63;
regions *49* (Cambridgeshire) 54;
(Kent) 56; (Lancashire) 56;
(London) 50; and social status
169, 172, 177; as sources of
information 5, 7–8, 162; urban/
rual comparisons 77, 79, *88*; *see
also* Tables of key goods
play 162
Pocock, Richard 52
population *62*; Carlisle 74; London
47, 73

potters: differing definitions 100–1;
inventories 34, 83, 170
pottery industry 37, 41, 58, 195, 197
Price, Rebecca 149
prices of goods 109–11
priorities *see* expenditure patterns
professions 14, 185, 189; incomes
100, 101; *see also* clergy, doctors,
lawyer's income, schoolmasters'
incomes

Ramsey, John 67, 153
regions sampled 43–7; attitudes to
spending 63–4; contrasting
patterns of consumption 60–1;
supply and trade 61–3; *see also
under* names of regions
Robertson, John 11, 58, 173
Rogers, Benjamin 104, 145

saffron 54, 104
St Andrews 85
Salusbury, John 145, 164
sample of inventories *see* inventories
Sandby, Paul 139; pictures 141, 148
saucepans 205; regions
(Cambridgeshire) 54; (London)
50; and social status 169, 179;
urban/rural comparisons 77; *see
also* Tables of key goods
Scarisbrick (Lancashire) *see*
Latham
schoolmasters' incomes 100, 102,
104
Scotland 59–60, 61, 166; beds 10,
11, 160, 175, 182; celebrations
and special occasions 67–8;
cooking 148–9; meals 153; size
of household 6, 94; size and use
of houses 10–11, 12 (illus.), 160,
173–4, 182; social status 167,
183–4; (cottars and sub-tenants)
175; (gentry) 171; (tenants) 172,
173–4; (tradesmen) 177, 178,
180, 182; *see also* Baillie
servants and services 123, 127,
139–42, 151; accounts *117, 125,
129, 133*

Shaw, Aaron (potter, Burslem) 83
shopkeepers 14, 100, 102, 187,
188; *see also* dealing trades, Stout
Shrewsbury 74
Shropshire: inventories (Lilleshall)
13, 33, 172; (Wellington) 83–4,
160, 166, 178; (other) 10, 84,
155, 170–1, 175, 181; kitchens
150; *see also* north-west Midlands
silver 28, 29–30, 66, 207; in taverns
157; in yeoman households 172;
see also Tables of key goods
Sinclare, George 174
sleep and rest 159–61; *see also* beds
and bedding
social emulation 20, 194–6
social meaning of environment 8–
13
social role of goods 137
social status as ownership factor 1–
2, *166–89, 168, 184, 212*;
difficulties of defining 167–9;
gentry 169–70; husbandmen
174–6; labourers 176;
professions 180–3; social
boundaries 183, 191–4;
tradesmen and craftsmen 176–
80, 185; yeomen 171–4
Society of Friends 128, 132
Somerville, Thomas 67, 173–4
special occasions *see* celebrations
spinning, home 114, 118, 119, 131,
145
Staffordshire 101; china 31;
earthenware manufacture 63, 87;
looking glasses 30; *see also*
Burslem, north-west Midlands
Stamford 86
Stanier, Richard 160
Stapley, Richard 145
Steventon, John 172–3
stoneware 87, 101, 206; *see also*
earthenware
Stout, Ellin 140, 149
Stout, William 84, 95, 144; family
and household 139, 162;
finances 99, 102; social status
172

Stout, William (nephew of above)
99
Stukeley, William 102, 163
sub-tenants (Scotland) 175
sugar 122, 126, 131, 149; in
household accounts *116, 124,
129*
supply and trade 61–3, 84–7, 197
Sussex 61
Swarthmoor Hall (Lancashire) *see*
Fell

table linen 28, 109, 156, 207; *see
also* Tables of key goods
tables 8, 109, 175, 177, 204–5;
settings 35; *see also* Tables of key
goods
taverns and alehouses 157
tea 28, 37–8, 41, 158–9; dealers
61–2; in Pengelly household 126;
see also hot drinks utensils
Telford inventories *see* Shropshire
tenants (Scottish farmers) 10–11,
172, 173–4
testaments, Scottish 59, 166, 233
textiles 55, 206–7; *see also* beds and
bedding, clothing and cloth,
curtains, table linen
Thomlinson, John 159, 162, 164,
165
Thornton, Alice 234
towns *70–90*; effect of density on
ownership 81, 83; integration
with rural areas 89, 90;
marketing and trade 84–7; nature
of urban communities 71–2, 89–
90; scope of sample 74–5; size
and type 72–4; urban/rural
comparisons 75–9, 83, 89–90
trade and supply 61–3, 84–7, 197
trades and occupations 77–9, 187,
188, 209–11, 213; *see also* craft
trades, dealing trades, tradesmen
and craftsmen
tradesmen and craftsmen: contents
and value of inventories 106;
incomes 99; social status (high-
status) 180–2; (intermediate

status) 178–80; (low status) 177–
8; yeomen as 171–2; *see also* craft
trades, dealing trades
transport and travel 127, 132; in
household accounts *117, 124,
129, 133*
Tusser, Thomas (quoted) 137

upholstered furniture 207
urban/rural comparisons 75–9, *80*,
83, *88*, 89–90

Van Aken, Joseph 8, 35, 150, 153,
159, 216; pictures 7, 82, 158
visiting 157–8, 164–5

wage-earners *see* labourers and
wage-earners
wages *see* incomes
Warley, Lee (Kentish yeoman) 64,
196; (quoted) 112
washing *see* cleaning and washing
Watkis, William (blacksmith) 84
wealth 96, 105–9; *see also*
incomes
weavers 83, 101, 131, 177
weddings 65, 68 (illus.)
Wedgwood, Josiah 1, 195
Wedgwood, Richard 170
Wellington (Shropshire),
inventories from 83–4, 160, 166,
178
Wentworth, Sir Thomas 171
Westminster 48
Westmoreland 52
wheat 56
Whitechapel, parish of 48
Whitehaven 58
whiteware 206
wholesalers *see* dealing trades
Wight, Isle of 56, 141 (illus.); *see
also* Hampshire
Wiltshire 61
Winchester (diocese) *see*
Hampshire
Winchester (town) 74
window curtains *see* curtains

women 164; contribution to
income 105; domestic role 137–
9; as educators 162; as heads of
households 182
wooden plates and dishes 156, 159
woodworking trades 33
wool 119, 145; accounts *116, 129*
Wrockwardine (Shropshire) 10
Wyat, Allen (Newmarket glazier) 66

yarn *see* spinning
yeomen *171–4*, 187, 189; incomes
98, 99–100, 101; inventory
values *212, 213*; size of
households 94; in status
hierarchy *168, 184*, 185
Yonge, James 102
Yorkshire 87; inventories 11, 166,
171, 179